Reading Colonial Japan

Reading Colonial Japan

TEXT, CONTEXT, AND CRITIQUE

EDITED BY

Michele M. Mason AND *Helen J. S. Lee*

STANFORD UNIVERSITY PRESS
STANFORD, CALIFORNIA

Stanford University Press
Stanford, California

The Hokkaido Former Natives Protection Law was previously published in *Race, Resistance and the Ainu of Japan* (Routledge, 1996), 194–96. Reprinted with permission.

"Officer Ukuma" © 2000 University of Hawai'i Press. Reprinted with permission.

Chapter Four develops material previously published in "Ethnography, Border, and Violence: Reading Between the Lines in Satō Haruo's 'Demon Bird,'" *Japan Forum, Journal of the British Association of Japanese Studies*, 19, 1 (2007): 89–110, and chapter 2 of *Tropics of Savagery: The Culture of Japanese Empire in Comparative Frame* (University of California Press, 2010). The author thanks the editors of both publications for allowing him to reprint portions of these works.

Manchu Girl translated and printed with permission of Koizumi Suzuko and Shirato Yoshiko.

The Adventures of Dankichi translated and printed with permission of Shimada Michio.

Printed in the United States of America on acid-free, archival-quality paper

Library of Congress Cataloging-in-Publication Data

Reading colonial Japan : text, context, and critique / edited by Michele M. Mason and Helen J.S. Lee.
    pages cm
 Includes bibliographical references and index.
 Includes Japanese texts translated into English.
  ISBN 978-0-8047-7696-7 (cloth : alk. paper)--ISBN 978-0-8047-7697-4 (pbk. : alk. paper)
  1. Japan--Colonies--History. 2. Japan--Foreign relations. 3. Japanese literature--20th century--History and criticism. 4. Japanese literature--Translations into English.
5. Colonies in literature. 6. Imperialism in literature. I. Mason, Michele, editor of compilation, translator. II. Lee, Helen J. S., 1968- editor of compilation, translator.
 JV5227.R43 2012
 325'.352--dc23   2011049958

Typeset by Bruce Lundquist in 11/14 Adobe Garamond

To our teachers,
who taught us to think and live beyond the books and walls of the academy.
We are happily forever in your debt.

Contents

Contributors

DAVINDER L. BHOWMIK is Associate Professor of Japanese at the University of Washington, Seattle, and the author of *Writing Okinawa: Narrative Acts of Identity and Resistance* (Routledge, 2008). She is currently working on a book on violence in contemporary Japanese literature.

KOTA INOUE is Assistant Professor at the University of Redlands. His research interests include the colonial logic of modernity, the critique of globalization, and psychoanalysis. He is currently working on a book manuscript, *Unsettling Suburbs: Colonization of Everyday Space in Imperial Japan*, which examines colonization of the everyday through critically reading the representations of suburban space in Japanese literature and cinema.

KAWAMURA MINATO is Professor in the Department of International Cultural Studies at Hosei University, Tokyo. Recognized as a pioneering figure in Japanese postcolonial studies, Kawamura is also a prolific scholar with more than thirty books to his credit. He continues to expand the field, researching on topics such as ethnic minorities and postwar Korean film.

KOMORI YŌICHI is Professor of Modern Japanese Literature in the Department of Language and Information Sciences at the University of Tokyo. He is widely known as a literary and social critic, activist, and public intellectual. Komori's large corpus of writing addresses a wide range of subjects, including modern literature, war and peace, postcolonialism, the Japanese imperial system, and modernity and capitalism.

KIMBERLY T. KONO is Associate Professor in the Department of East Asian Languages and Literatures at Smith College. She is the author of *Romance, Family, and Nation in Japanese Colonial Literature* (Palgrave Macmillan, 2010). Her current research focuses on Japanese women's writing on travel to the colonies.

HELEN J. S. LEE is Assistant Professor of Japanese studies at the Underwood International College, Yonsei University, Seoul. Her research focuses on Japanese settlers in colonial Korea, and her projects employ the popular media, such as satiric poetry (*senryū*), travel narratives, and cartoons to investigate the race relations between Japanese and Koreans in the colonial context. Her publications include "Voices of the 'Colonists,' Voices of the 'Immigrants': 'Korea' in Japan's Early Colonial Travel Narratives and Guides, 1894–1914" (*Japanese Language and Literature*, 2007), "Writing Colonial Relations of Everyday Life in *Senryū*" (*positions: east asia cultures critique*, 2008), and "Dying as Daughter of the Empire" (*positions: east asia cultures critique*, forthcoming).

MICHELE M. MASON is Assistant Professor of Japanese literature at the University of Maryland, College Park. Her research and teaching interests include modern Japanese literature and history, colonial and postcolonial studies, gender and feminist studies, masculinity studies, and the history and literature of Hiroshima and Nagasaki. Mason is the co-producer and interpreter for the short documentary film *Witness to Hiroshima* (2010). Her publications include "Nanshoku to kokka: Hara Hōitsuan no 'Anchu seijika'" (Male-Male Sexuality and the Modern Japanese Nation: Hara Hōitsuan's *Secret Politician*) (*Jendāshigaku*, 2009), "Writing Hiroshima and Nagasaki in the 21st Century: A New Generation of Manga" (*Asia Pacific Journal*, 2009), and "Empowering the Would-be Warrior: Bushidō and the Gendered Bodies of the Japanese Nation" (*Recreating Japanese Men*, 2011).

RICHARD SIDDLE is Professor in the Research Faculty of Media and Communication, Hokkaido University. His areas of expertise include Japan's indigenous Ainu, Okinawa, minorities, and multiculturalism in Japan. He is the author of *Race, Resistance and the Ainu of Japan* (Routledge, 1996) and co-editor of *Japan and Okinawa: Structure and Subjectivity* (Routledge, 2003).

ROBERT TIERNEY is Associate Professor of Japanese literature in the Departments of East Asian Languages and Cultures and Comparative and World Literatures at the University of Illinois at Urbana-Champaign. His recent publications include *Tropics of Savagery: The Culture of Japanese Empire in Comparative Frame* (University of California Press, 2010). He is currently researching the history of Japanese adaptations of Shakespeare and Japan's first anti-imperialist movement.

Acknowledgments

This project has been long in the making, and on our journey we have been supported and assisted by a great many people to whom we would like to extend our heartfelt thanks. To Tongfi Kim, Makiko Inoue, and Masayuki Shinohara, for their invaluable help with translations. To Setsu Shigematsu, for crucial guidance early on with the proposal. Thank you to Julie Koser and Leslie Winston for their excellent suggestions and unstinting encouragement. We would also like to thank Steven Chung, Katie King, Nina Leacock, D. Serrano Mateo, Connie North, Richi Sakakibara, Isao Shimizu, and Ilona Tsutsui. Michele's two years on Stanford University's Freeman Spogli Institute Fellowship (2005–2007) supplied the necessary intellectual engagement and practical assistance, which turned a sprout of an idea into an exciting project. Helen extends thanks to the Korea Foundation (fellowship, 2006–2007), Yonsei University (faculty research grant, 2008–2009), and the Korea Research Foundation (research grant, 32A-2009-1-A00127) for their generous support of her work. Helen wishes to recognize her students and colleagues at the University of Florida, who helped her grow as a teacher and scholar of postcolonial studies. Much of the conceptual groundwork and initial writing of this volume was done during her years in Gainesville (2003–2008), and she is indebted to the intellectual environment her first teaching job generously provided. Michele treasures her wonderful colleagues at the University of Maryland, who in so many tangible and intangible ways helped this work along. Our deepest gratitude goes to Stacy Wagner at Stanford University Press for her unflagging faith in the project. We greatly appreciate the three anonymous reviewers, who provided critical comments that have strengthened the volume. We are enormously indebted to Professors Kawamura and Komori, who not only graciously allowed us to translate their important works, but also have patiently mentored us for years. We would like to express our deepest appreciation to Shimada Michio, son of Shimada Keizō, and Koizumi Suzuko and Shirato Yoshiko, family members of Koizumi Kikue, for kindly granting us permission to translate and publish *The Adventures of Dankichi* and *Manchu Girl*. Michele offers an especially hearty thank you to Leslie Winston, without whom this project and her life would not have blossomed in the sweet way they did.

A special thanks to Jim Fujii and the late Miriam Silverberg, who first planted the seeds of knowledge about Japan's colonial period in us and whose intellectual energy and passion have inspired us.

Note on Japanese Names

Japanese names are rendered in this volume in the conventional Japanese manner, namely surname first and given name or pen name second. Typically, authors are referred to by their last names, but in certain cases they are called by their first names, usually a pen name. For example, Natsume Sōseki is commonly referred to as Sōseki rather than Natsume.

Reading Colonial Japan

Introduction

MICHELE M. MASON AND HELEN J. S. LEE

B y any measure, Japan's modern empire was formidable. The only major non-Western colonial power in the twentieth century, Japan controlled a vast area of Asia and numerous archipelagos in the Pacific Ocean. Its reach extended from Sakhalin Island north of the Japanese archipelago to the Solomon Islands in the South Pacific and expanded into Manchuria, areas of China, Korea, and much of Southeast Asia and Micronesia. Over the more than seven decades of Japanese colonial rule (1869–1945), Japan successfully naturalized two colonies (Ainu Moshir/Hokkaido and the Ryukyu Kingdom/Okinawa)[1] into its national territory. The massive extraction of resources and extensive cultural assimilation policies radically impacted the lives of millions of Asians and Pacific Islanders. The political, economic, and cultural ramifications of this era are still felt today.

Over the last thirty years, the field of Japanese studies has produced an impressive body of Japanese and English language scholarship on Japan's colonial era. Initially, solid groundwork was laid with works elucidating economic, legal, and agricultural policies produced in the imperial center and imposed on the colonial periphery.[2] More recently, critical work emphasizes that despite overwhelming unequal power relations, all colonial processes intrinsically demand a political, economic, and cultural *exchange* through negotiation, struggle, collaboration, and resistance. Excellent scholarship addressing the multifaceted exchanges among Japan's colonies and the metropole, the discursive construction of colonized and colonizing subjects, and key social, scientific, academic, and cultural institutions that bolstered Japanese imperialism is now available. Numerous books and essays interrogate the complex cultural and political negotiation of colonial identities and reveal the importance of the collective imagination and the role of ordinary Japanese in the colonial project.[3]

Building on this strong foundation, *Reading Colonial Japan* aims to deepen knowledge of Japanese colonialism(s), providing both an eclectic selection of translated Japanese primary sources and analytical essays that illuminate the specificities of Japan's many and varied colonial projects. The primary documents, which span a variety of genres, including legal documents, children's literature, cookbooks, serialized comics, as well as literary texts by well-known authors of the time, serve to highlight the centrality of cultural production and dissemination to colonial endeavors and to accentuate the myriad ways colonialism permeated every facet of life. In the essays, the contributors are primarily concerned with representation and rhetoric and how these intersect with operations of power. They investigate the workings of imperialist discourse through close readings of cultural representations in colonial narratives and imagery, revealing how the Japanese imperial project was understood, imagined, and lived. The scholars herein take as a premise that colonialism is not simply a military quest, legal process, or government-led project. Rather, it is a complex cultural system, both in the formulation of underpinning ideology and the execution of policies backed by those ideological beliefs. In addition to forming economic and political structures, colonial powers enlist the participation of various institutions, educational processes, and publication networks, which produce "knowledge" that rationalizes the colonial order. By making available and analyzing a wide range of sources that represent "media" during the Japanese colonial period, we engage in a dialogue with scholarship in cultural studies and highlight the powerful role language and imagination play in producing the material realities of Japanese colonialism.

No colonial project succeeds without substantial support from its citizenry. In fact, cultural production by a broad spectrum of "ordinary" Japanese citizens—for instance, a housewife in Manchuria, settlers in Korea, manga artists and fiction writers in mainland Japan—functioned effectively to reinforce the official political, economic, and cultural policies that controlled and violated the lives of the colonized throughout Japan's empire. Whether individual Japanese actively promoted the imperial project or quietly acquiesced to its demands, they were, to varying degrees, complicit with imperial ideology. Although a young man's volunteering for the army might have been a conspicuous expression of loyalty to the imperial state, the works herein show that no one was precluded from participating in the promotion and maintenance of the colonial campaign. Women, for instance, published "memoirs" that mobilized colonial rhetoric and their promotion of state policies in locally published cookbooks served imperial causes in significant ways well beyond the restricted domestic sphere of the home. Likewise, children's manga, such as *The Adventures of Dankichi*, included in this volume, showcase both unsettling manifestations of racialized colonial justifications and the unapologetic recruitment of Japanese children's imaginary world and minds. In fact, every mode of expression was mobilized to further the colonial agenda. If laws such as the Hokkaido Former Natives Protection Law dramatically impinged on and restricted the lives of the colonized, a variety of fictional works justified unequal power relations between Japan and its many colonial entities. Be it depictions of the naturescape in Hokkaido that erased the existence of the island's indigenous population, or the "retelling" of a violent legend of Taiwanese "barbarians," literary depictions of the Other joined forces with official arguments to shore up a colonial world order. Many Japanese citizens from all walks of life consumed, accepted, and reiterated the implicit and explicit messages of such texts, thereby participating in the imperial project in the most mundane, yet indispensible, ways.

Serving as the mainstay of the theoretical framework of this volume are the following two premises: that colonial discourse never marshals a totalizing persuasive power and that colonial powers do not exert their authority through a single, cohesive, and consistent ideology. As formidable as is the ideological capacity to determine reality, especially when backed by overwhelming military force and economic privileges, there always exist inherent contradictions, competing ideologies, and intersecting subjectivities. As the resistance movements in Taiwan and Korea suggest, not everyone was convinced of the "benevolence" of the Japanese imperial project. The experiences of a collaborating colonial elite in Korea, a Chinese "coolie" in Manchuria, an Okinawan police officer, or a Japanese female settler differed greatly as any individual's place within a group and the empire was determined by a number of shifting, and not infrequently incompatible, factors. In fact, one of the most laborious tasks of colonial authorities was to police various levels of slippage that potentially undermined the order of the empire. For instance, with growing numbers of Japanese citizens living in colonies abroad, a great deal of apprehension and suspicion was directed toward colonial settlers who were deemed morally bankrupt and sexually decadent. The barometer of these "perversities" came in the form of "news" of Japanese men and women becoming intimate in every way possible with colonial subjects, single women leading independent lives, and the free flow of drink, drugs, and wild sex. After the defeat, the distrust and disdain of the Japanese expatriates became evident when rather than a hearty welcome home, forceful internment and humiliating medical examinations greeted the returnees.[4] If the issue of Japanese expatriates evinces the instability of the rhetoric professing the inherent superiority and civilized nature of the Japanese colonizer, the imperial conscription of colonial male subjects reveals a bittersweet compromise of the colonial government. In lining up an impressive number of male bodies for the front lines, the colonial government succeeded, but whether to trust them enough with rifles was a matter that generated tremendous anxiety.[5] As is demonstrated by a few examples, multiple discourses and representations were circulated and modified, and sometimes collided, as various actors responded to changing political, economic, and social imperatives in the varying colonial contexts.

Disparate, even contradictory, ideas, ideals, identities, and imagery are the mortar of any colonial project. This is not to suggest that the discursive construction of, for example, the colonizer and colonized specifically or the colonial undertaking generally was generated without devastating consequences. There are important historical works that record the crimes and injustices of the Japanese empire and translated works by colonial subjects that lend personal perspectives on the tragic loss of livelihoods and lives. The critical readings in this volume, however, focus attention on how colonial logic in texts written by various members of the colonizing nation converts the obviously belligerent and violent facts of colonialism into a "palatable," even noble cause, greases the wheels of empire, and fans the fires of imperial desire. They expose and challenge the rhetorical mechanisms used to erase the voices of the colonized and monopolize the authority to define their cultures and histories. We hope to further fill in the picture of Japan's diverse empire and stimulate discussion among scholars concerned about the broader questions of colonialism in the past and present.

Re-Viewing Japanese Colonial History

Typically, Japan's age of empire is dated from 1895 to 1945, beginning when Taiwan was ceded to Japan following its victory over China in the Sino-Japanese War (1894–1895), and concluding with Japan's defeat in the Asia-Pacific War (1931–1945). What is commonly characterized as Japan's "formal" empire includes Taiwan, Southern Sakhalin, Korea, the Kwantung area of the Liaodong peninsula in China, and most islands in the South Seas.[6] Japan also wielded considerable political and economic influence over much of China through military threat and installed a puppet government in "Manchukuo," which allowed de facto Japanese rule in Manchuria. By 1945, after numerous military victories in the Pacific region, the imperial reach extended to Vietnam, the Philippines, Burma, Malaysia, Indonesia, Brunei, Timor, Hong Kong, and Singapore.

However, viewing Japan's forceful acquisition of the Ainu homelands and the Ryukyu Kingdom during the Meiji era (1868–1912) as obvious acts of colonialism, we date the inception of Japan's modern empire to 1869, when Japanese officials unilaterally laid claim to the island now known as Hokkaido, and firmly locate Okinawa within colonial history. Naturalized as "Japan proper" in colonialist rhetoric, both Hokkaido and Okinawa have commonly been dismissed as "internal colonies," which obfuscates the violent enterprise of territorial appropriation, economic exploitation, and cultural repression that enabled the "Japanization" of these lands and their people. The explicit inclusion of Hokkaido and Okinawa in Japan's colonial history in this volume functions to challenge the Meiji elite's self-interested characterization of the exploitation of these lands as "development" of "Japanese territory" and their subjugation of the indigenous inhabitants as "protection." Committed to a project of deconstructing imperialist discourse, the contributors herein offer criticisms of colonial euphemisms and justifications, reflecting on the ways the cases of Hokkaido and Okinawa both reinforce and complicate received notions of colonial operations generally, and Japan's empire specifically.

In an attempt to fill a gap, we include two chapters on Hokkaido, which to an even greater degree than Okinawa has been too often overlooked in scholarship.[7] In doing so, we also seek to emphasize the crucial role the colonization of Hokkaido played in constructing the modern Japanese nation and empire. It is our presumption that the fledgling nation-state of "Japan" (established in 1868) and the island now called "Hokkaido" (claimed in

1869) were constructed in tandem and that these processes were inextricably linked. Borrowing the words of Leo Ching, we affirm that "cultural and political identities, be they metropolitan or colonial, do not exist prior to the processes of colonialism."[8] Thus, Japan's identity as an "advanced," "civilized" nation endowed with a natural political, economic, and cultural superiority was forged in opposition to depictions of other Asian countries as "backward," "barbaric" and incapable of surviving in modern times. These differences between colonizer and colonized were not manifest realities, but rather products of colonial discourse employed to validate Japanese imperial expansion in Asia. Before Japan consolidated its political and economic infrastructure and embarked on imperial expansion through the Sino-Japanese War (1894–1895) and Russo-Japanese War (1904–1905), Hokkaido was fertile ground in which imperial ideology, legal rationalizations, assimilation policies, and settlement campaigns were conceived, implemented, and tested. The colonial experiments conducted during these early years of empire informed, in significant ways, the political, economic, and cultural strategies in the later "formal" empire.

Although not the focus of this work, the question of what should constitute the end of Japan's empire also deserves reconsideration. The year 1945 might mark the conclusion of the Asia-Pacific War and the liberation of Japan's colonial subjects, but residual effects manifest in many obvious and subtle ways to this day. The continued presence of U.S. bases in Okinawa with Japanese official sanction, the charged protests against prime ministers' visits to Yasukuni Shrine, territorial disputes over the Dokdo/Takeshima Islands and the "Northern Territories" with Korea and Russia respectively, and the ongoing debates about Japan's responsibility for Korean survivors of Hiroshima and Nagasaki are just a few examples of the ways the colonial past lives on in the present.

To help our readers, the next few pages present the broadest outline of Japan's complex imperial history that spanned more than seventy years. Richer detail provided in individual essays will build on this preliminary narrative and further contextualize each colonial case.

. . .

After the overthrow of the Tokugawa shogunate in 1868, which brought centuries of samurai rule to an end, the leaders of the newly installed government characterized their victory as a "restoration" of imperial rule. Scrambling to establish authority and consolidate a disparate population along the lines of a Western model of the nation-state, the elite quickly defined the most pressing tasks—foreign relations, the tax system, and the "development" (*kaitaku*) of Ezo, "land of the barbarians," the then Japanese appellation for the island of Hokkaido.[9] This last priority, making Ezo into "a little Japan," was understood to serve a number of goals, including generating much-needed revenue for the nation-building project, showing the emperor's "power and prestige to the world," and discouraging Russian designs on the territory. Elites soon realized that resettling disgruntled former samurai, who had lost their status and economic privileges, could also help dissipate pent-up dissatisfaction that had resulted in numerous violent uprisings. To that end, a colonial farming militia (*tondenhei*) was established, and general campaigns for migration to Hokkaido were pursued to alleviate worsening poverty in rural areas of the mainland. Already during the Tokugawa period (1600–1868) a certain degree of economic and political subordination at the hands of shogunal and Matsumae domain officials contributed to weakening Ainu communities. With the installation of the colonial government under the aegis of the Hokkaido Development Agency in 1869, Japan commenced full-scale economic exploitation of the island's resources and massive migration from the mainland so that by the end of the nineteenth century Japanese settlers greatly outnumbered the deprived and displaced Ainu population.

The Ryukyu Kingdom had its own long and troubled history with Japan. After nearly two centuries of political independence, vigorous maritime trade with much of Asia, and a flourishing of arts and architecture, the Ryukyu Islands were invaded by the Satsuma domain in 1609. For the next 270 years, Satsuma dispatched countless directives, injunctions, and judgments on matters of trade, governance, and cultural practices, forcing Ryukyuan kings to negotiate a delicate balance of power with Satsuma, the central shogunal officials of Japan, and the Ming and Qing courts in China. This quasi-autonomous status came to an end in 1879, a decade after the Meiji Restoration, when Japan officially, and unilaterally, annexed "Okinawa," in what is called the "disposition of Ryukyu" (*Ryūkyū shobun*).[10] Despite having proclaimed the Ryukyu Islands Japanese territory, the disregard for the Okinawan population was extreme, evidenced by Tokyo's rejection of Japanese governor Uesugi Shigenori's proposal that would have greatly alleviated poverty without necessitating either an increased tax burden on Okinawans or financial support from the central government. Impoverishment, unemployment, and illiteracy engendered by Japan's singular and oppressive economic policies toward Okinawa were then attributed to an inherent inferiority of the people of the islands. Those able to migrate to the mainland encountered fierce discrimination in employment and lodging. Assimilation rhetoric may have suggested that Okinawans could become national citizens and the emperor's subjects through the eradication of local customs and the adoption of the Japanese language, but economic, political, and cultural campaigns that ensured hardship, privation, and stigmatization made clear that they were not to be considered fully "Japanese." Okinawa's marginalized position in the nation was made alarmingly evident in 1945 by the Battle of Okinawa, one of the bloodiest battles fought in the Pacific, when the Japanese Imperial Army mercilessly and indiscriminately killed civilians and forced them to commit suicide.

After more than two decades of national consolidation and colonial exploits in Hokkaido and Okinawa, the Meiji leaders had established the foundation of Japan's political and economic infrastructure and inculcated nationalistic sentiment in its citizenry as deemed appropriate to a modern nation-state. The attempt to secure a colonial foothold in Taiwan in 1874 through the Taiwan Expedition had failed, but following triumph in the Sino-Japanese War in 1895, Japan ushered in its age of formal empire. The Treaty of Shimonoseki granted possession of Taiwan to Japan in perpetuity. As a measure to stave off anti-Japanese sentiment, Taiwanese were initially allowed to relocate to mainland China, yet for over ten years the colonial rulers met vigorous resistance to which they responded with violent repression. The colonial administration quickly embarked on plans to control and modernize police, transportation, communication, trade, and financial systems. It gradually promoted public education and health facilities and introduced agricultural innovations and new tax schemes. Although these did bring about various improvements in the lives of some Taiwanese, the colonial policies were crafted to benefit local Japanese settlers and the needs of the metropole. This was most evident in the policy of confiscating "untitled land" and selling it to Japanese migrants and corporate interests. With sugarcane and rice production dominating the economy, Taiwan proved to be a relatively profitable colony for the Japanese empire, evidenced by the fact that it did not receive governmental subsidies after 1904.[11] Nevertheless Taiwanese experienced double standards in education and employment as well as constant surveillance by an extensive police force that was charged with a variety of tasks, including suppressing dissidents, taking the census, collecting taxes, and promoting and enforcing economic, social, and cultural programs.

Long before Korea's official annexation in 1910, Japan jockeyed to promote its national interests on the peninsula. As early as 1873, a faction in the Meiji government advocated an invasion of Korea, but officials of the Iwakura clique quashed the idea, arguing that Japan was not yet prepared to take on such a costly and provocative endeavor. In 1876, using "gunboat diplomacy," a tactic to which it had previously fallen victim, Japan pressured Korea to agree to unequal trade, the opening of ports, and extraterritorial rights for Japanese. In the ensuing years, Japan incited numerous confrontations with Korea in which its covetous officials attempted to take advantage of the escalating factionalism within the Yi court. Still, it was the stunning victory over Russia in 1905 that lent Japan vital leverage in negotiations. Granted "permission" by major Western powers to make Korea a "protectorate," Japan steadily took over the political and economic reins in the peninsula. In 1910, the Korean emperor was forced to sign away absolute sovereignty to the emperor of Japan. Japanese official and commercial interests were favored through the seizure and allocation of fertile or useful land, protection of markets for Japanese products, and numerous structural and tax incentives. To deal with problems of a growing population and increased wages in the metropolitan center, the colonial government tightly managed the production and cost of food and the flow of labor. Opposition to Japan's rule, most notably the March 1st Movement in 1919, was met with overwhelming military repression.

More so than other colonies, Taiwan and Korea constituted "agricultural appendages" of Japan,[12] providing much of the staple foodstuffs, especially rice, for the main islands. As the war dragged on, imperializing (*kōminka*) policies that began in 1937 further impinged on everyday life as the colonizers tried to instill "Japanese spirit" in the colonized. Taiwanese and Koreans were urged to abandon their "backward" traditions and to adopt Japanese daily customs and cultural practices. Additionally, in the 1940s, they faced the most thorough assimilation campaigns, exemplified by, for example, compulsory Japanese language acquisition, name changes, and emperor worship at Shinto shrines. At the same time that the people of Taiwan and Korea were assured that they were Japanese citizens, a wide array of publications disparaged their histories, societies, and cultures, effectively maintaining the divide between colonizer and colonized. Taiwanese and Korean men were first encouraged to volunteer and then from 1945 drafted into military service. Slogans such as "Japan and Korea as One" (*nissen ittai*) aimed to channel all human and natural resources into the war effort and obfuscate the ever-increasing burden on colonial subjects in these occupied territories.

The 1905 defeat of Russia also allowed Japan to take possession of the southern half of Sakhalin, which Japan named Karafuto, and the Kwantung territory on the Liaodong peninsula. The latter aided Japan in making crucial inroads into Manchuria and China. Strategic military bases were built in Port Arthur and Dalian. Japan's control of Manchuria extended out from the network of tracks of the Southern Manchurian Railroad, over which Japan held absolute authority. Japan wielded considerable influence backed by the constant military presence of the Kwantung Army, strategic alliances with local leaders, and its ascendancy in the economy. In 1931, the Kwantung Army, ignoring the chain of command, sabotaged a section of the Southern Manchurian Railroad and then blamed Chinese radicals. This, now known as the Manchurian Incident, precipitated the full-scale invasion of Manchuria and establishment of Manchukuo, a puppet-state of Japan, in 1932. Responding to a growing economic and population crisis in the metropole, Japanese colonial administrators implemented a massive immigration campaign and diversified Manchuria's economy according to state and corporate interests.

Another feather in the cap of Japan's formal empire was acquired in 1914 when, taking advantage of the outbreak of hostilities in Europe, Japan demanded a transfer of Germany's mandate in the colonial territories of the Marshall, Caroline, and Mariana Islands in Micronesia. This distant and diverse collection of islands was known to Japanese as the South Seas (*Nan'yō*). Since the 1880s and 1890s, popular adventure novels and firsthand accounts by civilian attachments to naval training missions in the South Seas had fed the Japanese popular imagination fanciful images of a tropical paradise, enormous commercial profits, and exciting escapades in areas inhabited by "barbaric natives." First a naval and then, from 1922, a civil administration oversaw the typical political and economic integration of the well over 1,300 islands into the empire. Preferential support to Japanese individuals and companies generated substantial commercial profits, and an imported labor force of poor Japanese, Okinawans, and Koreans quickly outnumbered Micronesians. Material conditions may have initially improved for indigenous inhabitants, but social stratification clearly favored Japanese colonists, and in the last years of the war Micronesians endured some of the fiercest battles between Japan and the United States.

Beginning in 1940, the former Asian colonies and territories of Britain, France, Holland, Germany, and the United States fell into Japanese hands after bloody combat in the Pacific. For instance, Japan took over French

Indochina (Vietnam) in 1940, the Philippines and Hong Kong were under Japanese occupation soon after the attack on Pearl Harbor, and 1942 saw the invasions of Burma, Singapore, and Indonesia. Japan's defeat in 1945 meant liberation for most of its colonized and occupied territories. Still, the legacy of this history continues to fundamentally shape political and economic relations in Asia.

Connecting Texts, Contexts, and Critiques

Our project is two-fold: if the primary sources accentuate the wide array of representations of the empire, the critical essays illuminate the encompassing human involvement, underscoring that people of all walks of life were not merely implicated in but inevitably or willingly *participated* in the expansion and management of the empire. The contributors have uncovered a corpus of original materials that represent the profusion of discourse during the colonial era, and the project is conceived partly out of a desire to bring these previously unearthed sources to a wider audience of scholars, students, and individuals interested in thinking about the many forms colonialism and imperialism assume.

The primary sources included in this volume expound on a set of questions and dilemmas that were defining features of Japan's imperial policies and institutions. We feature a customary colonial tool—legal documents—that did not just restrict, regulate, and punish individuals and communities, but also played a crucial role in constructing colonial identities. The 1899 Hokkaido Former Natives Protection Law exemplifies the potency of legal doctrines for imperial conquest, which were deployed in Hokkaido under the pretense of "protection," echoing the "developmentalist" rhetoric employed by the United States in subjugating America's native peoples. Analysis of legal language and its underpinning logic offers insights into how laws masked violent and discriminatory practices.

In contrast to laws, sources such as manga and children's stories might at first seem innocuous and even unrelated to the colonial quest. The effects of these popular media are not directly linked to military actions. Rather, they help shape an imaginary realm, one that generates imperialist aspirations and builds a consensus for imperial conquests. Hence, the heroic tale of Dankichi's adventure in the South Seas in manga format, presented in the last chapter of this book, became an imperialist fantasy shared by many Japanese children and adults in the 1930s. In it, and many other colonial works, the theme of the "barbaric" Other looms large. Thus, juvenile publications, along with other popular and practical cultural texts such as literary texts and cookbooks, worked in tandem with political proclamations, economic treatises, and legal codes to construct the prevailing perceptions of and attitudes toward Japan's colonial subjects and imperial pursuits.

While the organization in this anthology generally follows a historical chronology of Japan's colonial aggression, its theoretical and thematic currents warrant discussion. Each primary source in translation is paired with an essay that suggests one of the ways to corroborate its meaning in relation to imperial discourse. Because any study of imperialism has to first identify the mechanisms of power, the point of departure for the contributors to this volume is an inquiry into the workings of power in a variety of cultural texts and contexts.

Compared to its European counterparts, Japan's empire as a main subject of postcolonial studies has had a shorter history, spanning just over three decades. The theories of colonial encounters modeled after the European experiences have thus served, to a certain degree, as points of reference and barometers for understanding the Japanese case. Drawing on intellectuals such as Michel Foucault, the contributing scholars in this volume investigate the processes of subjection, surveillance, and subordination that are underlying operations of power. The Althusserian notion of "ideological state apparatuses" and the significance of social practices in constituting the subject also inform the scholarship herein, which problematizes independent subjectivity outside of ideology. Edward Said's theorization of the Orient helps us understand how cultural productions of the Other both feed and feed off of the hierarchical relations between two entities. Examinations of the human psyche trapped in the colonial milieu benefit from the work of Albert Memmi and Homi Bhabha on identity formation. Contributors are inspired by and readily make use of the conceptual and linguistic tools that these and other theoreticians of postcolonial studies have advanced. At the same time, in addition to reinforcing such theories, the works in this volume shed new light on and complicate ideas and themes long studied in Western colonial contexts.

In addition to theoretical concerns woven through the essays, this anthology presents intertwining dialogues on intersecting subject matters. While Komori Yōichi showcases the juridical implementation of the expansionist aspirations in Hokkaido through a close analysis of the vocabulary and tone of colonial logic, Michele Mason's essay shows how fiction metaphorically emptied the space of Hokkaido, facilitating the incursion of Japanese settlers. Despite ample evidence that testifies to the history of the indigenous population, Japanese literary depictions of Hokkaido, such as "The Shores of the Sorachi River," primarily and consistently evoke an uninhabited and richly resourced island in need of human "development." These first two chapters speak to the way words and ideas bring into being very material and tragic realities, focusing sharp legal and literary lenses on Japan's earliest modern colonial project.

Komori's and Robert Tierney's essays emphasize the function of emerging educational institutions and disciplines in producing "knowledge" that underwrote and rationalized the empire. These scholars map the multidirectional pathways between the theories, histories, and conceptual frameworks formulated by intellectuals in fields such as archeology, linguistics, and anthropology and colonial policy and expansion. Although they treat two very different geographic locations, Hokkaido and Taiwan respectively, each conveys the disturbing fact of the complicity of academic institutions, scholarly research, and educational models in Japan's empire.

As brutal and oppressive as institutional and official colonial subjugation was, its more subtle and nuanced, but nevertheless lasting effects were inscribed in human psychology. Davinder Bhowmik most forcefully employs Homi Bhabha's theory of "hybridity" to discuss the split and straddling identities of an Okinawan policeman in the short fictional work "Officer Ukuma." The protagonist pursues access to power and prestige through state-sanctioned roles only to confront in the end how he is structurally alienated in the power hierarchy. Tierney's essay on the short story "Demon Bird," which simulates ethnographic recordings of the irrational, superstitious colonial Other, elucidates how the narrator repeatedly undermines his own credibility as purveyor of "objective" knowledge. When read carefully, Tierney argues, the story does not necessarily reinforce colonialist logic, but rather calls into question the "civilized" nature of the colonizer and exposes the unsettling, violent, and chaotic conditions of colonial reality. Read together, Bhowmik's and Tierney's essays highlight the precarious state of colonial subjectivities and inevitable contradictions in colonial rhetoric. Thus, Officer Ukuma's search for professional success proves futile in the end, and the narrator of "Demon Bird" cannot but betray the slippage in the colonial implementation of ethnography as a scholarly discipline.

Working with two unique texts, Kimberly Kono and Helen Lee focus attention on colonial collaboration in the gendered interior sphere of the home. Kono elaborates on women's participation in the empire by introducing the term "imperialist motherhood" in her treatment of *Manchu Girl*, a Japanese woman's "autobiographical" work that recounts her mission to assimilate a Manchurian maid. The colonizer-colonized relationship rests on a trope of intimacy between a "motherly guardian" and an "adoptive daughter" in a narrative that prioritizes the dilemmas and desires of the narrating Japanese colonizer even as she purports to report honestly the thoughts and voice of her house servant. Lee's essay delineates the challenging tasks of mothers who were called upon to maximize nutrition and produce healthy bodies for the state in colonial homes in Korea during the total mobilization era, the final phase of Japan's empire during which all imperial subjects were plagued by dire food shortages. *The Manual of Home Cuisine*, Lee notes, dishes up much more than just recipes and practical tips for procuring ingredients at a time of scarcity. Its prescriptions for spiritual nourishment are meant to harness patriotic sentiment and foster "Japanese-ness" in a community far removed from the "homeland." Kono and Lee link in important ways the seemingly immaterial realm of creating and maintaining national/colonial identities with material conditions and displays of national allegiance. Attempts by the narrator of *Manchu Girl* to "Japanize" her Manchurian charge through her coaching on proper manners, clothing, and language resonates with the cookbook's exhortations that Japanese subjects demonstrate their loyalty to the emperor and the colonial cause by performing daily proper prayers and etiquette at mealtimes.

The colonialist logic and imperial zeal that manifested mostly in the adult world also penetrated the realm of children's imagination, revealing how extensive the reach of colonial propaganda was at the time. Kawamura Minato's and Kota Inoue's essays investigate two distinctly different children's works. Kawamura offers a nuanced reading and contextualization of the serial manga *The Adventures of Dankichi*, whose protagonist lives out the adventurous imperialist dream by traveling to an unknown island in the tropical South Seas and subjugating the savage Other, becoming their king. Here, imperialist ambitions are unabashedly exhibited, even glorified. Extremely racialized visuals, shocking to today's reader, work with a storyline that bolsters the natural superiority of the little Japanese leader who recruits the "barbarians" into his "elite army corps." In contrast, Inoue's primary text, "Wolf Forest, Basket Forest, and Thief Forest," seems a rather benign, even humorous, chronicle of a group of human farmers who carry out tension-filled negotiations with mischievous inhabitants of the surrounding forests. Inoue's close reading, however, excavates a not-so-obvious critique of colonial usurpation illustrated in the tale. Though the tone of the original works vary on a spectrum ranging from outrageously jingoistic to subtly critical, Kawamura and Inoue each point to the broad circulation of such sources that collectively incubated ideas endorsing the foundational ideologies of imperialism and belied the violation and violence inherent in colonial processes.

In *Reading Colonial Japan: Text, Context, and Critique*, we have endeavored to draw some of the cultural and historical contours of Japan's age of empire. Revealing operations of power in the intersections of cultural production and colonial practices has been an overarching goal. Needless to say, each essay in this collection represents just one reading of its paired primary source. We imagine there is much more to say about these original texts when viewed through different theoretical or disciplinary frameworks or approached with different intellectual interests. We invite readers—both Asian specialists and scholars and students of colonialism—to articulate additional interpretations and critical commentary. It would be gratifying if these primary documents and analytical essays stimulated further discussion of the serious and persisting questions of colonialism of the past and inspired meaningful reflection on the implications for our present moment.

Notes

1. Ainu Moshir, literally "the land of humans," is the Ainu name for their native land, which was populated by many independent Ainu communities. The Ryukyu Islands were unified in 1429 by King Shō Hashi of the central region (Chūzan), and were thereafter known as the Ryukyu Kingdom. In this volume, we will follow the custom of writing the the word "Ryukyu" without long vowels.

2. The first two volumes of the trilogy on Japan's modern empire were instrumental in launching Japanese colonial studies. See Ramon H. Myers and Mark R. Peattie, eds., *The Japanese Colonial Empire, 1895–1945* (Princeton, NJ: Princeton University Press, 1987), and Peter Duus, Ramon H. Myers, and Mark R. Peattie, eds., *The Japanese Informal Empire in China, 1895–1937* (Princeton, NJ: Princeton University Press, 1989).

3. The list of such works is ever growing, and while not exhaustive, here are some examples that have come out in just the last decade or so. Jennifer Robertson's *Takarazuka: Sexual Politics and Popular Culture in Modern Japan* (1998), Louise Young's *Japan's Total Empire: Manchuria and the Culture of Wartime Imperialism* (1998), Leo T. S. Ching's *Becoming "Japanese": Colonial Taiwan and the Politics of Identity Formation* (2001), Faye Yuan Kleeman's *Under an Imperial Sun: Japanese Colonial Literature of Taiwan and the South* (2003), Sabine Früstück's *Colonizing Sex: Sexology and Social Control in Modern Japan* (2003), Prasenjit Duara's

Sovereignty and Authenticity: Manchukuo and the East Asian Modern (2003), Alexis Dudden's *Japan's Colonization of Korea: Discourse and Power* (2005), Miriam Silverberg's *Erotic Grotesque Nonsense: The Mass Culture of Japanese Modern Times* (2006), Michael Baskett's *The Attractive Empire: Transnational Film Culture in Imperial Japan* (2008), Mark E. Caprio's *Japanese Assimilation Policies in Colonial Korea, 1910–1945* (2009), and Mark Driscoll's *Absolute Erotic, Absolute Grotesque: The Living, Dead, and Undead in Japan's Imperialism, 1895–1945* (2010). Consider also the works of contributors to this volume, including Davinder Bhowmik's *Writing Okinawa: Narrative Acts of Identity and Resistance* (2008), Kimberly Kono's *Romance, Family and Nation in Japanese Colonial Literature* (2010), and Robert Tierney's *Tropics of Savagery: The Culture of Japanese Empire in Comparative Frame* (2010).

4. Lori Watt, *When Empire Comes Home: Repatriation and Reintegration in Postwar Japan* (Cambridge, MA: Harvard University Press, 2009).

5. Miyada Setsuko, *Chōsen minshū to kōminka seisaku* (Koreans and Kōminka Policies) (Tokyo: Miraisha, 1985).

6. Taiwan, Korea, and Southern Sakhalin were sovereign colonies over which Japan had exclusive control. Japan first "leased" Kwantung in 1905 and in 1915 extended the lease until 1998. Japan was accorded a mandate in the South Seas in 1914, and this mandate nominally fell under the authority of the League of Nations Council, until Japan withdrew from the league in 1933. We have not included Tsingtao (Qingdao) of the Shandong peninsula, as it was under Japanese control for the relatively short period of four years.

7. Okinawa's distance from the mainland, its sacrifice during World War II (exemplified by the Battle of Okinawa), and the continued presence of U.S. military bases with the Japanese state's approval make the legacy of Japanese colonialism there manifestly clear. Excellent scholarship on Okinawan history and politics and collections of translated works by Okinawan authors and poets published over the last ten years have expanded on the many ways colonial relations live on in Okinawan politics and society today. See, for example, Laura Hein and Mark Selden, eds., *Islands of Discontent: Okinawan Responses to Japanese and American Power* (Lanham, MD: Rowman and Littlefield, 2003), Glen D. Hook and Richard Siddle, eds., *Japan and Okinawa: Structure and Subjectivity* (London: RoutledgeCurzon, 2003), and Mike Molasky and Steve Rabson, eds., *Southern Exposure: Modern Japanese Literature from Okinawa* (Honolulu: University of Hawai'i Press, 2000). In contrast, the contemporary repercussions of Hokkaido's colonial era are much less obvious, and scholars have taken longer to turn their attention to its colonial history. An excellent contribution to this subject, however, is Richard Siddle's *Race, Resistance and the Ainu of Japan* (London: Routledge, 1996).

8. Leo T. S. Ching, *Becoming "Japanese": Colonial Taiwan and the Politics of Identity Formation* (Berkeley: University of California Press, 2001), 11.

9. These are laid out in the Iwakura Proposal (*Iwakura teigi*, February 28, 1869). Tanaka Akira, *Hokkaidō to Meiji ishin* (Hokkaido and the Meiji Restoration) (Sapporo: Hokkaidō daigaku tosho kankōkai, 2000), 26.

10. For a helpful explanation of the "disposition of Ryukyu," see the "Epilogue

and Conclusions" chapter of Gregory Smits' *Visions of Ryukyu: Identity and Ideology in Early Modern Thought and Politics* (Honolulu: University of Hawaiʻi Press, 1999), 143–62.

11. In contrast, in Korea and Manchuria subsidies were necessary until Japan's defeat in 1945. Samuel Pao-San Ho, "Colonialism and Development: Korea, Taiwan, and Kwantung," in *The Japanese Colonial Empire, 1895–1945*, eds. Ramon H. Myers and Mark R. Peattie (Princeton, NJ: Princeton University Press, 1987), 358.

12. Ibid., 350.

CHAPTER ONE

TEXT

The Shores of the Sorachi River

KUNIKIDA DOPPO

CONTEXT

Hokkaido

CRITIQUE

Writing Ainu Out/Writing Japanese In: The "Nature" of Japanese Colonialism in Hokkaido

MICHELE M. MASON

KUNIKIDA DOPPO (1871–1908) is widely regarded as having played a formative role in the creation of modern Japanese literature. A child born out of wedlock to a former samurai and a servant, Doppo grew up in rural southwestern Japan, which is said to have imbued him with a love of nature. He converted to Christianity in 1891 after he gave up his dream to be a politician. He studied English literature at university and was later active in various literary and poetic circles in Tokyo. He was a war correspondent for the journal *The Nation's Companion* (*Kokumin no tomo*) during the Russo-Japanese War (1904–1905). Doppo died at the age of 36 from tuberculosis.

Not unlike many of his contemporaries, Doppo, for a time, envisioned Hokkaido as a utopian space. He convinced his lover, Sasaki Nobuko, to elope and "escape" to Hokkaido where, it was imagined, the restrictions of Japanese traditions did not reach. The marriage and his stay in Hokkaido were short-lived. Doppo's "Unforgettable People" (*Wasure'enu hitobito*, 1898) and "Musashino" (*Musashino*, 1901) have attracted much scholarly attention, although later works, for instance those in his collection entitled *Fate* (*Unmei*, 1906), earned him critical acclaim during his life.

In "The Shores of the Sorachi River" (*Sorachigawa no kishibe*, 1902), the male protagonist travels to Hokkaido to buy some land. His endeavors to find local officials, who can advise him about property along the Sorachi River, force him to travel about the "newly opened" island. From his train and lodging windows, from atop a horse-drawn wagon, and during his walks in the mountains and through a rugged mining outpost, "I" observes the unfamiliar landscape of the northern island and muses on the relationship between humans and nature. The narrator's inner dialogue chronicles his mercurial moods, ranging from ecstatic to despondent according to the ever-changing weather, and reveals his sense of alienation from both society and nature.

The Shores of the Sorachi River

KUNIKIDA DOPPO

TRANSLATION BY MICHELE M. MASON

Part One

I stayed in Sapporo for five days. It was only five days, but in that time my fond feelings for Hokkaido multiplied many times over.

Even the wilderness of the northeast inspired devotion in me, a person who grew up in the densely populated central region of our country's mainland and was accustomed to scenery of mountains and fields that had been conquered by human power. Upon seeing Hokkaido, the northernmost part of the country, how could my heart not be moved?! Sapporo is said to be the Tokyo of Hokkaido, but I was all but bewitched by the many sights there.

I set out alone from Sapporo for the shores of the Sorachi River on the morning of September 25. Had it been Tokyo, it still would have been warm, but here I was wearing my Western winter clothing. Autumn was waning and the bare trees told me that winter was chasing close behind.

My goal was to meet a prefectural official who had surveyed the shores of the Sorachi River and to consult with him about choosing some land. However, I was completely in the dark about the geography. Also, since I didn't know where the prefectural official was stationed, and neither did any of my acquaintances in Sapporo, I boarded the train headed for Sorachibuto feeling disheartened.

The fields of Ishikari were lost in the low-lying clouds, and as I stared out from the train window onto the fields and mountains, I was overwhelmed by the frightening power of nature. Here there was no love, no compassion. To look out on this savage, lonely, heartless, and yet magnificent sight, it appeared to me all the more that nature scorns the powerlessness and fragility of humans.

I wondered what several people in the same train car were thinking about me, a young man silently sitting in the corner next to a window with his white face buried in the collar of his overcoat. The passengers' conversations included crops, forestry, the soil, and how to extract gold from the unlimited natural resources of the area. Some were talking loudly while they sipped alcohol, and others joked around as they smoked their pipes. Most of them had met for the first time on the train. I was the only one who didn't join in, and I kept myself apart from the rest, sinking into my own thoughts. I had never put any thought to the question of how you are supposed to get along in society. I simply went from moment to moment concentrating on how to make my own way. Therefore, my fellow passengers seemed to be of another world, and I could not help but feel that between them and me stretched an impassable, deep valley. I thought to myself that even today, with me isolated in a corner of this train car full of people passing through the Ishikari plain, was like any other day of my life. Ah, the loneliness! Even though I willingly walk outside of society, in the depths of my heart I cannot bear the loneliness.

If it had been a fine, fall day and clear on the high peaks, I could have escaped my gloomy mood and relaxed. But the clouds hung increasingly lower, and the forest was enveloped in the mist so that no matter where I looked there was not even a flicker of light. I fell into a nearly unbearable state of melancholy.

The train arrived at a certain stop that splits off to the coal mine at Utashinai, and most of the passengers disembarked to transfer to other trains, leaving behind just two others besides myself. The train ran on a straight line, piercing the huge forests in which not one person has tread since the beginning of time—thousands of years. Layer upon layer of ash-colored mist, appearing and then disappearing as if a living being, was silently wafting and floating.

All of a sudden a man asked me, "Where are you headed?" He was around forty years old, with a masculine build, long hair, a square face, sharp eyes, and a big nose—a man who seemed a rogue at a glance. His manners suggested he wasn't an official or a craftsman. He wasn't a farmer or a merchant either. In fact, he was the kind of man whom you would only see in a place like Hokkaido. He was the adventurer type that always first dominates any unopened land.

"I plan to go to Sorachibuto."

"On the business of the prefecture?" He took me for a minor official for the Hokkaido prefectural office.

"Oh no, I'm here to buy some land."

"Oh I see. I don't know where you plan to look in Sorachibuto, but it seems there isn't anything valuable there anymore."

"I wonder, can I get to the shores of the Sorachi River from Sorachibuto?"

"I think you should be able to, but I can't be sure without knowing where on the Sorachi River you are headed. . . ."

"In the area where the group of settlers from Wakayama prefecture are, there are supposed to be two prefectural officers. That's where I'm aiming for. At any rate, I'm planning on going out as far as Sorachibuto and asking there."

"Is that so? Well then, when you come to Sorachibuto you should go to the lodging house called Miura Inn. The owner knows a lot about those things, so asking him would be a good idea. Since the roads aren't open yet, you have to take roundabout ways to get to places that are even fairly close. So, for someone who doesn't know the area getting around will be very difficult."

Then, he talked about various things: the difficulties of clearing land; the very different challenges depending on the quality of the land; the fact that you can't easily get to the markets with a valuable harvest because of the inconvenient transportation; and the way to use tenant farmers. I had heard some of these things from my friends in Sapporo, but taking in all that this man spoke of, I could only thank him for his kindness.

Finally, the train arrived at a desolate station. I noticed that altogether there were no more than twenty travelers who got off the train with me. The train returned from whence it came.

I saw that this small station, surrounded by forest, was nothing more than a lonely island. Besides two or three small buildings in the vicinity of the train stop, there was nothing that had any connection to humans. The long-reverberating whistle of the train echoed in the forest, and when the sound diminished and finally died out, suddenly the silent, desolate island was left behind.

Three horse-drawn wagons were waiting. Silently people boarded them. I also got on board along with the man who had been in the train with me earlier.

Two stocky, Hokkaido-bred horses, one sturdy young man, and six passengers set off without knowing the particular destination. I had the sense that I was "in the middle of nowhere." Really, it was the case that had I asked myself where I was going, I couldn't have answered.

The three horse-drawn wagons were separated by about one hundred yards, and because mine was at the tail end of the line, I could see clearly how the others bumped along as they traveled the road filled with potholes. The mist swept over the forest, cut across the road, and then entered the forest again. The tree leaves, dyed a deep red, fell from the branches, two or three dancing behind one of the wagons. The driver gave a strong lash to the horse, and shouted out, "We'll arrive soon!"

The man from earlier called out "Please stop in front of the Miura Inn" and looked back at me. I nodded and thanked him for his kindness. No one in the wagon spoke a word, and with anxious faces they all fell deeply into thought. Because the driver once again applied a forceful snap of the whip and sounded a bugle, the small-bodied yet robust and hardy horse of the north galloped off.

Slowly the forest opened up, and just as I noted that two or three of the colonists' houses had appeared, all of a sudden we came out onto a plain. On both sides of the wide road, what looked like merchant houses flew by and the area had the characteristic look of a town in newly cleared land. The wagon ran through this stretch with its bugle valiantly announcing its approach.

Part Two

I arrived at Miura Inn and immediately called for the owner. I asked him the way to the shores of the Sorachi River and told him the details of my plan. However, the proprietor suggested that it would be much more convenient for me to go back to Utashinai and approach and cross the mountains from there.

"The next train would get you into Utashinai before sundown, so if you stay tonight in Utashinai, tomorrow you can ask around and head out. Utashinai is different from here in that some people from the prefectural office are there. They might know where the man named Ida is."

Hearing this, I agreed. However, I had come to Sorachibuto believing that it was best to advance along the Sorachi River in order to know the whereabouts of the prefectural agent, Mr. Ida, whom I hoped to meet. However, to get to the shores of the Sorachi River from Sorachibuto without a guide would be impossible, and from the owner of Miura Inn I heard for the first time about the lack of proper roads. So, I heeded the caution of the owner and decided to go around to Utashinai. Lonely and alone on the second floor of the Miura Inn, I waited for the train, which was due more than two hours later.

Looking about, I saw a field in front of the inn. Sticking up here and there were a few trees that had been left when the others had been cut down. Perhaps because of the strong wind the trunks were naked with only a few yellow leaves sticking to the branches. Even those, in the time that I watched, fell randomly to the ground. On top of the wind came the rain. The rain clouds closed off the distant view, but close-by there stood an oak tree about thirty feet tall. The thick leaves made strange sounds as they were hit by the rain and quivered in the wind. Not one person passed on the road.

It was certainly not enjoyable there, knowing not a soul and without anyone with whom to talk, to be resting against the window of the inn and staring out on the falling autumn rain. I unexpectedly remembered my mother, father, younger brother, and good friends in Tokyo and presently felt what great warmth of human love I had been surrounded by until then. As I yearned to muster up my manly spirit and follow my ideals—there in the forest to search for a land of freedom—I roused my heart so that I definitely would not become womanly. However, in short, ideals became cold and human feelings became warm. Nature is brutal and intimacy with it is difficult; society is dear and is the appropriate place to make a nest.

I passed the two hours forlornly. Just when I thought the rain was letting up, the sound of a bugle-horn rang from afar. When I stuck my head out to look, there came a horse-drawn wagon nearing at a gallop that was being struck by a thread-like rain that fell at a slant. I boarded the wagon and once again set off for the train station, leaving Miura Inn behind.

There were just a few people on the train. I was the only one in the cabin I entered, but being alone wasn't pleasant and I was thinking I should change my cabin. Leaving that thought aside, I leaned my body against the corner of the train car that had become dark from the rain and fog. I was gazing out on the movement of the clouds in the darkening sky, and I absent-mindedly stared at the forest as trees passed by one after another. In times like these, you can attain a perfect serenity of mind—if you have no thoughts of self-interest and no thoughts of final destinations—if you are without feelings of love and without malicious feelings of hatred—without disappointment and without hope—only absently looking and listening. When traveling to a place where there are no familiar bonds, your body and soul tires, and finding yourself swaying with the movement of the train, occasionally you can fall into such a mental state. At times like these, by chance the scenery that comes before your eyes is etched deeply into the depths of your brain, and you are unable to forget it over many years. Now, next to the train-car window, I was just like that, watching the movement of the clouds and the birch forests.

When the train arrived in the valley of Utashinai, the rain had stopped completely and the weather had cleared. I was without a destination for lodging, and when I left the train station, two or three representatives of local inns were waiting to greet potential guests, which is understandable for such a place with a few thousand miners and several hundred crowded houses in a narrow ravine. Led by one of these men from a local inn, I walked through the stone-strewn, darkly lit town and entered a two-story building. When the wife spoke in dialect with grace and charm and welcomed me sincerely, I couldn't help smiling.

Because the proprietor came to my room without being called after the evening meal had finished, I straight away spoke of my plans and asked whether he could be of any help to me. He listened all the while smiling.

"Wait one moment. I have an idea," he said over his shoulder as he left the room. After some time, he returned.

"Luck is a strange thing. No need to worry. I've figured it out." Pleased with himself, he sat down.

"You figured it out?"

"Yes I did. I've got it all sorted. As of four days ago there has been a guest staying here. This person is someone who deals with imperial estates, and for some time he had been surveying the forest area. He did a lot of sleeping outdoors, so eventually his health broke down, and now we are taking care of him. His name is Shinohara. Since I heard that he'd been in the area of the Sorachi River the day before he showed up here at our place, I thought maybe he'd know something. So I asked him and he did. He said that there is a small cabin straight below where you cross the mountain, and a prefectural office representative is there. You can relax. This place is about two and a half miles from here, so it will be easy to get there. If you go in the morning you can come back before the afternoon."

"Thank you for everything. That's a relief. But I wonder if it's any good to go to the cabin now. They change locations so often, even at the prefectural office they didn't know where the representatives were."

"Don't worry, he'll be there. And if he's moved on, just ask whoever happens to be there. He won't have gone far."

"Well then, since I'll set out early tomorrow morning, could you ask someone to be my guide?"

"Oh, that's right. That mountain road has many forks, so you should take a guide. I'll have my son take you. He's a young boy of fourteen, but he knows his way to Sorachibuto. He should be able to guide you." The innkeeper said all these kind things, and I didn't know how to thank him. Luck is strange indeed! If I had stayed at another inn, things would not have been taken care of so expediently and kindly, for sure.

The owner was an extremely jovial man and seemed fearless and to care little for what others thought of him. The kindness he generously showed me, whom he had never seen or known before, was in keeping with what appeared to be his natural character. It was as though he made the world his home and discovered a homeland every place he traveled. He seemed to consider the people he met his friends wherever he went. I imagined that, because of this, when he saw a person in trouble, no matter who it was, as long as there was no history of malice, it was normal for him to show the sympathy of a longtime friend. After I had heard a brief story of his life from him, I found that his personality was close to what I had guessed.

In his hometown, he had had a proper estate, but when his two younger brothers grew to strongly covet his sole right to the inheritance, a contentious battle erupted among the siblings. His seventy-year-old, aging father, who loved his younger two sons, tended to agree with them about dividing the estate among the three. But if the estate were divided among them, none of the brothers would be able to maintain a family. "So I thought about it. What pettiness to be fighting with my brothers over such a trifling amount of money. All right, I'll give it to you two. I would like just one-fifth, and I'll use that to take off to Hokkaido. At that time my boy was nine. The three of us came here just like that. Well, human beings can live anywhere. Ha, ha, ha," he said laughing. "It's ironic, but both of my brothers have wasted most of the portions I gave them. I have written letters countless times encouraging them to emigrate to Hokkaido, but they don't come thinking that their tiny village on the mainland is better than anywhere else."

I learned a great deal watching what this man did and listening to what he said. Even if this owner of a small inn is not the man I think he is, and even if the figure I conjure up by adding my own imaginings is better than this owner, the following can be said: He is supremely free and independent. While living in society, he is not oppressed by it. He faces alone the limitless, natural world, yet he is happy. He strides in a lordly manner, as though master of the oceans, mountains, plains, and towns, and is not troubled in the least. No matter where he goes he enjoys the fragrance of the flowers and lives with a warm heart. Isn't he the kind of man a true man is supposed to be?!

As I felt this, my heart opened wide. From the time I left Sapporo until arriving in Utashinai my heart had been bound up with the clouds and wilted with the rain. But now there came to me a feeling of boundlessness like the limitless, deep blue sky.

At around ten that night when I went out to walk, I could see the stars between the streaks of clouds. I passed through the dark town, and when I got away from the buildings, a distance from the valley, there stretched out horizontally in front of me a black timbered forest, like a folding screen, over which the moon appeared. The floating clouds grazed the mountains and slowly erased this picture. The air was heavy and wet and in the sky was a wind, but on the ground there was a solemn silence. I could hear only the faint sound of a mountain stream. On one side of me were the mountains and on the other side an uphill path along a cliff. When I came out onto a slightly elevated open space, all of sudden raucous singing reached my ears.

Following the base of the mountains was a strip of long buildings and facing these was another strip. The songs were coming from these buildings. On one strip a few of the doors were divided, and because they were all papered doors, the light shone through brilliantly. Amid the cacophony of the *shamisen* and the harsh voices belting out melodies without care, promiscuous laughter would burst out. Who would imagine that these buildings, just like cattle sheds, made up the entertainment frontier sought out by miners in this little nook of rugged country?!

There were those who after a life of wandering became miners and prostitutes. There were people who were there to buy and others to sell. This was a dream world with crazy songs and disorderly dances. I kept going and entered an alley along one of the long buildings.

The road was muddy from the rain, and the puddles reflected the lights. The buildings turned out to be even more pathetically constructed upon a closer look. Since it was newly opened land, the papered doors on the fronts of the houses had unvarnished wood, which even in the dark could be seen clearly. The floors and roofs were low. I wondered if the papered doors extended directly from the ground to the eves, and then from a distorted gap I saw the shade of a hanging lamp. A rough, naked man was reflected like a phantom devil. A barmaid with disheveled hair and a head like a female demon was caught in the light. I heard a sound that made me think the floor had collapsed, but only sudden laughter came from the house. The shouts of "Drink!" "Sing!" "I'm gonna kill you!" "I'm gonna punch you!" and the loud laughter, harsh language, cursing, shouts of joy, scolding, and short verses of songs of romance were enough to break your heart. The tearful tunes of the *shamisen* were in one instant like a violent storm and in the next a spring rain. Amid the merriment was bloodthirstiness and amid the bloodthirstiness were bitter tears. Was it crying or laughing? Was it laughing or crying? Was it anger or singing? Was it singing or anger? Ah, life is fleeting! These people fell into this valley where until a few years ago bears slept and wolves lived. Here they stagnated. Here they became enraged. Here they sank to the bottom. The shadow of the moon chillingly illuminated it all.

I walked on past and was standing there a bit when all of a sudden the papered door of a house close by opened up and a man appeared. "Hey, the moon is out!" he cried. Looking at his upturned face, I thought he seemed to be a robust young man of twenty-six or twenty-seven, tall and with wide shoulders. He was looking all around him, but then blowing out a breath reeking of alcohol he clicked his tongue and staggered back in again.

Part Three

With the innkeeper's son faithfully guiding me, I finally set off for the shores of the Sorachi River at nine in the morning on September 26.

The weather couldn't make up its mind whether to be fine or cloudy. Just as I thought a few thin sunrays would shine through, the fog would roll in and envelop the mountaintop, the forest, and the roads. The mountain road was easier than I thought it would be, and talking with the innkeeper's son about various things as I walked along made my body and heart light.

The forest was all fall leaves, and the turning ivy leaves were dyed a deep scarlet. When the fog rolled in, the mist formed a screen, which made it seem you were seeing flowers. When the sunlight shone directly, all the leaves tinged with dew radiated like millions of strands of pearls and jasper, and I felt the entire mountain was on fire. The innkeeper's son told me about bears along the shores of the Sorachi River. Then he enthusiastically narrated several bear tales he had heard and committed to memory with his child-like heart. Descending a slope, we came to an area thick with bear grass and he stopped for a moment.

He said, "Can you hear it? The sound of the river?" He cocked his ear and continued, "You can hear it, right? That's the Sorachi River. It's just over there."

"Seems like we should be able to see it from here."

"It's not something you can see from here. It runs in the middle of the forest."

The two of us traveled a bit on a very narrow path with our heads hidden by bear grass when an old farmer-type came by. I asked for directions to the prefectural official's cabin.

"If you go just about one hundred yards, then you'll come out onto a wide, newly opened road. He's in the first cabin on the right-hand side," he said over his shoulder as he walked away.

Coming thus far from Utashinai, that old man was the only person we met. Along the way, we hadn't seen anything that looked like a cabin. Meeting this old man, I realized that there were already some pioneers who had come and settled on the shores of the Sorachi River. When we came out from the path of bear grass, there was a wide road that you would not expect to find penetrating the forest in one straight line. It was probably wider than thirty feet. Moreover, on both sides a dense thicket grew wherein there were many trees whose diameter ranged from over six to nine feet, and due to the ditches passing through, this expansive road seemed like a railroad track. However, seeing this road, I understood how great the difficulties were for the prefectural office's earnest plans for colonization.

Looking again, I saw on the right side of this road a strange makeshift cabin, which you would never see on the mainland. All around this cabin the forest had been cut and a small flat area opened up. I had successfully made it to this cabin to meet the prefectural agent, Mr. Ida, and another man.

Thanks to the polite introduction by the colonial office head, the men were friendly and accommodated my requests for consultation. Moreover, what surprised me was that they had heard of my name and had already known of me—even my jumbled writings. It turned out that, completely unbeknownst to me, I had readers in this unexpected place of Hokkaido.

After the two men listened to my plans, they opened up a map of the Sorachi River, and with their great experience appraising land, they suggested around six plots, here and there, from the twelve-acre plots of land that had been parceled out for emigrants.

Business having been completed, we moved on to small talk.

The cabins are never more than eighteen feet by twenty-four feet, and the roofs and surrounding walls are a weaving of wide shakes of bark from whole logs. The only place wood planks are used is on the floor, and you lay straw matting on that. As for the entrance, a single door, also fashioned out of the woven bark, is hung on one side. This becomes the settler's nest, the settler's house, or, you could say, his castle. In a corner a large rectangular chimney is cut, and a brazier, oven, tobacco tray, and in the winter a stove, are used there.

"When the winter comes, I wonder if I can bear it to be in such a cabin."

"Well, all of the pioneers live in these kinds of cabins. What do you think, can you tough it out?" Ida asked as he smiled.

"I'm resolved to see it through, but when the time comes, it'll probably be fairly difficult."

"It's not what you think it is. If winter comes and it seems like you're just not going to be able to hack it, well, sir, because of your situation, it would be better for you to escape to Sapporo. For that matter, hibernating in the winter is the same no matter where you are."

"Ha ha ha ha ha. If that's the case, it would be best if you left things up to the tenant farmers from the beginning and lived in Sapporo," said the other agent.

"Yes, yes, you're right. If I'm going to take off to Sapporo in the middle of the winter, I might as well stay in Tokyo and open land there." Then, showing my resolve, I said, "Whatever comes, I can bear it."

Ida said, "That's right. First the snow will come, and you'll be filling up this stove. Firewood, well, you get that by hand. Then, a person like you will study the numerous books you've brought up, right?"

"Is the idea that I transform into a great scholar by the time the snow melts?" I laughed unexpectedly.

As we were talking, all of a sudden there was a sprinkling sound, and I went outside. The sun was shining dimly as the clouds were passing silently over the quiet deep forest, and a rain shower passed over.

Leaving behind the innkeeper's son, I left the cabin to walk around the area alone.

Returning to the wide road, I realized just how strange it was. They had chosen to make it in this extreme no-man's-land, destroying the thick forest that had been here for thousands of years and using human power to defeat nature. As far as anyone could see on both sides, only forest enveloped the road. Without even one shadow of a human, without even one thread of smoke, and without even one person to speak to or to listen to, it stretches out desolate and lonely.

I am aware of the loneliness of the sound of rain, but still I have never felt such loneliness as when the rain shower stealthily passed over that vast primeval forest. This is, in fact, the quiet murmuring of nature. Anyone who should hear this sound from the forest floor could not help but feel the power of limitless nature that disdains living creatures. Tumultuous waves, windstorms, sharp claps of thunder, and flashes of lightening are nature's threats. Yet, it oppresses people most when it is most quiet. When the faraway blue sky looks down upon the earth, silently, not saying a word, and when in a place deep in the forest that has never permitted a human footprint, a leaf from a tree in one corner dies and falls without any wind, nature yawns and says, "Ah, another day has come to an end." And in this instant a thousand human years fly by.

When I looked at both sides of the forest, I discovered that there was a place where the forest thinned on the left side. Parting the grasses, I proceeded through, and suddenly turned back to see I was standing on the deep forest's floor. I sat down on a large, fallen rotting tree.

When I realized that the forest had become dark, the rain shower started again, making pattering sounds on the high branches. Just when I thought, "Ah it's come again," in the next moment it stopped and all was silent in the forest.

I sat still for some time, watched the depth of the forest become darker, and sank into my thoughts.

Where is society? Where is "history" that humans are so proud to pass on? Here people are only creatures of "survival" and feel only that they are at the mercy of one breath of nature. A Russian poet once said that having sat down in a forest, he felt the shadow of death press upon him, and this is very true. He also said, "When the last person from the human race disappears from this earth, not even one tree leaf will tremble."

The death-like silence, the frigidness, the gloominess—sitting in the deep forest, there isn't a soul who would not feel this oppressive feeling. Forgetting myself, I was sinking into frightful visions when . . .

"Mister! Mister!" Someone called from outside the forest. I hurried out and saw the innkeeper's son standing there.

"Everything's taken care of, so shall we head back?"

First, the two of us returned to the cabin, and Ida said, "Would you like to spend the night to test it out and see how it feels?"

In the end, I've come to this day having never stepped foot on the land of Hokkaido again. And, although a family matter forced me to cancel all my plans to open land there, even now when I think of the shores of the Sorachi River, I feel as though I am being pulled in by that brutal nature. I wonder why.

Writing Ainu Out/Writing Japanese In: The "Nature" of Japanese Colonialism in Hokkaido

MICHELE M. MASON

Today, Hokkaido, Japan's northernmost island, takes hold in the Japanese imagination in a number of telling ways. It is a popular summer tourist destination renowned for its natural beauty and outdoor activities. Hokkaido's harsh winters are tamed into massive ice sculptures of architectural wonders and popular cartoon characters in the Sapporo Snow Festival every year.[1] Designated national landmarks, Meiji-era (1868–1912) red brick buildings and the Sapporo clock tower, built with Euro-American designs, lend the island a Western air. Hokkaido's most famous local specialties—potatoes, corn, and beer—strengthen this foreign flavor. Moving family dramas, fantastic samurai-pioneer adventures, and romantic narratives of the indigenous population, the Ainu, are produced for popular consumption in television and films.[2] At the same time, the specter of Abashiri Prison, the Alcatraz of Japan, looms large in the national consciousness as the cruelest punitive fate.[3]

Diverse and sometimes conflicting contemporary representations of Hokkaido constitute invaluable traces of the historicity of the island's recent incorporation into Japanese territory. Known for centuries as "Ezo," Land of the Barbarians, the area was first unilaterally claimed in 1869 by the fledgling Meiji government, which had yet to even suppress the last of the resistance to its takeover of power. Later that same year, officials renamed the island "Hokkaido," and declared that the emperor should "show His power and prestige to the world" by making it into "a little Japan."[4] To that end, the Hokkaido Development Agency (Kaitakushi) was established to manage the colonial project. The emperor did his part to bring Hokkaido into the strong embrace of the emerging Japanese nation and empire by casting his gaze over this northernmost reach of his realm twice on his historic imperial tours of 1876 and 1881.[5] The 1875 Sakhalin-Kurile Exchange Treaty with Russia accorded international legitimation of Hokkaido's position within Japan, and by 1882, Hokkaido had been officially integrated into the emerging Japanese national body through its prefectural status. At the century's end, Hokkaido could boast of several substantial townships, and with emigration increasing annually, Japanese settlements pushed further inland and toward its eastern coast.

Even as the island became more firmly incorporated within the nascent Japanese nation, the collective imagination of "Hokkaido" drew from historical associations and modern propaganda, the contents of both comingling, shifting, and conflicting. It was at once a natural part of the Japanese archipelago and a remote foreign land; a fount of untouched natural resources and an empty wasteland of snow and ice; a utopian escape and a desolate dead end. This space called "Hokkaido" inspired government officials, literary figures, and intellectuals to draw their own designs and desires upon it as they produced narratives that shaped the future of this once Ainu homeland and Japan's modern national identity.

At the heart of both romantic and dystopian fantasies of Hokkaido in the Meiji period lay the island's awe-inspiring natural world. Hokkaido's majestic mountains, sweeping plains, and vast "virgin" forests collectively constituted what seemed an infinite "empty" expanse that beckoned adventurous Japanese settlers. In its rugged and undeveloped state, Hokkaido was characterized as a limitless source of hitherto untapped natural resources awaiting Japanese ingenuity and civilization. Such images of Hokkaido as a pristine and primitive wilderness served the state's goals by not only justifying the extraction of unfathomable profit to fuel "modernization," but also by acting as a foil to confirm "Japan's" superior status and rationalize the colonial expropriation. At the same time, individuals unconnected to officialdom also found uses for Hokkaido's natural world. In particular, representations of its forbidding landscape and climate were deployed to express an alienated and disoriented Japanese psyche that struggled to cope with the dramatic and traumatic transformations of the Meiji era, which seemed to redefine every aspect of personhood and society.

In this essay, I offer a reading of "The Shores of the Sorachi River" (*Sorachigawa no kishibe*, 1902) by novelist and poet Kunikida Doppo (1871–1908), which highlights the implications of the protagonist's engagement with and musings on Hokkaido's nature.[6] In Doppo's short story, a man, identified as a writer, journeys from Tokyo to Hokkaido to investigate purchasing a tract of land to open and cultivate. While trying to locate prefectural officials who can provide him with information on possible plots along the Sorachi River, he observes the scenery of Hokkaido and the Japanese who make their home there. He ultimately meets and consults with the experts. His trip, however, turns out to be so disconcerting due to the hostile landscape that, as he confesses in the last lines, he never buys land or returns to Hokkaido again.

"The Shores of the Sorachi River" foregrounds the "battles" of Japanese colonists confronting Hokkaido's unfamiliar landscape in such a fashion that the very real consequences of Japan's colonization on the Ainu, who had lived on the island for centuries, are supplanted by metaphors of Japanese modern malaise. Doppo's use of Japanese colonialists' struggle with oppressive natural forces in Hokkaido to signify modern angst effectively rewrites colonial history so that the subjugation of the Ainu is displaced and replaced by the victimhood of the colonizer who is "subjugated" by a cruel and indifferent nature. This short story exemplifies how literary texts of the period, while not officially connected to the colonial administration, both reflected and reinforced the state's colonial project. Working in tandem with policies penned by the political elite, fictional narratives like "The Shores of the Sorachi River" further naturalized Hokkaido as Japanese territory and facilitated Japanese settlement by incorporating the island into the social imaginary of the nation.

The "Nature" of Colonial Hokkaido and the Naichi/Nation

From the earliest Meiji writings on Hokkaido, nature played a prominent role in defining both the northern island and the "Japanese" *naichi* (mainland/homeland). The difference between Hokkaido and the mainland is commonly expressed through dichotomies of nature/culture and wild/tamed. On the one hand, Hokkaido is a "no-man's-land" (*mujinchi, mujin no sakai*) and a "savage land" (*mikaichi*).[7] On the other hand, official, intellectual, and popular writers attribute to the *naichi*/nation a domesticated landscape, comforting human ties, literary significance, and rich, enduring history—signifiers of Japan's advanced technological expertise and enlightened civilization. Held up to the mirror of Hokkaido's perilous, primeval natural world, the mainland appeared to be a place of orderly cultivated landscape inhabited by civilized, harmonious communities enveloped in time-honored traditions.

Justifications for the colonial project in Hokkaido were often, implicitly or explicitly, articulated through notions of promoting agriculture—that age-old practice of taming nature. By the 1890s, representations that aligned "Japanese-ness" with agricultural production had taken root, and what Carol Gluck calls the "agrarian myth," which asserted that the rice-producing villages were "the communal foundations of Japanese national experience"[8] and "the repository of ancestral custom,"[9] was a staple of officials and scholars alike. Hokkaido-born literary critic Ogasawara Masaru observes how the idea of the "civilized" *naichi* was anchored in traditional practices of cultivation, which lent the mainland a hospitable feeling.

> *Naichi* [homeland] was not merely a word that signified a discreet geographical area—the Japanese mainland to the south of the Tsugaru Straits—but rather it was a vital symbol that measured a distance in spiritual topography. In other words, *naichi* meant home, native country, a place of unchanging configuration. It was the lands of one's beloved, of affecting mountains and streams, of a history that spanned the generations; a land that could make one forget if only for an instant the bodily fear and uncertainty that was Hokkaido. *Naichi* reminded one of harmony brimming with reassurance . . . the truth and poetry of a birthplace was *there*. Here, in Hokkaido, there was none of that. Here there was only a savage nature, not cultivated land. Here nature was an object to be fought. Survival depended on its continual destruction.[10]

Associations with history, harmony, and poetics reinforced the cultural plenitude of the *naichi* in contrast to Hokkaido's "cultural vacancy."[11] In Hokkaido, in place of "cultivated land," stood "savage nature," which had to be destroyed in order to bring it under the control and into the service of society as the many generations of Japanese had done on the mainland. Thus, agri*culture*, as the locus of Japan's "advanced" society, confirmed Hokkaido's distance in spatial and temporal registers from a "cultured" *naichi*/nation.

The use of "mainland" in this context should not be read simply as the English translation of *naichi* (or *hondo*), but rather these original Japanese terms should be understood as metonyms for the Japanese nation. Using Hokkaido as the antithesis of the *naichi*/nation allowed the new nation-state of Japan to legitimize the "development" of Hokkaido as it simultaneously endeavored to consolidate its political and economic infrastructure, create imperial subjects, shape national identity, and negotiate a stronger position vis-à-vis the West. In challenging the characterization of the Boshin War (1868–1869) as a "bloodless coup" and assumptions that the Meiji Restoration represents a smooth transition into nation-statehood, historian James Edward Ketelaar rightly warns against naively accepting narratives that "equate the 'declaration' of the Meiji era with its production."[12] In a similar fashion, a critical eye should be leveled at statements that posit the existence of a Japanese nation-state prior to the process of appropriating the island called "Hokkaido." Hokkaido was claimed, named, and colonized in tandem with the establishment and consolidation of the power of the Meiji imperial state, and these two processes mutually defined each other. In a dialectical relationship, images of and policies toward Hokkaido were constructed by and contributed to the discursive and material creation of the modern Japanese nation and empire.

For the first-person narrator in "The Shores of the Sorachi River," the initial impression of the uncultivated spaces of Hokkaido is thrilling, immediately inviting comparisons with the mainland; "Even the wilderness of the northeast inspired devotion in me, a person who grew up in the densely populated central region of our country's mainland and was accustomed to scenery of mountains and fields that had been conquered by human power. Upon seeing Hokkaido, the northernmost part of the country, how could my heart not be moved?!"[13] Although no specifics are given, we are to infer from the description of the mainland that Hokkaido represents the opposite of a land that has "been conquered by human power" (*ningen no chikara de tairage tsukushitaru*). The landscape becomes increasingly unfamiliar to the narrator as the distance from the nation's center increases, with Hokkaido signifying the extreme periphery. Thus, Hokkaido's wilderness is even more breathtaking than that of the northeast (Tōhoku), which still lies within the confines of the main island, Honshu. To further stress the difference between the center and periphery, the narrator debunks a rumor from the mainland that likens Sapporo to Tokyo. "Sapporo is said to be the Tokyo of Hokkaido, but I was all but bewitched by the many sights there."[14] Here, even the largest and most populated city of Hokkaido, constructed as peculiar yet alluring, offers nothing familiar to the eye of the mainland traveler.

As delighted as the protagonist of "The Shores of the Sorachi River" may be with the wild landscape of the north, it still remains that he imagines himself participating in the colonial project of "domesticating" Hokkaido. He has journeyed there to consider buying land to farm, and when he meets two officials in a cabin next to the Sorachi River, the three pour over maps and discuss and evaluate at least six plots that have been parceled out for Japanese immigrants. He is considering becoming a colonist or literally a "person who opens land" (*kaikonsha*). In such an undertaking, he will have to destroy the wilderness that fascinates him to imprint the agricultural model of the mainland on Hokkaido.

Doppo's protagonist also undercuts his reverence for Hokkaido's natural wonders in one of the rare scenes that overtly acknowledges the colonial project. "I" admires a road in the middle of the forest and appreciates the power that could achieve such a feat.

> When we came out from the path of bear grass, there was a wide road that you would not expect to find penetrating the forest in one straight line. It was probably wider than thirty feet. Moreover, on both sides a dense thicket grew wherein there were many trees whose diameter ranged from over six to nine feet, and due to the ditches passing through, this expansive road seemed like a railroad track. However, seeing this road, I understood how great the difficulties were for the prefectural office's earnest plans for colonization (*takushoku*).[15]

With the core meaning of "increasing or multiplying reclaimed land," the word *takushoku* emphasizes humans' mastery over nature.[16] The narrator appears sympathetic to the state's goals to inscribe colonial ambitions onto the "empty" space of Hokkaido and to integrate the wilderness into the national economy. The towering trees along the road—with diameters up to nine feet—are evidence of the difficulty of the operation, and the accomplishment of transporting civilization to the unruly natural space of Hokkaido is all the more significant and impressive to the narrator in light of the scale of such an enterprise where one would not "expect" it. This road, possibly soon to be converted into a railway that will further carry out the economic goals and settlement of the island, symbolizes the achievements of the Japanese state as it pursues imperial expansion.

Notably, in this scene where the protagonist is astonished by a wide and straight road piercing the dense forest, "I" characterizes the colonial process with the phrases "by destroying the thick forest" and "using human power to defeat nature."[17] *Horobosu* (to destroy) and *uchikatsu* (to conquer or defeat), the two verbs used, most readily evoke images of a hero vanquishing his foe. In this particular formation, the "battles" Japanese men have with Hokkaido's nature are converted into tales of adventurous warfare not unlike those found in romantic battlefield stories.[18]

The ultimate failure, however, of the narrator from Tokyo to become the "pioneer" he dreams of is foreshadowed in a passage that reveals his increasingly alienated feelings toward the forbidding scenery. His unease is detected by the two officials with whom he consults. When the topic of the harsh winters comes up, one prefectural officer proposes, "If winter comes and it seems like you're just not going to be able to hack it, well, sir, because of your situation, it would be better for you to escape to Sapporo."[19] Following this logic the other man suggests lightheartedly, "If that's the case, it would be best if you left things up to the tenant farmers from the beginning and lived in Sapporo."[20] Finally, in a comic moment, the narrator himself jokes, "Yes, yes, you're right. If I'm going to take off to Sapporo in the middle of the winter, I might as well stay in Tokyo and open land there."[21]

In the end, taking refuge in his library writing this story, the narrator tells us he has returned to the safe, orderly mainland and "cancelled all plans to open land" in Hokkaido.[22] Even though an actual relationship with Hokkaido proves to be too daunting, he cannot help but be intrigued with his romantic imagination of what Hokkaido is and offers. "I've come to this day having never stepped foot on the land of Hokkaido again. And, although a family matter forced me to cancel all my plans to open land there, even now when I think of the shores of the Sorachi River, I feel as though I am being pulled in by that brutal nature. I wonder why."[23] The "real" Hokkaido turns out to be too fierce, but from the safety of his study on the mainland his fantasy of the task of pioneering in Hokkaido is forever powerful and seductive.[24]

Writing the Ainu Out of Hokkaido

A panoply of Meiji-period narratives myopically concentrated on colonists' noble campaigns against nature, suppressing the story of the Ainu struggle with the emerging powerful Japanese nation-state and the policies and laws that violently denied them the right to their own culture, language, and means of subsistence. In the opening of a promotional booklet written in English for the 1893 World's Columbian Exhibition in Chicago, scholar and politician Nitobe Inazō extols the accomplishments of the Imperial Agricultural College in Sapporo, Hokkaido.[25] This short work typifies some of the central contradictions in the discourse on the colonization of Hokkaido.

> The War of Restoration over, the Japanese Government turned its attention to more peaceful pursuits. It began to divert the overflowing energies of the warrior class and the superabundant strength of the oppressed peasantry into new channels of industrial warfare and conquest. A field well suited for enterprises of this kind was not wanting. . . . The northern islands of Japan, vaguely called Yezo, were for centuries a terra incognita among people; all that was told about it, and unfortunately most readily accepted by them was that the region was the abode of a barbarian folk known as the Ainu,

and that it was a dreary waste of snow and ice, altogether unfit for inhabitation by a race of higher culture.

To Yezo, then, the northern frontier of the Empire and a land endowed with magnificent natural resources as yet untouched by human hand, the new Imperial Government wisely began to extend its fostering care.[26]

In the first sentences Nitobe depicts the "peaceful pursuits" of the Meiji leadership as "industrial warfare and conquest." The dissonance between the two contrasting notions in Nitobe's own language unintentionally exposes the historicity of the persistent characterization of the colonization of Hokkaido as merely "peaceful pursuits" when it would be more aptly defined as violent "industrial warfare and conquest." Still, in this celebratory pamphlet, these phrases, along with "fostering care," fortified the prevailing colonial trope in this context, namely that the advanced nation of Japan was "developing" Hokkaido.

Not surprisingly, Nitobe acknowledges the Ainu of Hokkaido with the derogatory term "barbarian" and implicitly describes the Japanese as a superior race. Tapping into the vein of Social Darwinism, which buoyed the belief in the moral, intellectual, and racial ascendency of the Japanese, Nitobe simultaneously ignores and legitimates the dispossession of Ainu. Immediately after mentioning that Hokkaido was the longtime homeland of the Ainu, Nitobe empties Hokkaido entirely of Ainu existence and history and describes the island solely in terms of its "natural resources *yet untouched by human hand*" (emphasis mine). Echoing the logic of Christopher Columbus' "discovery" of the "New World," Nitobe declares that Hokkaido is a "terra incognita," or unknown land, contrary to evidence of the Ainu's intimate knowledge of the flora, fauna, land, and climate, which made possible their longtime survival and rich cultural inheritance.

The figurative erasure of the indigenous Ainu in this and other texts was not a benign act. In *The Rhetoric of Empire: Colonial Discourse in Journalism, Travel Writing, and Imperial Administration*, literary and colonial scholar David Spurr elucidates twelve rhetorical modes employed by European colonialists, emphasizing the important connection between colonial discourse and colonial subjugation. Prominent among these is "negation," a rhetorical strategy that empties an inhabited space, making room for the envisioning and fulfillment of national and individual desires. Negation requires the construction of the Other as "absence, emptiness, nothingness and death."[27] The frequent characterization of Hokkaido as a "no-man's-land," a "blank slate," and a "vast void" during the Meiji era exemplifies this linguistic turn that justifies colonial projects through ostensible enterprising plans to convert a "vacancy" into a model of "civilization." The colonial project removed Ainu from their ancestral lands, which were vigorously exploited, for instance, surveyed, divided into plots (reserved for Japanese), mined, and deforested to make way for cultivated fields, towns, and railways. The discursive and physical erasure of Ainu from Hokkaido made way for the inscription of agricultural, economic, social, and political practices of the Japanese mainland onto the landscape there and the realization of imperial desire to claim the island as a symbol of Japan's advanced status.

Spurr specifically highlights the role of writing in colonial expansion. To begin, he cites Derrida's provocative premise that "the writer is the original and ultimate colonizer, conquering the space of consciousness with the exclusionary and divisive structures of representation."[28] Moving from this metaphorical instance, Spurr recognizes the wide range of texts, from legal to literary, that function to authorize, execute, and sustain colonial domination. Examples include not only edicts and laws, correspondence between various offices of government, corporate contracts, and surveys of land, people, and resources, but also journalistic reportage in newspapers and popular magazines, fictional works that imagine the colonial "frontier," and children's adventure stories.

In the case of Hokkaido, written laws eradicated the sources of the traditional Ainu diet (salmon, deer, and grain crops) and produced the emptiness of the lives of the Ainu forbidden to speak their language and conduct their own governance and rituals. Reinforced and justified by a large body of texts, the legal system was at the root of Ainu deaths caused by dislocation, disease, and desperation. As early as 1871 the Hokkaido Development Agency announced policies proscribing common Ainu customs, such as tattooing, wearing earrings, and burning the residences of the dead even as the officials, in the same document, encouraged "mainlanders" (*naichi jinmin*) to cooperate and live peaceably with the indigenous people.[29] In terms of basic survival, the intermittent laws that forbade spring-bow traps and poisoned arrows or fishing in certain regions during the Meiji era (usually precipitated by the radical depletion of herds of deer and stocks of fish because of the reckless hunting and fishing practices of the Japanese) delivered a crushing blow to Ainu subsistence.

In his incisive analysis of language in Ainu "protection" laws, Komori Yōichi, a leading cultural studies scholar, traces the Hokkaido Development

Agency's utilization of the legal theory of "ownerless land" (*terra nullius*, *mushu no chi*), first used by Western colonial powers, to claim "ownership" of Hokkaido.[30] Despite knowledge of Ainu communities' existence and historical land-use rights, Japanese colonial policies dismissed both the indigenous people and their conceptualization of their relationship to the land. Additionally, the Regulations for the Sale of Hokkaido Land (*Hokkaidō tochi haraisage kisoku*, 1886) and the Law for the Disposal of Undeveloped National Land in Hokkaido (*Hokkaidō kokuyū mikaichi shobunhō*, 1897) were the legal linchpins that made Japanese ownership possible, furthering the settlement of Japanese who were to "make Hokkaido a little Japan."[31] Thus, the deft application of the term *terra nullius* facilitated the practical aspect of colonizing and settling Hokkaido and the greater goal of the imperial project to expand the territorial boundaries of the Japanese empire.

If written law ensured the subjugation of the Ainu people and the appropriation of their homelands, then fictional works set in Hokkaido greatly assisted in "conquering the space of consciousness" of the Japanese citizenry. Adventure stories and heroic tales set in the "frontier" allowed the reading public to participate in the illusion that Japan was "developing" this backward, empty space. "The Shores of the Sorachi River," a representative literary work of the time, is replete with phrases that paint Hokkaido as nothing more than a vacant, "vast primeval forest." The narrator declares at different moments, for instance, that "the train ran on a straight line, piercing the huge forests in which not one person has tread since the beginning of time—thousands of years," that the forest "has never permitted a human footprint," and that a strange road was made in a "no-man's-land."[32] Standing on this road, he reflects, "As far as anyone could see on both sides, only the forest enveloped the road. Without even one shadow of a human, without even one thread of smoke, and without even one person to speak to or to listen to, it stretches out desolate and lonely."[33]

Yet, this vision was only possible because readers were not allowed to imagine people already living in Hokkaido. The "footprints"—the historical traces—of Ainu are erased and what is imagined in this space is only the impressive "progress" of enterprising Japanese. For centuries, Ainu had built their homes, gathered around their hearths, and paid respect to the reigning god of their pantheon of gods, the Fire Goddess, as they passed down their knowledge, customs, and philosophy in oral tales (*yukar*). By 1902, when Doppo's text was published, the many Ainu communities that had for generations dwelled along the banks of the Sorachi River, a rich source of fish and an excellent place to plant their rotating crops, had succumbed to the fatal colonial polices or been relocated, and their land turned into parceled plots reserved for Japanese immigrants.[34] The Tokyoite of the story confers with officials over the maps detailing the surveyed tracts that ignore the indigenous presence, drawing over their many lost communities.

The seemingly innocuous idea that the bounty of Hokkaido lay patiently waiting for the proper race to use it was the seed with which Japan's ambitious plans for Hokkaido's "unlimited natural resources," quite irrespective of Ainu livelihood, was propagated. Elucidating another rhetorical strategy common to colonization in a chapter entitled "Appropriation," Spurr asserts, "This appeal may take the form of chaos that calls for the restoration of order, of absence that calls for affirming presence, of natural abundance that awaits the creative hand of technology."[35] In the case of Hokkaido, the justification of colonial exploitation was bolstered by the assumption that the Ainu had not used the land correctly, as is indicated in the booklet *The Imperial Agricultural College of Sapporo, Japan* quoted above, wherein Nitobe implies that "a race of a higher culture," the Japanese, unlike the Ainu, understood "that the fertile virgin soil could be made to yield its richest treasures."[36] Moreover, Komori avers that the act of colonizing Hokkaido and the subjugation of the Ainu are rewritten so that the Japanese are cast as benevolent protectors. Words such as "protection" (*hogo*) and "emigrant" (*imin*) mask the maltreatment of Ainu inherent in the Japanese colonization and settlement of Hokkaido. Komori writes, "the term 'protection' in the Hokkaido Former Natives Protection Law not only suppresses the over thirty years of history of the Japanese invasion and looting of 'Ainu Moshir,' but also, in the end, contains the intention to invert the situation so as to make it appear that it was the Ainu's fault."[37]

The "failure" of the Ainu to have marked the natural landscape in a way that showed mastery over or subjugation of the land confirmed their "barbarity" in the eyes of Japanese. This was not unlike Western imperialistic interpretations of Africans and their relationship to nature. "History" is signified by leaving a permanent record of one's existence—of one's victory over nature. Because the Ainu had left no lasting disfigurement on their natural surroundings, Doppo is able to have his narrator in "The Shores of the Sorachi River" contend, quite contrary to evidence, that in the forest along the banks of the Sorachi River "not one person has tread since the beginning of time."[38] Thus, for the narrator, the road-cum-potential-railroad-track described earlier marks a break between human prehistory and history. Since any faithful history of the Ainu homelands is rejected, this character is able to wistfully ponder near the end of the story, "Where is society? Where is 'history' that humans are so proud to pass on? Here people are only creatures of 'survival.'"[39] For him Hokkaido is wholly without the landmarks of civilization and history. In this context, Ainu are invisible, and the Japanese who live there are reduced to a level far below that of the civilized world of the *naichi*, only struggling to survive.

Although no grand Ainu monuments imbued Hokkaido's landscape with historical or cultural significance, Ainu did leave more subtle clues of their longtime connection to the place through the meaningful names they assigned to the natural landmarks and localities of Hokkaido. Most names of regions, cities, and natural formations (mountains, rivers, etc.) dotting the maps of Hokkaido today were originally Ainu designations that derived from careful observations of the topography and characteristics of the island. To give just one example, the name of the largest city in Hokkaido today, Sapporo, comes from the Ainu *sat poro pet*, large dried up river.[40] Long accustomed to traversing their densely forested homeland for seasonal hunting and fishing, Ainu lent invaluable assistance to the survey teams that mapped the land and its natural resources. Countless appellations were passed on to Japanese, who assigned Chinese characters whose meaning typically had no connection to the original Ainu connotation and whose pronunciation was, and is, difficult to discern for many Japanese.[41] Ignoring the fact that these names constitute strong evidence of Ainu groups' centuries of inhabitation in the region, Meiji-era Japanese writers, official and otherwise, equate the commencement of the island's "history" with the commencement of Japanese "development" of "Hokkaido."

The dominant narrative, during the Meiji era and today, depicts Hokkaido's integration into Japanese territory as a natural process without the language of colonization. Thus, the historical reality that Hokkaido is Japan's first modern colony, the seed of its age of empire, is replaced by the prevalent view that Japan "developed" (*kaitaku*) the island. Likewise the Ainu are not recognized as the victims of a violent colonial project, but the benefactors of Japan's assistance. Richard Siddle is one Western scholar who places the proper import on the nature of Hokkaido's colonization in the Meiji era. As Siddle points out, this legacy survives today in the way Hokkaido's history is recounted. For example, commenting on a 1968 celebration of the one hundred years of Hokkaido "history," Siddle observes, "Almost no mention was made of Ainu history or their role in the colonisation of Hokkaidō.

This was not a mere oversight; such historical amnesia was integral to the legitimizing narrative of Hokkaidō kaitaku [development] that served to mask the violence of the colonial enterprise by casting it in terms of the application of the beneficial effects of 'progress' to a 'natural' extension of Japanese territory."[42]

The official, journalistic, and literary writings that erased the Ainu existence from Hokkaido altogether greatly contributed to the "success" of the colonial project there, so that today few question the status of Hokkaido as "one of Japan's four main islands." Importantly, the discursive evacuation of the presence and history of the Ainu in Hokkaido reflected and reinforced their actual dislocation and decimation. The characterization of the Ainu as "barbarians" and the rhetoric that emphasized the need to fill the "empty" space of Hokkaido with cultivated plots of land and other markers of "civilization" was not just a harmless distortion of history. It was (and is) a strategic obfuscation of how Japanese colonization usurped Ainu land and lives. Japan's imperial triumph in Hokkaido, facilitated by this process of writing the Ainu out, was, moreover, accompanied by the equally crucial colonial imperative of writing the Japanese in.

Writing the Japanese In

Many Meiji depictions of the northern territory go beyond merely emptying out any trace of Ainu from Hokkaido. The struggles of the Ainu are, in fact, repressed and replaced by the struggle of Japanese against a personified hostile natural world in Hokkaido. In such narratives, Hokkaido stands as the signifier of modern angst and the *colonizer* is recast as the victim of an oppressive, cruel, and indifferent nature. In Meiji literary works set in Hokkaido, characters are commonly impressed by its supernatural power and grandeur that bring to the fore a palpable sense of the insignificance of humans. The vastness of Hokkaido's seemingly unruly and uncultured landscape, which engendered fear and isolation, was converted into a symbol of the conflicted, turbulent nether regions of the mind.[43] Hokkaido became a useful tool with which writers could speak to Japanese feelings of disempowerment and disorientation in modern Japanese society.

The Meiji era brought about one of the most dramatic transformations in all of Japanese history. After over 250 years of rule by the Tokugawa shoguns, a thorough re-engineering of political, legal, educational, and religious practices redefined almost every aspect of society. The new rulers mobilized enlightenment principles, with an emphasis on models of rationality, to drive and define their new policies. An incipient native capitalist system was reworked and bolstered to facilitate modern Japan's rapid industrialization, drastically reconfiguring individuals' relationship to labor. With the deterioration of earlier modes of constructing identity—the Tokugawa status system and regional affinities—much of the population was unmoored, even as new definitions of an essential "Japanese" national identity were offered via state and popular media and reinforced through a variety of invented traditions. Daily rhythms and rituals were profoundly reshaped through, for example, the institution of "modern time," dictated by advanced mechanical clocks, and the state's appropriation of local shrines as the symbols of a "unified Japanese nation." At the same time, urbanization and imperial expansion molded new relationships between people within the emerging nation-state and with their neighbors in the larger region. These vast and bewildering changes caused a great number of people to lose not only their livelihoods but also traditional notions of selfhood.

As modernity reconstructed the everyday lives and perspectives of Japanese citizens in countless ways, the understanding of what constituted nature and humans' relation to it also changed. In the modern configuration of the relationship between man and nature, the latter was increasingly perceived as both the antithesis and antagonist of man. The exaltation of science, as a means by which man could control the unpredictable natural world, took root in both lofty and mundane ways in new academic disciplines and in people's private lives through the formation of "knowledge" and programs that confirmed Japan's "progress." The notion that humans were connected to and must cooperate with nature was replaced by an ever-widening gap between the conceptualization of "nature" and "culture."

In *Natural Space in Literature*, literary and cultural critic Tom Henighan treats Western literature depicting the sense of estrangement that emerged from a new relationship between inner experience and the outer world in the nineteenth century. Oceans, deserts, and other impressive landscapes were reinterpreted within modern notions of the "self" and "inner life."

> Natural sublime in modern literature, at any rate, is an image of man's perception of open space, a perception which involves a particular emotional response, an inner reaction. In the face of the wild landscape man may feel himself diminished, and the scale may become radically inhuman. The psyche is pressed upon by the immensity and a kind of agoraphobia of the spirit occurs. The inner is not equal to the outer dimension.[44]

The alienation of man from nature lies in his "discovery" that despite nature's beauty and splendor it lacks "humanity." Looking at nature, man can find nothing of himself and little to confirm his own sense of importance.

Functioning much like the open spaces in Western literature of this period, the landscape of Hokkaido consistently inspired the twin reactions of awe and fear. Confronted with the incommensurability of the space, people are simultaneously bewitched and distressed. For instance, viewed from the window of a train, the natural scene evokes an acute awareness of vulnerability in the narrator of "The Shores of the Sorachi River."

> The fields of Ishikari were lost in the low-lying clouds, and as I stared out from the train window onto the fields and mountains, I was overwhelmed by the frightening power of nature. Here there was no love, no compassion. To look out on this savage, lonely, heartless, and yet magnificent sight, it appeared to me all the more that nature scorns the powerlessness and fragility of humans.[45]

"I" is conflicted in that he is both impressed and frightened by the natural world he sees, which is invested with emotions and not only aloof from, but hostile to humans. The protagonist's feeling of being "overwhelmed" by the open space resonates with Henighan's notion of "agoraphobia of the spirit." The original verb, *afureru*, denotes "to be deluged, flooded, or overflowing" and accentuates the extremity of his powerlessness. Here Hokkaido's natural world does not stand as a backdrop to Japanese cunning and determination, but only punctuates the impotence of man.

Nature's indifference to humans is manifested in its timelessness as well as its immensity. The scale of human time is dwarfed or rendered insignificant in the "eyes" of nature. Reflecting on this, the protagonist explains:

> When the faraway blue sky looks down upon the earth, silently, not saying a word, and when in a place deep in the forest that has never permitted a human footprint, a leaf from a tree in one corner dies and falls without any wind, nature yawns and says, "Ah, another day has come to an end." And in this instant a thousand human years fly by.[46]

In this scenario an anthropomorphized nature observes detachedly but pays no heed to the vicissitudes of humanity. Nature's expansiveness, of space and time, reduces human reality to a meaningless fleeting moment. Moreover, given nature's constant threats to life, humans are forced to face their deaths "at the mercy of one breath of nature."[47] The narrator of "The Shores of the Sorachi River" reflects:

> A Russian poet once said that having sat down in a forest, he felt the shadow of death press upon him (*semaru*), and this is very true. He also said, "When the last person from the human race disappears from this earth, not even one tree leaf will tremble."
>
> The death-like silence, the frigidness, the gloominess—sitting in the deep forest, there isn't a soul who would not feel this oppressive feeling (*ihaku*).[48]

Here I have translated *ihaku*, which literally means "threat" or "menace," as "oppressive feeling." Coupled with the verb *semaru*, which means "to press down on," the distinctive impression is made that humans are the "victims" of the power and impunity of nature. In the context of this story specifically and in literature on Hokkaido in general, humans refer to Japanese not Ainu. These sentiments are, after all, voiced by the same narrator, who never once acknowledges the existence of Ainu.

In the context where modern thoughts and practices divided Japanese from their natural surroundings, Hokkaido proved a useful tool with which Japanese writers could display *their* apprehensiveness and anxiety. The denial of Ainu subjectivity and history—even their presence—worked in tandem with depictions of Japanese men's sometimes courageous, sometimes pitiful battles with Hokkaido's nature. In such formulations, the violent nature of Japan's colonization of Hokkaido is subsumed under the ostensibly benign projects of "developing" the island and modern nation-state-building. The Ainu of Hokkaido, however, were the ones who most acutely suffered. Not because of Hokkaido's natural world, which they had found ways to cope with over the years, but from Japan's policies of subjugation and the colonization of their homeland. In a cruel twist, the victimhood of the Ainu is denied, while national progress and modern angst are the frameworks by which Hokkaido in Meiji Japan is understood.

Conclusion: The Legacy of Colonial Hokkaido

Doppo's short story represents a much larger body of narratives that produced a national imaginary of "Hokkaido" *and* "Japan." Given that Meiji leaders claimed possession of the island so soon after the Meiji Restoration that brought to an end the long-lived Tokugawa shogunate (1600–1868), we cannot assume that Japan was a fully formed modern nation-state *prior* to imperial expansion into Hokkaido. In fact, the very process of appropriating Hokkaido lent life to the new rulers and their newly established authority. The documents that formalized the incorporation of Hokkaido in the emperor's name were the first in a long line of steps taken to link Japanese imperial and national prestige with military and territorial expansion. Hokkaido settler campaign materials encouraged potential colonists to protect Japan's agrarian essence by emigrating to the northern island. Economic exploits were soon paying off, for instance in coal mining, which funded economic growth on the mainland and fueled further imperial expansion. The fundamental colonial ideologies and policies tested in those early years would be reappropriated and refined in Japan's later colonial projects throughout Asia. Thus, Japan's nation-building project was initially staged on the discursive landscape of Japan's first modern colony, Hokkaido.

Coupled with adventure tales of Japanese "pioneers" and newspaper reports that championed the "progress" of "development" in Hokkaido, literary works like "The Shores of the Sorachi River" interpolated individuals into a mode of thinking that allowed them to see themselves as one member among many of the Japanese nation and empire. Without ever touching foot on the island of Hokkaido, newly anointed Japanese citizens could imagine themselves sharing a common responsibility for and pride in national consolidation and imperial expansion. Naturalizing Hokkaido as an integral part of Japan allowed Meiji elites to foster domestic support for their rule and to campaign for international recognition of "Japan" as a legitimate nation-state. As such, the claiming and settlement of Hokkaido and the representations of that colonial project during the Meiji period also played an important role in forming modern subjecthood and nation-state-hood.

The legacy of the colonization of Hokkaido can be seen most strikingly in contemporary museums that function to reproduce and valorize national history and values. Until recently the Asahikawa Northern Defense Museum (Asahikawa hokuchin kinenkan) was located inside the Self-Defense Forces base in Hokkaido's second largest city, Asahikawa, the former site of a large contingent of *tondenhei* (farming-militia) during the Meiji period. Before its recent renovation, when one entered the small, cramped museum, the first thing to capture the visitor's eye was the large oil painting hanging on the wall facing the front entrance. Therein two Ainu guides in traditional clothing accompany uniformed farming-militia soldiers and Development Agency officials who survey the lay of the land.[49] However, as one progressed through the exhibit there was no comment on the fact that Ainu had lived for generations on the land confiscated for Japanese settlers. Instead, it was emphasized that the settlers lived in "bear country," one placard reading, "Building their homes in a world where bears lived, enduring hardships (*kon'nan*), the farming-militia worked hard to achieve the utopia they saw in their dreams." Now, the completely remodeled Northern Defense Museum is located outside the base for easy access to the public in a much larger and improved exhibition space. The painting has been quietly integrated into the exhibits, but when the sergeant who guided me through a personal tour stopped to give an extended explanation of two officials in this artistic work, she failed to mention the presence or significance of the Ainu figures. Moreover, the sign that effaces the long history of human inhabitation on the island by referencing only the subtle, but seemingly more riveting, prospect of bears remains. Although the Ainu guides in the impressive painting are a testament not only to the existence of Ainu but also their role in introducing and acclimatizing Japanese to the island, such exhibits imply that the colonization of Hokkaido was and is wholly unconnected to Ainu.

The Asahikawa Tondenhei Village Museum (Asahikawa heison kinenkan) is another example of what one longtime curator in Hokkaido calls the "pioneer banzai" narrative. Today, just as when the museum opened in 1982, the re-created *tondenhei* home, farming implements, exotic clothing, and household items present a picture of the struggles and accomplishments of the colonists. A distinguishing feature of this museum is its focus on the difficulties of rice cultivation in Hokkaido as a symbol of the Japanese settlers' "extraordinary hardships" and resourcefulness. Technological innovations in agriculture, such as the "octopus legs" (*tako ashi*), a rice-planting tool invented by colonist Suetake Yasushijirō, become emblematic of the story of Japanese transplanting civilization in the northern territory.

These two museums, by no means unusual in their approach, represent the disassociation generated by the grand narrative that writes out the colonial violence in Hokkaido just over a century ago. Despite a recent success in the long-fought Ainu battle for recognition as an indigenous people of Japan, in society at large "pioneers" remain prominent fixtures in narratives that celebrate the Meiji colonialists' triumph over the wild, natural landscape of Hokkaido as part of Japan's miraculous modernization.[50] Fictional works, such as Doppo's "The Shores of the Sorachi River," certainly play their part in establishing and perpetuating this version of history. Thus, active members of the Ainu nation continue to push for another victory, which will be won when this story is rewritten to acknowledge the less flattering realities of the history of colonial Hokkaido.

Notes

I am greatly indebted to Masayuki Shinohara for his patience with my endless questions about Japanese minutia. Thank you to Julie Koser, Helen Lee, and Kota Inoue for extremely productive reading, listening, and questioning. As always, thank you to Leslie Winston for her exacting editorial eyes and support.

1. The 2011 festival featured, for example, snow exhibits of the famous cartoon character Sazae-san and her family, the Lion King menagerie, Darth Vader, and the 2010 Noble Prize winner in chemistry, Suzuki Akira, as well as impressive ice replicas of the Chinese Temple of Heaven and a historic pavilion in Kyoto's Honganji Buddhist temple.

2. The extremely popular drama *From the Northern Country* (*Kita no kuni kara*, 1981–2002), the film *Year Zero of the North* (*Kita no reinen*, 2005), and Miyazaki Hayao's 1984 animated *Naushika* come to mind.

3. Abashiri Prison was first constructed in 1890 and modeled on Jeremy Bentham's panopticon model. It continues to function, although in modern buildings, as a high-security correctional facility. I borrow Dani Botsman's analogy to Alcatraz. See *Punishment and Power in the Making of Modern Japan* (Princeton, NJ: Princeton University Press, 2005), 186.

4. This phrasing comes from the Iwakura Proposal (*Iwakura teigi*, February 28, 1869), which delineated what Iwakura Tomomi, one of the new government's most powerful officials, believed were the three most urgent issues facing the government: foreign relations, the tax system, and the "development" (*kaitaku*) of Ezo. Iwakura notes that the "development" of Hokkaido would reap unprecedented profits for the domestic sphere and stop Russia from "watering at the mouth" over the island. Tanaka Akira, *Hokkaidō to Meiji ishin* (Hokkaido and the Meiji Restoration) (Sapporo: Hokkaidō daigaku tosho kankōkai, 2000), 23–26.

5. During the decades he undertook six imperial tours, the Meiji emperor stopped in Hakodate on the Tohoku Tour (1876) and traveled to Sapporo on the Yamagata-Akita-Hokkaido Tour (1881). Today you can visit the Hōheikan Hotel where the emperor stayed on this latter trip.

6. "The Shores of the Sorachi River" appeared in the November and December 1902 installments of the magazine for youths, *Seinenkai*.

7. At this time, there was also liberal use of the phrase "virgin land" (*shojochi*), which lacks the antagonistic association, but carries fraught gendered implications that function to justify colonial plunder.

8. Carol Gluck, *Japan's Modern Myths: Ideology in the Late Meiji Period* (Princeton, NJ: Princeton University Press, 1985), 180.

9. Ibid., 181.

10. Paul Anderer, *Other Worlds: Arishima Takeo and the Bounds of Modern Japanese Fiction* (New York: Columbia University Press, 1984), 29 (italics in the original).

11. Ibid., 30–31.

12. James Edward Ketelaar, "Hokkaido Buddhism and the Early Meiji State," in *New Directions in the Study of Meiji Japan*, ed. Helen Hardacre (Leiden: Brill, 1997), 534.

13. Kunikida Doppo, "Sorachigawa no kishibe" (The Shores of the Sorachi River), in *Hokkaidō bungaku zenshū: shintenchi no roman* 1 (The Collected Literary Works of Hokkaido: Novels of the New World, Vol. 1), eds. Ogasawara Katsu, Kihara Naohiko, and Wada Kingo (Tokyo: Rippū shobō, 1979–1980), 256–65.

14. Ibid., 256.

15. Ibid., 263.

16. This character combination is slightly different in nuance from the homonym, which emphasizes planting the opened land.

17. Doppo, "Sorachigawa no kishibe," 264.

18. Use of the word "men" here is deliberate. Women's (and children's) existence and labor are often overlooked in the history of colonial Hokkaido, even though, for instance, the men recruited for the Hokkaido farming-militia (*tondenhei*) and other state-supported male settlers were required to be married and bring their extended family with them to the island.

19. Doppo, "Sorachigawa no kishibe," 263.

20. Ibid.

21. Ibid.

22. Ibid., 264.

23. Ibid.

24. It is notable that the Meiji settlement programs in Hokkaido were initially a colossal failure since a majority of would-be settlers returned to the mainland unable to bear the severe climate and rigors and privations of colonial life.

25. The 1893 World's Columbian Exhibition commemorated Christopher Columbus' voyages four hundred years earlier. The displays of "native villages" and "Buffalo Bill's Wild West Show" were evidence of the prevalence of Western imperialism throughout the world which was, in large part, the legacy Columbus' violent invasion of indigenous communities throughout the southern hemisphere. For an excellent pictorial tour of a similar fair, see Eric Breitbart, *A World on Display: Photographs from the St. Louis World's Fair, 1904* (Albuquerque: University of New Mexico Press, 1997). One chapter, "Ainu and Pygmy," includes pictures of the nine Ainu who traveled to be part of an exhibit of "native peoples."

26. Nitobe Inazō, *The Imperial Agricultural College of Sapporo, Japan* (Sapporo: Imperial College of Agriculture, 1893), 1.

27. David Spurr, *The Rhetoric of Empire: Colonial Discourse in Journalism, Travel Writing, and Imperial Administration* (Durham, NC: Duke University Press, 1993), 92.

28. Ibid., 93.

29. *Meiji nyūsu jiten* 1 (The Meiji News Encyclopedia, Vol. 1) (Tokyo: Mainichi komyunikēshonzu, 1983), 668.

30. Komori Yōichi, "'Hogo' toiu na no shihai: shokuminchishugi no bokyaburarii" (Rule in the Name of "Protection": The Vocabulary of Colonialism) in *Media, hyōshō, ideorogii: Meiji sanjyūnendai no bunka kenkyū* (Media, Representation, Ideology: A Study of the Culture of the Third Decade of Meiji), eds. Komori Yōichi, Kōno Kensuke, and Takahashi Osamu (Tokyo: Ozawa shoten, 1997), 352. See also Chapter Two of this volume.

31. For more information on land and settler policy, see Siddle's chapter "Development and Immigration Policy" in *Race, Resistance and the Ainu of Japan* (London: Routledge, 1996), 55–60.

32. Doppo, "Sorachigawa no kishibe," 257, 264.

33. Ibid., 264.

34. For more discussion of agricultural settlements, see Siddle, *Race, Resistance and the Ainu of Japan*, 57.

35. Spurr, *The Rhetoric of Empire*, 28.

36. Nitobe, *The Imperial Agricultural College of Sapporo*, 2.

37. Komori, "'Hogo' toiu na no shihai," 329. The territory designated by the Ainu term *Ainu Moshir*, or "The Land of Humans," in fact, extends to the Kuriles and southern Sakhalin. See Honda Katsuichi, *Harukor: An Ainu Woman's Tale* (Berkeley: University of California Press, 1993), 287.

38. Doppo, "Sorachigawa no kishibe," 257.

39. Ibid., 264.

40. Siddle, *Race, Resistance and the Ainu of Japan*, 57.

41. This accounts for existence of the Hokkaido Place Name Card Game (*Hokkaidō chimei karuta*), which includes a set of 212 beautifully illustrated cards, each with a town's assigned Chinese characters, a pronunciation guide, an indication of its location on a map of Hokkaido, and a short blurb, which frequently explains the Ainu meaning of the name. See also Kitamichi Kunihiko, *Ainugo chimei de tabisuru Hokkaidō* (Traveling Hokkaido through Place Names in the Ainu Language) (Tokyo: Asahi shinbun shuppan, 2008).

42. Siddle, *Race, Resistance and the Ainu of Japan*, 163.

43. Arishima Takeo (1878–1923) is another writer who is frequently associated with Hokkaido. Anderer presents a nuanced reading of Arishima's "The Descendents of Cain" (*Kain no matsuei*, 1916), which is set in Hokkaido, commenting that "Just as Hokkaido represents some 'other world' where the traveler sees around him nothing familiar and so is assaulted by the discordance or at least the difference of a new milieu, so does Arishima's fictional journey toward the interior of the mind reveal hitherto unknown areas of division and conflict." Anderer, *Other Worlds*, 37.

44. Tom Henighan, *Natural Space in Literature: Imagination and Environment in Nineteenth and Twentieth Century Fiction and Poetry* (Ottawa: Golden Dog Press, 1982), 36.

45. Doppo , "Sorachigawa no kishibe," 256.

46. Ibid., 264.

47. Ibid.

48. Ibid.

49. You can see a reprint of this painting in *Tondenhei emonogatari: Asahikawa bunko* 2 (A Pictorial Narrative of the Tondenhei: The Asahikawa Collection, Vol. 2) (Asahikawa: Sohokkai, 1982), 80.

50. In 2008, concerned about the international attention that would be drawn to the Ainu because of the G8 Summit held in Toyako, Hokkaido, the Japanese government formally recognized the Ainu as an indigenous people of Japan. Much credit for this should go to the Ainu who scheduled the Indigenous Peoples Summit to meet immediately before the G8 Summit. For more on this topic, see Annelise Lewallen, "Indigenous at Last! Ainu Grassroots Organizing and the Indigenous Peoples Summit in Ainu Mosir," *Asia-Pacific Journal* 48-6-08 (Nov. 30, 2008).

CHAPTER TWO

Hokkaido Former Natives
Protection Law

TRANSLATION BY RICHARD SIDDLE

CONTEXT
Hokkaido

CRITIQUE
Rule in the Name of "Protection":
The Vocabulary of Colonialism

KOMORI YŌICHI

THE HOKKAIDO Former Natives Protection Law (*Hokkaidō kyūdojin hogo hō*), enacted in 1899, was ostensibly drafted to stabilize the lives of Ainu, who had lost their means of livelihood because of incursions into their homelands by Japanese colonizers. The law endorsed individual land grants and the adoption of Japanese agricultural practices as the best means to rescue Ainu from poverty. For those Ainu who complied there were also provisions for medical treatment and education for children. It might be better understood, however, as a program of forced assimilation, which worked in tandem with other laws to undermine the ability of Ainu communities to support themselves in traditional ways and to suppress their language, history, and cultural practices.

In 1984, the Ainu Association of Hokkaido (Hokkaidō utari kyōkai) completed a draft for far-reaching legislation, the New Ainu Law (*Ainu shinpō*), as part of a growing grassroots movement agitating for the repeal of the Hokkaido Former Natives Protection Law and the promotion of meaningful redress of the legacy of colonization and discrimination. The New Ainu Law not only called for support in economic, educational, and cultural realms, but also official acknowledgment of Japan's colonial actions in Hokkaido and the allocation of seats in the Diet for ethnic groups. Due to the Ainu Association's efforts, the Hokkaido Former Natives Protection Law was abolished in July 1997. In its place the Ainu Cultural Promotion Law was enacted, which many Ainu consider only a marginal victory given that it ignores the most important and pressing concerns addressed in the New Ainu Law.

Komori Yōichi, professor of Japanese literature at the University of Tokyo, is a prolific and dynamic scholar of literature who frequently ventures far beyond the normal confines of the field. He is sometimes considered an institutional and intellectual outsider, due to having received his Ph.D. from Hokkaido University, his sharp criticism of political, economic, and social injustice, and his on-going activism against changing Article 9 of the Japanese constitution. While Komori is famous for his trenchant readings of canonical writers, such as Higuchi Ichiyō, Natsume Sōseki, and Miyazawa Kenji, he is also firmly grounded in a school of literary studies committed to providing historical contextualization and understanding the power of language to determine and shape history. Notable among his many works are *Narrative as Structure* (*Kōzō toshite no katari*, 1988), *"Oscillations" of Japanese Literature* (*"Yuragi" no Nihonbungaku*, 1998), and his autobiographical work *Komori Yōichi Discovers Japanese* (*Komori Yōichi Nihongo ni deau*, 2000). Komori has edited numerous works, including the thirteen-volume Iwanami Literary Studies series (2002–2003), which examines literature through a wide range of lenses, such as history, politics, media, sex, performance, nature, the nation, and more.

Komori's essay "Rule in the Name of 'Protection': The Vocabulary of Colonialism" (*"Hogo" toiu na no shihai: shokuminchishugi no bokyaburarii*, 1997) is significant as an early, and still rare, example of scholarship that clearly recognizes Hokkaido as a modern Japanese colony. Komori's liberal use of scare quotes in the original chapter functions to disrupt conventional meanings, emphasize the power of naming, and highlight how words determine and obfuscate reality and history. In order to improve readability, we have eliminated some of the scare quotes in the translation after a term has been sufficiently established as deserving critical analysis.

Hokkaido Former Natives Protection Law (Law No. 27, March 1, 1899)

ADAPTED BY RICHARD SIDDLE
FROM JOHN LIE'S TRANSLATION FOR THE
HOKKAIDŌ UTARI KYŌKAI[1]

ARTICLE 1

Those Former Natives of Hokkaido who are engaged, or wish to engage, in agriculture shall be granted free of charge no more than 12 acres of land per household.

ARTICLE 2

The land granted under the preceding Article is subject to the following conditions on rights of ownership.

1. It may not be transferred except by inheritance.

2. No rights of pledge, mortgage, lease or perpetual lease can be established.

3. No easement can be established without the permission of the Governor of Hokkaido.

4. It cannot become the object of a lien or preferential right. The land granted in the preceding Article shall not be subject to land tax or local taxes until 30 years from the date of grant. Land already owned by Former Natives shall not be transferred except by inheritance, nor shall any of the real rights (*jus in rem*) referred to in paragraphs 1 to 3 be established upon it without the permission of the Governor of Hokkaido.

ARTICLE 3

Any part of the land granted under Article 1 shall be confiscated if it has not been cultivated within 15 years from the date of the grant.

ARTICLE 4

Hokkaido Former Natives who are destitute will be provided with agricultural implements and seeds.

ARTICLE 5

Hokkaido Former Natives who are injured or ill but cannot afford medical treatment shall be provided with medical treatment or expenses for medicine.

ARTICLE 6

Hokkaido Former Natives who are too injured, ill, disabled, senile or young to provide for themselves shall be granted welfare under existing legislation and if they should die at or during the period of assistance funeral expenses will be provided.

ARTICLE 7

Children of destitute Hokkaido Former Natives who are attending school will be provided with tuition fees.

ARTICLE 8

Expenses incurred under Articles 4 to 7 shall be appropriated from the proceeds of the communal funds of Hokkaido Former Natives, or if these are insufficient, from the National Treasury.

ARTICLE 9

An elementary school will be constructed with funds from the National Treasury in areas where there is a Former Native village.

ARTICLE 10

The Governor of Hokkaido will manage the communal funds of the Hokkaido Former Natives.

The Governor of Hokkaido, subject to the approval of the Home Minister, may dispose of the communal funds in the interests of the owners of the communal funds or may refuse to expend them if he deems it necessary.

The communal funds managed by the Governor of Hokkaido shall be designated by the Governor of Hokkaido.

ARTICLE 11

The Governor of Hokkaido may issue police orders with regard to the protection of the Hokkaido Former Natives and may impose a fine of over 2 yen but no more than 25 yen or a period of imprisonment of over 11 days but no more than 25 days.

By-law

ARTICLE 12
This Law will become effective from April 1, 1899.

ARTICLE 13
Regulations relevant to the implementation of this Law shall be set by the Home Minister.

Rule in the Name of "Protection": The Vocabulary of Colonialism[2]

KOMORI YŌICHI

TRANSLATION BY MICHELE M. MASON

Two "Protection Laws"

Building on the Emigrant Protection Regulation of April 12, 1894 (Ordinance No. 42), the Emigrant Protection Law (Law No. 70) was enacted on April 7, 1896. Then, the Hokkaido Former Natives Protection Law (Law No. 27) was officially announced on March 1, 1899. This law, which had been presented as a government-sponsored proposal in the preceding year, was based on the Hokkaido Natives Protection Law Proposal submitted by Diet members Chiba Tanehide and Suzuki Mitsuyoshi in 1895. This article aims to interrogate why these "protection laws" were enacted like bookends on the Sino-Japanese War (1894–1895) and what precise kind of act the word "protection" denotes.

To begin, there is one place in the Emigrant Protection Law where the word "protection" is clearly used. Article 4 of the law reads, "To *protect* emigrants, maintain public order, or when deemed necessary for diplomatic purposes, the government may prohibit emigrant voyages or revoke permission to take such voyages" (italics added). Moreover, Article 1 of the Emigrant Protection Regulation states, "By this decree the definition of emigrant is a person who for the purposes of labor travels abroad, and the term emigrant agents designates those people whose occupation it is to run agencies that recruit emigrants and arrange for the emigrants' travel abroad regardless of what they are called." In a similar fashion, the Emigrant Protection Law sought to supervise the relationship between "emigrant agents" and "emigrants" through the licensing of national "administrative" agencies. That is to say that the principal objective of this protection law was to "protect" emigrants from emigrant agents whose aim was commercial gain.

"Emigrant services" emerged as a particular industry, and the reason the state could ill afford to ignore it concerned the rapidly increasing numbers of "emigrants" at the time. For instance, comparing the numbers of Japanese residing in foreign countries in 1885 and in 1895 reveals a dramatic jump; in the United States the number of Japanese rose by almost 5,000, from 1,090 to 6,156 persons, in Hawai'i by 21,000 Japanese, from 1,949 to

23,102 persons, and in Korea by 8,000, starting at 4,521 and reaching 12,303 persons. Then, during the five years between 1896 and 1900, the United States suddenly saw an increase of 26,000 Japanese, in Hawai'i an increase of 34,000, in Korea 3,000, and in China 3,000, which amounts to a precipitous growth exceeding the preceding ten years. After the Sino-Japanese War, Japan was facing a true overseas "emigration era." Consequently, the emigrant service industry came into being, and numerous problems emerged between emigrant agents and emigrants and even more so between the nation called "Japan" and the countries to which the emigrants traveled.

The crux of the trouble becomes evident from matters prohibited by the law. The aims of the regulations included preventing people from traveling abroad without government permission, attempting to gain permission by lying about one's destination, conducting the business of emigrant services without governmental permission, and "recruiting emigrants by means of deception." What we must remain cautious about is the seventh article of the Emigrant Protection Law wherein it is stipulated that "only imperial subjects and, alternatively, commercial companies that conduct the main part of their business within the imperial nation and whose stockholders or employees are solely imperial subjects can be considered 'emigrant agents or agencies.'" First, we understand that emigrant services were chiefly conducted by commercial companies, and, thus, an era arrived when humans as labor commodities, in the form of emigrants, became the objects of commerce in the same way things become goods.

However, we also notice an excessive insistence on the issue of the interior of the "imperial nation." The important point is that commercial companies permitted to undertake emigrant services had to be managed by imperial subjects only. Companies that were involved with foreigners or foreign capital were denied emigrant service status. Here, the memory of one incident involving emigrants, which occurred at the beginning of the Meiji era, must have had an impact. In 1868, 148 Japanese were transported to what was at that time the Kingdom of Hawai'i by an American consul general, Eugene Van Reed. In the Kingdom of Hawai'i there were vast fields of sugarcane, and toward the middle of the nineteenth century the technological innovations in sugar production suddenly made advances, necessitating a massive labor force of obedient farm workers. These Japanese, really labor commodities, were taken to Hawai'i in a manner equal to the slave trade. The Japanese government, angered by this, called off all emigration to Hawai'i, a ban that would last for seventeen years, until 1885. When Walter

Murray Gibson, who had been appointed premier in Hawai'i in 1882, peti-
tioned to the Meiji emperor to reopen Japanese immigration to Hawai'i, the
offer was accepted, and the first group of government-contracted emigrants
was sent in February of 1885. By 1894, when the 26th group arrived, close to
30,000 Japanese had crossed over to Hawai'i.

In 1885, when Minister of Finance Matsukata Masaoshi's deflation policies
reached their extreme, poverty and starvation in rural farming communities
reached an all time high due to overpopulation in the post-Meiji-Restoration
era. Japanese farmers who could not make a living within the borders of the
nation of Japan, and who until that point had been forbidden to go abroad,
left, favoring Hawai'i and California. The Republic of Hawai'i was established in 1894 because of an intervention carried out by the combined efforts
of U.S. ministers and pro-American forces the preceding year. From this year
on, the Japanese system of government-contracted emigration was abolished
and replaced by private companies, which functioned as go-betweens for contract emigrants. Consequently, situations exactly like those feared in the Emigrant Protection Law actually developed in the year that this law was enacted.

In November 1896 the arrival of emigrants on the ship *Tōyōmaru* occa-
sioned a lawsuit, and in February of the following year, 534 Japanese were not
allowed to disembark when they landed in Honolulu aboard the *Shinshūmaru*.
Again, on March 20 the 163 immigrants transported on the *Sakuramaru* were
denied entrance into Hawai'i. The basis for these denials on the Hawaiian
side was the fact that the Japanese emigrants lacked the fifty dollars needed for
status verification, as stipulated in Hawaiian immigration regulations. What
the private emigration companies had been doing upon docking was to lend
fifty dollars cash to those emigrants who lacked such funds and then collect
the fifty dollars once the emigrant arrived ashore. In other words, it was cam-
ouflaged "show money." In this way, according to the Hawaiian officials, the
number of delinquent emigrants continued to grow. At the time the Japanese
Emigrant Protection Law was issued, one could count nineteen such special-
ized emigrant companies in the nation.

On the one hand, protecting Japanese who emigrated abroad meant, first
of all, protecting imperial subjects from the profit-driven emigrant enterprises that committed illegal activities in both Japan and the destination
country. On the other hand, the emigration problem was also a phenomenon that arose out of a rivalry between the United States, which was modi-
fying its colonial policies toward Hawai'i and developing its naval military
power in the Pacific Ocean, and Japan, which formed colonial strategie in

opposition to these moves. In the ten years following 1886—the year an immigration agreement was signed by the Japanese foreign minister, Inoue Karoru, and Hawai'i's foreign minister, R. W. Irwin—over 30,000 Japanese so-called emigrants were transported to Hawai'i. In Hawai'i, the populations of Americans, Hawaiians, Chinese, and Japanese became roughly even. The politically cozy relationship between King Kalakaua and Chinese merchants provoked in the United States a sense of impending danger that Hawai'i would be taken over by Chinese immigrants. In 1890 a tax law that was to protect domestic American sugarcane business interests was enacted, and agitation by American owners of Hawaiian sugarcane fields for the annexation of Hawai'i became stronger. In 1898, Hawai'i became incorporated as a territory into the United States.

At this time, Japan's central colonization policy was based in Taiwan's colonial economy. On April 17, 1895, the peace treaty for the Sino-Japanese War was signed in Shimonoseki, and it was decided that China should pay the sum of 300 million yen in reparations and cede the Liaodong peninsula, Taiwan, and the Pescadores Islands. Then on April 23, as is common knowledge, there was the so-called "Triple Intervention" by Russia, Germany, and France over the Liaodong peninsula. On May 5 Japan accepted the recommendation to "return" the Liaodong peninsula. Five days later, on May 10, Admiral Kabayama Sukenori was appointed Taiwan's first governor-general, and Imperial Guards, under the division commander Prince Kitashirakawa, landed in Taiwan. On June 2 China handed over Taiwan to Japan, but a resistance movement that opposed the ceding of Taiwan fought until October, extending into the central and southern areas. Prince Kitashirakawa died from an illness contracted in battle. Subsequently, Japan reformed the governor-general mandate and a civilian system replaced it on March 31, 1896.

Given that failed domestic governance forced Japanese unable to make a living within Japan to other countries, threatening the livelihoods of the inhabitants of those countries, it could be said that wars of colonial invasion and "emigration" fall under the same logic, namely as policies that attempt to solve problems through incursion. At the same time, the Emigration Protection Law was a necessary strategic move by Japan to address international discord caused by both of these varieties of Japanese invasions. It was the case that efforts to exclude Japanese immigrants, which had begun at the end of the nineteenth century, grew even stronger in the twentieth century. Under the pretext of "emigrant protection," the nation-state called Japan actually sought to "protect" its interests vis-à-vis major Western powers, and it is within this context that the term "protection" gains meaning.

This history notwithstanding, in actuality, from the beginning of the Meiji era in 1868 until the twentieth century the majority of Japanese "emigrants" settled in the island Ainu Moshir, homeland of the indigenous Ainu, which was unilaterally named "Hokkaido" by Japan in 1869. As we will see, the word "protection" in the Hokkaido Former Natives Protection Law fulfilled rather remarkably the role of concealing traces of that invasion from the Japanese populace on the mainland.

Invasion in the Name of "Development"

Ainu Moshir was designated a strategic bulwark against Russia's southern expansion policies by the new Meiji government. An 1869 imperial inquiry reads:

> Ezo is the northern gate of the imperial nation. It is close to Santan and Manchuria, and although its boundaries are roughly settled, in the northern area there is a place where locals and people from abroad live together. The Japanese administrators there, who have enslaved the natives until now, have been cruel in the extreme. The foreigners have been exceedingly amiable; therefore, the natives are sometimes hostile to our countrymen and instead have reverence for the foreigners.[3]

At this point in history, the Japanese appellation for Ainu Moshir was "Ezo," or the Land of Barbarians, and the Japanese understood the geographical scope to include Sakhalin. The vague phrase "a place where locals and *people from abroad* live together" indicates the presence of Russians. Japanese are referred to as "our countrymen," while the term "natives" is chosen for the Ainu.

However, in September of that same year, in a letter by Sanjō Sanetomi addressed to the Hokkaido Development Agency we can see several significant changes.

September 1869

Development Agency:

1. Hokkaido is the imperial nation's northern gate and is an extremely valuable area. In accordance with the recent command to develop Hokkaido, we must carry out the deepest wishes of the imperial will. To that end, one must follow the path of caretakers, spreading civilization and deepening moral customs.

2. As mainlanders gradually emigrate, they must cooperate with natives, be productive in their occupations, and devote themselves to the civilizing mission.

3. As for Sakhalin, where mainlanders live among Russians, one must be wholly decorous, devote oneself to reason, and not behave in a thoughtless manner or take up vices. Even in the case that Russians are arrogant or do unjust things, one cannot respond as an individual. In all decisions, one must choose rightly and consult with the consul. Moreover, in those cases where one experiences difficulties, one must go through government agencies, using all of the nation's resources appropriately, enduring trifling matters peaceably, and endeavoring not to subvert our larger mission.

4. Especially when building a new country in a distant place, if one does not work in solidarity with government officials, far-reaching projects will never succeed. One should not debate who is noble and who is not, but should approach everything with consideration and sincerity and obey orders and not just pretend to do so.

Minister of the Left[4]

In August of 1869 Ezo was renamed "Hokkaido," and what the Japanese called "Karafuto" (Sakhalin) was deemed to be a separate entity. Since this decision was predicated on Russia's encroachment upon Sakhalin Island, this area was referred to as a "Russian mixed-residential quarter," and a logical framework different from the one applied to Hokkaido was followed. Given that Sakhalin was a space where two nations, Russia and Japan, confronted each other, "individual personal conduct" was impermissible, and in the case that trouble should arise, "one must go through government agencies" and "consult with the consul" of Russia. In those situations when matters still could not be resolved, then "all of the nation's resources" would be brought to bear. In contrast, the area named Hokkaido was viewed as a territory without any such preconditions. There, Japanese officials employed the legal terminology "ownerless land" by which European and American powers had earlier established the "sovereignty" of their modern nation-states by pushing through colonial strategies that ignored indigenous peoples.[5]

The "development" of Hokkaido was at the heart of an employment scheme for former samurai whose previous special privileges were rescinded through the process of abolishing feudal domains and establishing prefectures in 1871. After the creation of the Hokkaido Development Agency in

1869, "regulations for emigrant assistance" in the Sapporo area were put into place. These stipulated:

> Farmers will be provided housing, a small stipend, farming implements, household items, a three-year food supply, and even expenses for opening land, in addition to travel expenses. For merchants and artisans, capital for building a house and a pecuniary allowance will be granted or lent. Some of these privileges will be available not just to individuals recruited by the Development Agency but also to those who voluntarily resettle. Moreover, we will establish facilities for those who are approved and relocate to their designated posts.[6]

With the promulgation of the Family Register Law (*Kōsekihō*, 1871), the Ainu were incorporated into the category of "commoners," and at this time it became practice to enter them into the record as "former natives." The Hokkaido Development Agency carried out blatant assimilation policies, issuing most notably an order that strictly abolished "customs" that were deeply rooted in Ainu livelihood.

Announcement to Natives:
1. Those people who engage in opening land will be provided with a house, farming implements, and other things, and it is forbidden to burn the house of a deceased person and change residences, as has been hitherto the custom.
2. It is strictly forbidden for girls born hereafter to be tattooed.
3. Hereafter, the custom of wearing earrings is strictly forbidden for men, but for the time being, women may do as they wish.
4. One must make every effort to learn spoken Japanese, of course, but also the rules of written Japanese.

Development Agency[7]

In the first place, in the phrasing "people who engage in opening land" there lies a notion that denies the fundamentals of Ainu life. Only people who open land and undertake farming are recognized. However, Ainu livelihood relied primarily on hunting and fishing, not to mention the fact that they did not have the concept of owning land or private ownership. According to the Ainu, Ainu Moshir, or the Quiet Land of Humans, was a collectively shared natural world. Still, the Hokkaido Development Agency passed the Land Holdings Regulation in September of 1872, and land that had already been "opened and planted" was converted into privately owned land, while, with the exception of areas that had previously been designated for government use or private "lease land," all of Hokkaido, as a government-owned entity, was put up for sale to interested private parties. This regulation was for the sake of none other than "mainlanders." Vast areas where Ainu were once able to hunt and fish were expropriated as land for Japanese settlers.

In a similar fashion, the rituals related to Ainu traditional views on life and death were denied, and Ainu were even forced to adopt the gendered customs of the so-called mainlanders. It goes without saying that the language of the Hokkaido Development Agency's announcement is Japanese. The Ainu language, which did not have a writing system, was not acknowledged as a language. Thus, Hokkaido became a place where only mainlanders could live and prosper, and "cooperating with natives" there was fundamentally impossible.

This was not, however, solely the idea of the Hokkaido Development Agency's director Kuroda Kiyotaka. Kuroda, who had traveled to the United States, invited Horace Capron, commissioner of the Department of Agriculture under the authority of the victorious Civil War general President Grant, as a foreign consultant to assist in "developing Hokkaido." The offer to Capron set his yearly salary at 10,000 dollars and included housing. Capron, after arriving in Japan in 1871, ordered a survey by forestry agents and chemists who had accompanied him from the United States, instructing them to search for appropriate farming, logging, and mining locations. America's putative development path after the opening of the transcontinental railroad was put into practice in Hokkaido. That is to say, the strategic aggression against and encroachment upon American indigenous peoples by Anglo-Saxon "immigrants" were replicated by Japanese immigrants in Hokkaido, the homeland of the Ainu. Capron, who advocated free migration and foreign capital, but opposed to the bitter end the Meiji administration's commitment to "development" through government channels, returned home in 1875.

Then, in that same year there was a turning point in Hokkaido's development due to the signing of the Russo-Japanese cooperation agreement called the Sakhalin-Kurile Exchange Treaty. The states known as Russia and Japan unilaterally divided up the territory of Ainu Moshir and drew the countries' borders in such a fashion that people of the same ethnic group were made to hold differing citizenship. Once the national borders were fixed, 854 Ainu living in Sakhalin were forcibly moved to Hokkaido, and there were even cases in which Ainu were coerced into relocating to interior areas because authorities feared they would escape back to their homeland.

In 1876, William Smith Clark came to Japan on a contract to establish the Sapporo Agricultural College.[8] In the short period of one year, he taught agricultural practices suited to Hokkaido's climate and lifestyle, converted students to Christianity, and attempted to shape Hokkaido's landscape into the likes of a rural farming community in New England.

Thus, the origins of the development of Hokkaido, to put it simply, lie in a system of invasive immigration as relief for the former samurai who had lost privileges that they had had as military personnel and government officials under the shogunal system during the Tokugawa period (1600–1868). For example, in 1873, the Hokkaido *tondenhei* farming-militia system was created, which until 1890 mainly recruited former samurai as a crucial means to provide them aid. By 1899, when the Hokkaido Former Natives Protection Law was issued, 7,337 households totaling 39,911 people were sent as "emigrants" to Hokkaido under this program.

In 1883, the year after the abolition of the Hokkaido Development Agency, the central government decreed that every year 150,000 yen could be lent to former samurai who applied to migrate and settle in Hokkaido, and the Regulation for the Settlement of Former Samurai (1885) in Hokkaido was issued. This regulation gave extremely privileged and favorable treatment to former samurai from all prefectures who could not shoulder the resettlement expenses, loaning them interest-free capital for opening land and even offering payment plans that allowed a deferment for seven years and thereafter twenty annual installments. Each household was provided with approximately 8 acres of land, and after this had been opened it could be purchased at a low price. Under this Regulation for the Settlement of Former Samurai, 300 samurai households "emigrated" to Hokkaido. Not only that, there were numerous legal devices put into place to "protect" the "emigrants," who were mostly samurai. Of course, in the background, the livelihoods of Ainu, which were fundamentally rooted in nature, were destroyed by this process.

Thus, the term "protection" in the Hokkaido Former Natives Protection Law not only suppresses the over thirty years of history of the Japanese invasion and looting of Ainu Moshir, but also, in the end, contains the intention to invert the situation so as to make it appear that it was the Ainu's fault. We should not forget, moreover, that the Hokkaido *tondenhei* farming-militia fell under the Ministry of the Army's administration and participated in both the Sino-Japanese War and Russo-Japanese War (1904–1905) as part of Japan's imperial regular army. These ostensible emigrants were therefore also an invading army.

The Discourse of "Ruin"

Article 1 of the Hokkaido Former Natives Protection Law reads, "Those Former Natives of Hokkaido who are engaged, or wish to engage, in agriculture shall be granted free of charge no more than 12 acres of land per household." As mentioned above, this law applied only to those who "engage in farming" or those who "wish to engage in farming." Thoroughly permeating this law is the idea that without converting to the practice of farming, one cannot be recognized as a Japanese "citizen," which completely disregards the *habitus* of the Ainu, who for many centuries had lived by hunting and fishing. To force the practice of farming on a people who live by hunting and fishing is none other than an act of violence against their very right to a livelihood. Thus, this law constituted an attack on the Ainu's entire arena of life, ranging from issues of physical health and nutritional balance based on daily foodstuffs to worldviews, cosmology, and religious beliefs.

Article 5 of the law reads, "Hokkaido Former Natives who are injured or ill but cannot afford medical treatment shall be provided with medical treatment or expenses for medicine" and Article 7, "Children of destitute Hokkaido Former Natives who are attending school will be provided with tuition fees." Article 9 states, "An elementary school will be constructed with funds from the National Treasury in areas where there is a Former Native village." For the Ainu this law meant ultimately to be controlled by the science of hygiene and made into Japanese citizens through a "civilizing" mission executed through the educational system. In other words, to be subjugated in the name of "protection."

This colonial law claims its purpose is to make "former natives" independent by converting them to farming according to "the Emperor's wish for universal benevolence" and to "bestow the honor of becoming imperial subjects" on Ainu through assimilation and advancement via the educational system. However, this assertion is made possible only because the law presents "national duty" within an assumed "logic" of "survival of the fittest."[9] It goes without saying that it was the Japanese putative development of Hokkaido that precipitated the crisis of Ainu society and that it was not caused by the Ainu themselves. Moreover, we must pay attention to the fact that the policies of "protection" and "assimilation" themselves, essentially policies of "imperialization" (making Ainu into imperial subjects) deployed in colonial law, hastened their "ruin" and not the other way around.

Still, at this time when the Meiji government was creating modern "citizens" (by abolishing the former four hierarchal statuses—samurai, farmers, artisans, merchants—and making all Japanese equal), the process of turning Ainu into "citizens" through the phrase "former natives" paralleled the new designation of the outcaste class (*hisabetsu burakumin*) as "new commoners," positioning both groups on the periphery of the concept of citizenship by fixing their difference. Afterward, Japan's imperial rule over foreign peoples proceeded apace and Japanese leaders applied their experiences subjugating the Ainu and took as their reference the Hokkaido Former Natives Protection Law in these new contexts. For example, consider the Korean Name Change Order (1939), which forced Koreans to take Japanese names, or the suppression of "Takasago aborigines" in Taiwan. Also, the "aboriginal school houses" built in the mountainous regions of Taiwan were modeled on the "former natives' schools" set up by the Protection Law.[10]

In practice, the enforcement of the Hokkaido Former Natives Protection Law, which lacked any budgetary support, did not proceed as planned. However, as Murai Osamu rightly points out, the emerging ideology found in it can be said to have formed the foundation of the colonial policies of the Greater Japanese Empire. Not only did the promulgation of the Imperial Rescript on Education (1890) represent a critical opportunity to establish the ideology of assimilation centered on compulsory schooling, but rapidly growing new academic discourses at the time also played a significant role in the establishment of this ideology. The emerging scholarly disciplines were anthropology, archeology, and linguistics. The symbol of the "ruin" of the Ainu people was comprehensively formulated by these three academic fields, which mutually drove each other on. Those who created the fundamental premises of this new scholarship, as it turns out, were foreign diplomats and foreigners hired to work in Japan.

There was, for example, English consul Walter Dening's research on Ainu vocabulary, the study of Ainu poison arrows by Dr. Stuart Eldridge, who was Horace Capron's underling in the Hokkaido Development Agency, geological surveyor Benjamin Smith Lyman's measurements of Ainu bodies, the Ministry of Industry's geologist John Milne's survey of the customs and language of the Sarudani Ainu, Austria's legation's official translator Heinrich von Siebold's research on folk customs, zoologist Edward Morse's scientific surveys, and Isabella Bird's reports on Ainu life. Even Basil Hall Chamberlain, professor at Tokyo Imperial University, visited the Ainu village Biratori in 1887. Chamberlain developed the new academic fields of "Japanese national language studies" and "Oriental comparative linguistics," and he undertook comparisons of Ainu and Japanese languages, myths, and place names and even extended his efforts to the Ryukyuan language, hypothesizing a theory of the genealogy of the Japanese language based on the theory of evolution.

Of course, it goes without saying that at the center of Ainu research was the missionary John Batchelor. After Batchelor came to Hakodate in 1877 on a mission for the Anglican Church, he began the study of the Ainu language and continued proselytization for the "salvation of the Ainu." As the numbers of converts increased, Batchelor established the Airen Charity School in Horobetsu village in 1890 and endeavored to teach Ainu youths, but this became untenable since such activities were illegal according to treaty stipulations. In 1892 he set up a school in the Yachigashira area of Hakodate and educated Ainu children who boarded there, and again in 1895, he taught twenty Ainu girls, who were living with him in his home in Sapporo. In 1892 he built an Ainu hospital in Sapporo, and, cooperating with the head of the Sapporo hospital Sekiba Fujihiko, provided medical treatment to approximately four hundred Ainu over the course of four years. In addition to Batchelor, Englishwoman Miss Lucy Payne set up a charity school in 1891 in Harutori village in Kushiro and built "native schools" adjacent to a number of churches.

The state of education in Hokkaido after the promulgation of the Imperial Rescript on Education points to the nationalistic backlash against the activities of foreigners. A report by the 1893 investigative committee on the Former Natives Education Law claims, "Ainu schools have not yet been set up, so students begin their education in vain with foreigners. There is a school in Horobetsu that is managed by Batchelor. More than twenty Ainu accept his absolute control. The schoolhouse in Harutori was built by Payne. Over forty children are being raised there. It will be a national disgrace if we continue to look on as spectators."[11]

To somehow extract the Ainu from the care of foreigners was an idea passed on since the days of the Matsumae domain's domination in Ezo during the Tokugawa era. This thinking was not in the least bit different from when the 854 Ainu were forcibly removed once Sakhalin became Russian territory. Without a doubt, one of the goals of the Hokkaido Former Natives

Protection Law was to extricate Ainu from the educational and medical activism of foreigners and to place them under the auspices of the state then called the Greater Japanese Empire. At the same time that the word "protection" functioned to simultaneously separate the indigenous people of this internal colony from the "foreigners" and segregate and distinguish them from Japanese under the control of the Greater Japanese Empire, this term also concealed the fact that the successful Japanese colonial invasion known by the monikers "immigration" and "settlement" thoroughly destroyed the roots of indigenous culture and society.

Then, according to evolutionary theories, the Japanese were positioned as early adopters of "civilization" and superior to the Ainu, and the discourse of cultural anthropology, which reasoned with the oft-repeated idea that Japanese needed to protect the racially inferior and distinct Ainu race since it was suffering a crisis of "ruin," gained footing through the work of Japanese anthropologists.

In 1893, the first courses in anthropology at Tokyo Imperial University were launched. The "Koropokkuru Debate" that developed between Tsuboi Shōgorō (1863–1913), who adhered to the Edward Morse school of thought, and Koganei Yoshikiyo (1859–1944) of the Erwin von Bälz school, was quite famous, and in 1894 the Hokkaido Anthropological Society came into being and the colonization of knowledge continued.[12] The following is a portion of a speech given by Koganei in the year before the Hokkaido Former Natives Protection Law was proposed in the National Assembly:

> So then, as scholars from Japan and abroad have said, the people called Ainu *are not capable of acquiring civilization,* the same as the world's ordinary barbarian races. As for the reason for this—that these barbarian races are unable to acquire civilization—there is the argument that civilization is *like a poison to them, and barbarian races that come in contact with civilization gradually become extinct,* which is a claim that can likewise be made regarding the Ainu. When we think carefully, however, *it still retains some vagueness. We must try to think of what could bring about a successful meeting of Ainu and civilization.*
>
> So, if someone should say the Ainu are steadily becoming extinct because the Japanese have imparted civilization to them, well, that is an explanation hard to swallow. To be sure, since the Meiji Restoration, the development of Hokkaido has progressed yearly, and the more Hokkaido improves, the more worsening hardships are created for the Ainu. This may be obvious. As the land is further reclaimed, the animals they hunt [bear] and the fish they catch [salmon], among other things, decline. This is perhaps undeniable. Compared with civilized people, barbarians generally need a great ex-

panse of land. That is to say, since the barbarians do not know how to adopt farming of their own accord, taking and eating that which is produced by nature, they require quite a large area of land. As more Japanese come to settle and open land, from a perspective of people-to-land ratio, the land area decreases, and, owing to this, the Ainu's struggle to survive becomes increasingly difficult. This is for the Ainu a considerable hindering obstacle. Whether Ainu can overcome this obstacle or not—this is a matter of life or death. In other words, because survival will become more challenging, I believe that if Ainu cannot manage to survive through work, they will inevitably gradually decline.[13]

Koganei's speech is replete with contradictions. He starts by stating that "As Hokkaido progresses" via "development," "worsening hardships are created for the Ainu." It is none other than the Japanese, who, under the name of development, usurp Ainu hunting and fishing grounds, privatize their territory, and convert it into farmland by "reclaiming" the forests. Up to this point, his argument is founded upon the historical realities of Hokkaido and its colonization. However, the argument that the responsibility of "imparting civilization" to the Ainu falls to the "Japanese" affirms the colonization of Hokkaido and the Japanese settlement there. Not only are the Ainu a "barbarian race," it is asserted, they are also "incapable of acquiring civilization," the latter being a common characteristic of the "world's ordinary barbarians." Therefore, it is suggested, the Ainu barbarian race is fated to "extinction."

This is Koganei's irrational logic. The impoverishment of Ainu livelihood caused by Japanese colonization and emigration is attributed to problems with the Ainu "race." On the one hand, we have the "Japanese race," which was able to adopt civilization, and, on the other hand, the "barbarian race" of Ainu, who naturally go "extinct" when they come into contact with "civilization." As a result, within this discourse there operates an unfounded assertion that the Japanese are civilized. Based on this definition, Koganei produces a logic that assumes that the so-called civilized Japanese race has been charged with the mission to protect the barbarian Ainu race that is becoming extinct.

Once colonial invasion is justified under the rhetorical devices of "civilization" and "race," the schema wherein the Japanese did the protecting and the Ainu were the ones protected towers as if a scientific truth. This logic was not applied just to the Ainu race. It was shared by the linguist Kindaichi Kyosuke, who tried to "protect" the literary heritage of the Ainu traditional oral epics (*yukar*) from "ruin." In this way, hidden behind the language of protection, the colonial crimes of the Greater Japanese Empire and the truth of the circumstances forced on the Ainu, wherein the Japanese were obliged to protect the Ainu who were destined to extinction, were concealed and erased from historical memory.

Notes

1. [Translator's Note] The original translation can be found in the Ainu Association of Hokkaido (Hokkaidō utari kyōkai), *Statement Submitted to the Fifth Session of the United Nations Working Group of Indigenous Populations* (Geneva, August 1987), 117–19.

2. [Translator's Note] Komori's essay first appeared in the book *Media, hyōshō, ideorogii: Meiji sanjyūnendai no bunka kenkyū* (Media, Representation, Ideology: A Study of the Culture of the Third Decade of Meiji), eds. Komori Yōichi, Kōno Kensuke, and Takahashi Osamu (Tokyo: Ozawa shoten, 1997), 319–34. I would like to thank Kim Tongfi, Inoue Makiko, Masayuki Shinohara, and Leslie Winston for their invaluable help with this translation. A special thank you to Komori Yōichi for allowing us to include this essay in our volume.

3. [Translator's Note] In previous centuries Japanese were under the mistaken notion that Hokkaido was geographically close to Manchuria and Santan, an area in China. It is true that historically Ainu conducted what Japanese called "Santan trade" with various groups on Sakhalin for Chinese goods, such as silk and colored beads.

4. *Kaitakushi nisshi* 4 (Journal of the Development Agency 4) (Tokyo: Tōkyō daigaku shuppankai, 1987).

5. Hanasaki Kōhei, "Ainumoshiri no kaifuku: Nihon no senjyūminzoku Ainu to Nihon kokka no taiainu seisaku" (The Restoration of Ainu Moshir: Japan's Indigenous Ainu and the Japanese State's Policies toward the Ainu), in *Iwanami kōza gendai shakaigaku 15: sabetsu to kyōsei no shakaigaku* (Contemporary Sociology Vol. 15: Sociology of Discrimination and Coexistence), ed. Inoue Shun et al. (Tokyo: Iwanami shoten, 1996), 93–108.

6. Takakura Shinichirō, *Ainu seisaku shi* (The History of Ainu Policy) (Tokyo: Nippon hyōronsha, 1942), 401.

7. *Kaitakushi nisshi* 2 (Journal of the Development Agency 2) (Tokyo: Tōkyō daigaku shuppankai, 1987).

8. [Translator's Note] Smith was a professor of chemistry and president of the Massachusetts Agricultural College from 1867 to 1879. He is most famous in Japan for his parting words, which were, according to legend, "Boys, be ambitious!"

9. Utari mondai konwakai (Ainu Issues Discussion Group), 1988.

10. Murai Osamu, "Kindai Nihon ni okeru *nation* no sōshutsu" (The Construction of the Nation in Modern Japan), in *Iwanami kōza, gendaishakaigaku 24: minzoku, kokka, esunishitei* (Contemporary Sociology Vol. 24: Race, the Nation-State, and Ethnicity), ed. Inoue Shun et al. (Tokyo: Iwanami shoten, 1996), 117–38.

11. Takakura, *Ainu seisaku shi*, 571.

12. [Translator's Note] This debate emerged out of a larger discussion of the "racial" origins of the Japanese. Tsuboi argued for the existence of a non-Ainu Neolithic people, based on his discovery of an Ainu legend that spoke of a "dwarf-like people" (*kor-pok-un-kur* in Ainu, *koropokkuru* in Japanese) who had preceded Ainu settlement, while Koganei suggested that the Jomon people, known through archaeological evidence, were in fact Ainu. See Richard Siddle's discussion in *Race, Resistance and the Ainu of Japan* (London: Routledge, 1996), 81–84.

13. "Ainu no hanashi" (Stories of the Ainu), *Kokumin shinbun* (Kokumin Newspaper), Mar. 27, 1894 (emphasis added). [Translator's note: The interpolations "bear" and "salmon" were added by *Kokumin Newspaper*.]

CHAPTER THREE

TEXT
Officer Ukuma

IKEMIYAGI SEKIHŌ

CONTEXT
Okinawa

CRITIQUE
Subaltern Identity in Okinawa

DAVINDER L. BHOWMIK

A N I N V E T E R A T E W A N D E R E R, Ikemiyagi Sekihō (1893–1951) was born in the historic Kume section of Naha, Okinawa, where early Chinese immigrants and their descendants settled. He studied at Waseda University in Tokyo. Upon Ikemiyagi's return to Okinawa in 1917, he worked as a newspaper reporter and a Japanese-language teacher in a middle school.

In addition to his fiction published largely in the 1920s, Ikemiyagi crafted widely acclaimed *tanka* poetry and gifted translations of French, Russian, and American works. He is also respected for his collection of Ryukyuan historical tales. "Officer Ukuma" (*Ukuma junsa*), a prize-winning story selected from more than four hundred manuscripts, won Ikemiyagi seventy yen when it appeared in the journal *Kaihō* in 1922.

"Officer Ukuma" centers on the figure of a low-ranking officer, Hyaaku, from a disenfranchised segment of Okinawan society, who craves confidence and social acceptance in spite of his "impure" background. As an Okinawan of Chinese heritage, the protagonist achieves a modicum of status through his hard-earned position as a policeman, only to be marked as "other" in both his professional and personal worlds: his background prevents him from becoming a full-fledged member of the Japanese police force, and his peremptory behavior results in his estrangement from family and community. Alienated, Hyaaku seeks comfort in the red-light district, where he befriends the prostitute Little Kamarū. When Hyaaku's conflicted position becomes further exacerbated, he discovers that he cannot escape the pain of his fractured life.

Officer Ukuma

IKEMIYAGI SEKIHŌ

TRANSLATION BY DAVINDER L. BHOWMIK

On the outskirts of Naha, the capital city of Ryukyu, is a certain village I'll refer to as "X." Its residents are of Chinese descent, and most of them—no, I should say nearly all—are poor and do menial work. Frog catchers go out to the rice fields to hunt for frogs, which they skin and take to market. Frogs are considered a delicacy by people in Naha and in the nearby town of Shuri. There are also fishermen and weavers among the villagers. Their work is humble, and people in other parts of Naha look down on them as "those X'ers," but they enjoy a simple, communal life with few worries.

Their village is thickly shaded by towering subtropical trees—banyan, *deigo*, and *fukugi*. Low bamboo hedges encircle each shabby house made from thatched miscanthus reeds. In the morning the village men walk to the rice fields carrying fishing poles and nets, while the women spread straw mats under the cool shade of the trees and weave hats and sandals, singing the mournful melodies of Ryukyuan folk songs. In the evening, after the men come home from the fields, their wives and daughters go to market to sell the freshly caught frogs and carp. With the little money they make, they buy fish and one square wooden container each of *awamori*, then return holding lighted torches so they won't be bitten by poisonous *habu* snakes. At home they are greeted happily by the men who, after finishing the meager evening meal, stretch out, quietly sipping *awamori*. So accustomed are the villagers to this life that they never find it sad. Though poor, they pool their money so that in bad times they can help each other out. And in this southern clime, no day, even winter, is too hard to bear. They live simply and in peace.

But when one of their own, Ukuma Hyaaku, attained the highly respected position of policeman, it was not only an honor for the Ukuma family but for the entire village. For these Chinese descendants, who barely eked out a living with their menial labor, becoming a government official was no small feat. Indeed, it was close to a miracle.

When word had spread of Ukuma Hyaaku's ambition to be a policeman, all the villagers rejoiced as though his good fortune would be their own, and everyone prayed fervently for his success. The young man's father excused him from his daily chores to encourage him in his studies and his mother engaged a shaman, traveling with her to many sacred sites to pray that Hyaaku would pass the qualifying examination. The day before the exam, Hyaaku's mother took him to the family's ancestral tomb, where she recited a lengthy prayer.

The hopes of Hyaaku, his family, and the village were realized when he passed the examination with flying colors. It was considered a triumph for all, and everyone took half a day off from work for a banquet celebrating Hyaaku's success. The village men gathered on the shaded lawn in front of Hyaaku's home, where they passed away the afternoon drinking *awamori* and plucking the three-stringed *jabisen* while nearby the youngsters played at imitating actors in Ryukyuan dance dramas.

It had been May in the early 1920s, a time of year when one didn't feel cold even wearing an abaca-cloth kimono. Red *deigo* flowers were just beginning to bloom and white lilies were opening here and there in the grass of shady groves. Absorbing the fierce southern sunlight, hibiscus flamed brightly among the hedges.

The village men, stripped to their waists, sang, danced, and played the *jabisen* while the women gathered around to watch with obvious pleasure. Our Ukuma Hyaaku looked odd amid all this noisy merrymaking as he sat in a chair someone had brought out for him, like some victorious general, wearing a uniform and cap and carrying a glistening sword. The women stared with admiration and awe at his strangely imposing figure.

The banquet went on this way until dawn, with music and boisterous laughter echoing through the forest on what would ordinarily have been a quiet night in the village.

After he finished his training, Officer Ukuma started working alternate days at the main police station, where he'd been assigned because of his high marks. He spent every other day at home reading books, and his family was proud to see him leave and come back from the station wearing his cap and uniform. When told by visitors from time to time that their son had been seen walking somewhere in his uniform, his family could scarcely contain their delight. And the visitors, too, spoke joyfully, as if seeing him had been some special event, and a few said they hoped their own sons would become policemen someday.

On the twenty-fifth of the month, Hyaaku left for home with his wages in his pocket. His heartbeat had quickened with joy when he held this money for the first time, and now he fingered the thick envelope tucked inside his right pocket as he walked along briskly. Arriving at home, he barely managed to calm his excitement, then went into the living room and tried to look nonchalant as he took out the envelope and handed it to his mother.

"Well, now!" His mother spoke happily as she took the envelope and examined its contents. "Twenty-three yen," she said after counting the bills. "It's not much." Though she'd already heard that this was all his salary would be, she seemed surprised when she actually saw the money.

The next two or three months went by peacefully, but Hyaaku's family began to feel that he was growing distant from them. He rarely spent time with other young people in the village anymore and they seemed to have lost interest in him as well. He thought only about how he might succeed as a policeman and how he could use his present position as a stepping-stone to something higher.

Hyaaku grew more and more short-tempered. Whenever he came home he complained, "This house is dirty. It's filthy!" And, blaming his sister, he bawled her out constantly. After his fellow officers dropped by one day, he got even more upset about the house. Hyaaku's mother cried at the sight of him railing at his sister and wondered what had caused her good-natured son to change so drastically.

But things only got worse, and Hyaaku began meddling in the lives of his fellow villagers. One day during a local festival he stood up in front of the crowd gathered in the village square and, looking as if he'd been waiting for just such an opportunity, began to speak. At first the villagers thought Hyaaku would be announcing good news of some benefit for them. Since Hyaaku was a policeman and a fellow villager, they expected to hear that, through him, the city government would be making improvements in their living conditions. They imagined he would say something about lower taxes, road repairs, or perhaps free medical care. What Hyaaku told them, however, completely betrayed their expectations.

"From now on the sewers must be cleaned thoroughly every day. When it's hot in the summer, many of you go around without clothes. This is a crime punishable by law, so if a policeman sees you, expect to be fined. I'm a policeman, too, and from now on I won't let you get away with anything just because you say you're from this village. We public officials value nothing more than impartiality. So we can't look the other way even if a member of our own families or a relative does something wrong or vulgar."

He went on to chastise them for things that, until now, they had done without a second thought. "Furthermore," he said, "drinking until late at night and singing is forbidden. You must drink less, work harder, and save your money so you can get more respectable jobs."

Hyaaku continued this loud and heated harangue while the villagers stared at him, looking very uncomfortable. They could not bear the thought that Hyaaku now saw himself in a position different from their own. So when the festival ceremonies ended and the drinking and merrymaking began, not one person offered him a cup of *awamori*.

During those days Hyaaku's fellow officers often visited him at home. He would offer his guests *awamori*, and some of them stayed on from afternoon late into the night, drinking and raising a ruckus. These tough, brawny young men were loud and rude. Unlike the local people, they didn't play the *jabisen* or sing Ryukyuan folk songs, but would bang on their plates and bowls, singing incomprehensible songs from Kagoshima and reciting Chinese verse. Occasionally one of them would stand up all of a sudden, brandishing a stick, and do a sword dance. Their wild behavior frightened Hyaaku's quiet family, who did not even want these men in their house. They were especially upset at Hyaaku for joining in their carousing.

From olden times these villagers had instinctively feared the police. Nevertheless, at first they rejoiced when Hyaaku became a policeman. But now they were worried about his dramatic change in attitude; and on top of that, the other policemen's frequent comings and goings from Hyaaku's house also made them uneasy. These officers, staggering through the streets on their way home, would shout insults at the villagers who wore few clothes when they worked. As such things occurred more often, the villagers began to curse the very presence of Hyaaku's house, which they only rarely visited, in their midst.

Gradually, even Hyaaku himself began to sense the changed attitude of those around him. At home he was always irritated. And the cold looks of villagers he encountered on the street made him hostile. It angered him that he was now the village outcast, and to make matters worse, he discovered that his fellow officers were making fun of him because he came from this village. When he overheard them call him "that X'er," he could feel his face grow hot. Hyaaku was so ashamed of his birthplace, where he still lived, that he talked to his family about moving, but they could not agree. Nothing hurt them more than the thought of leaving this village—not only because they had grown so used it, but also because moving was sure to make them even poorer.

Thus Hyaaku could find no relief from the hostility he felt toward the village, and he grew increasingly lonely. Among his fellow officers he could not find a single true friend. Since most of them were from other prefectures—Kagoshima, Saga, and Miyazaki—their lives and feelings differed sharply from his own. Although he could join them for drinking and merrymaking, he was unable to speak with them from the heart. Even when they talked at the police station, he sometimes found himself murmuring, "They are strangers." And he sensed that they also viewed him as an outsider. Yet even though Hyaaku's feelings of isolation were becoming unbearable, his fellow officers continued visiting his house to drink and were every bit as rambunctious as before.

Summer that year was very hot, and there was a long drought. Every day dazzling sunlight filled the clear, bright Ryukyuan sky. The sultry scent of earth and weeds wafted up into the parched air as the powerful sunlight reflected off Naha's red-tiled roofs and bore down on people's eyes and skin. The grass that grew above the high stone walls around houses became withered and crackling dry. One moment a lizard with gleaming silver skin could be seen dashing out from a wall only to hide itself again seconds later inside a crack in the stones. In the afternoon hours, the sun made the road seem like a desert, filling the air with its silent, piercing rays.

Sometimes a waft of clouds would appear in one portion of the sky like shimmering layers of mica, and people thought how wonderful it would be if the clouds turned to rain. In the late afternoon, the setting sun would blaze through the layered clouds, and when the villagers saw its rays shining on the green hills and forests, they would hope for rain the next day. The dream-like voices of children singing echoed in the quiet sky that glowed as the sun set.

The fabled monkey's home has burned. To fix it let's buy a bit of birdlime.

The children would sing this song happily, though they didn't understand the words, at any hour of the evening. But when the sun finally set, the layers of clouds vanished and the sky seemed to envelop the earth with throngs of stars glowing brightly like sweeping grains of silver dust.

As the days and nights dragged on this way, Hyaaku seemed to wilt like the withered grasses and trees, growing utterly downcast. He could find no relief even in his work, and life had become unbearably dreary.

One night, when he was fed up with these doldrums, a fellow officer from Kagoshima invited him to go for a walk along the seashore. Even those who had lived here long admired the beautiful evening hues on the beaches of this coral island. The reef looked like it had been whittled down here and there, and in some places the tide had gnawed out deep, dark hollows. The wave crests surging toward the beach would seem about to melt away, then reemerge, ashen and white, beneath the pale blue moonlight. Sorrowful melodies came flowing like a mountain stream from the hills or the shore where prostitutes sang love songs. Their alluring voices seemed to beckon Hyaaku as cool breezes wafting off the ocean danced over his skin. Near where he sat, from time to time, he could see in the moonlight the fair-skinned face of a prostitute dressed in a thin *tonpyan* kimono as she swam by expressionlessly. On his way back that night, invited by his fellow officer, Hyaaku went for the first time to Tsuji, Naha's renowned brothel district.

Facing its streets were long rows of two-story houses surrounded by high stone walls. From inside drifted the plucked notes of *jabisen*, the echo of drums, and the high-pitched voices of young women. Hyaaku's friend entered through the roofed gate at a certain house, knocked on the door, and gave a signal. At length a girl's voice asked, "Who is it?" and the door opened. The girl, seeing Hyaaku's friend, smiled broadly. "Come in," she said, and the two men were led to a six-mat guestroom. Inside was an alcove decorated with a scroll of Chinese poetry, and a black lacquered koto lay nearby. In front of one wall sat a long lacquer chest, its brass fittings gleaming brightly. The cupboard beside it also seemed very new, its varnish still fragrant. Across the room stood a large folding screen on which was painted a *deigo* tree with a white parrot perched on one of the branches that bloomed in a profusion of red blossoms.

To Hyaaku it all looked beautiful and exotic. After a time some women came in carrying liquor and food on red lacquer trays. While the two men drank, the women played the *jabisen* and sang. Presently a geisha, who seemed to be about fourteen or fifteen, appeared wearing a flashy red-patterned kimono and performed dances grasping a halberd and waving a fan.

At first Hyaaku was shy, but as the *awamori* began to take effect, even he eased into a rare, rollicking mood. At last he was telling jokes that had the women laughing and was beating with surprising facility on some drums in the room.

That night Hyaaku bought a woman for the first time. The girl he was matched with, a prostitute called Little Kamarū, seemed scarcely out of puberty—probably seventeen or so—with a round, doll-like face. Something in her sweet, childlike manner captivated him. When the party ended and they went together to her room at the rear of the house, Hyaaku sobered up all at once and felt strangely uneasy. He leaned against the wooden tray around the hibachi while she hung the blue mosquito netting and pretended not to notice her changing out of her kimono. But as she disrobed he caught a glimpse of her white shoulders, and the sight of her long arms moving gracefully caused his eyelids to tremble.

The girl, now dressed only in a thin nightgown, entered the mosquito netting, fastened down on three sides, and slipped over beside Hyaaku. Silently, he poured water from a clay pot into a teacup and drank it. The girl picked up a round fan but made no effort to fan herself as she leaned over beside him against the charcoal brazier and stared down at the white ashes inside. Every now and then Hyaaku could hear her breathing deeply.

·   ·   ·

The next morning Hyaaku found himself sleeping next to the girl under the blue mosquito netting. Though mildly surprised and embarrassed, he was secretly delighted. But when she awoke, the girl seemed to be in a very bad mood. Later she saw him out to the front gate. "Please come again tomorrow," she said. Hearing this, Hyaaku imagined he might be followed and left hurriedly, returning home on a road few people traveled. That day, when he faced his family, he felt awful. No matter how much he told himself that what had happened last night was of no consequence, he continued to feel he had done something terrible.

Hyaaku vowed he would never stay in Tsuji again. His fellow officer had invited him that first time and arranged for the girl. But Hyaaku had not paid her and thought he'd better go back just to give her the money. So on the evening he received his salary, Hyaaku went alone to her house. He said little after entering her room and remained standing as he downed two or three cups of the Chinese tea Ryukyuans like to drink. Then, very awkwardly, he took out a five-yen note from his wallet and handed it to the girl, but she refused to take the money. And, thinking he wanted to leave, she asked him to stay. Just then another girl, her companion, came into the room. "Please stay and visit a while," she also urged him. So that night, too, he drank *awamori* and slept in Kamarū's room.

The next day, when Hyaaku returned home, he gave his mother the remaining eighteen yen from his salary and told her he had deposited five yen in his postal savings account. Then he explained in great detail how the postal savings system worked. His mother nodded silently.

Without planning to, Hyaaku visited the girl's place two or three times after that, and the more he saw her the more something about her attracted him. He wasn't sure if it was her soft, beautiful body, her kind, gentle demeanor, or the glittering, gay surroundings in which she lived. But he felt drawn to her like a magnet.

This girl, Kamarū, was the daughter of a family who had once owned many acres of farmland in the countryside. But after her father died, her none-too-bright older brother had been deceived by swindlers and lost the family fortune. After squandering all of their property, he fell deeply in debt, and to repay the family's losses, his sister was sold into prostitution. The intimacy with which she confided this to Hyaaku, so different from her attitude toward him on their first meeting, caused him to feel even more drawn to her.

The relentless drought that year brought bad times for everyone. In the pleasure quarters, all the houses lost customers. Only two or three regulars showed up at Kamarū's place, and even their visits became more infrequent. No matter what time Hyaaku went to visit Kamarū, he always found her waiting impatiently for him. And the more she showed her feelings for him, the more his feelings for her deepened, and he no longer tried to control them.

When Hyaaku went to see Kamarū on the evening of his next payday, he boldly handed her two ten-yen bills.

"You'll be in trouble if you give me this much. One is enough," she said, returning the other bill to him.

"Take it," he insisted, handing it back to her. "I should give you more. Next time I will."

When Hyaaku went home the next day, he told his mother he had loaned his month's salary to a fellow officer in a financial emergency who would pay it back the following month. Even as he spoke, he could feel his face growing hot and his voice trembling. His mother looked at him suspiciously but said nothing.

On the afternoon of September 27 a cold wind began to blow. Hyaaku was working at the police station and had just started wondering if it was going to rain when a typhoon warning arrived from the weather bureau. "Violent winds expected locally. Caution advised in coastal areas." A low-pressure system had formed in the ocean 160 knots southeast of Ishigaki Island and was said to be moving in a northwesterly direction toward Okinawa.

By evening the storm was raging. The thick branches of the huge trees in front of the police station swayed in the wind. Baby sparrows, lost and confused, flew in circles, beating their wings. Yellow dragonflies, swept this way and that by the gale, swarmed around the mulberry trees. And in the sky far above the town could be heard the shrieking cries of seagulls seeking refuge.

That night Hyaaku changed at the station from his uniform into his street clothes, then went to Kamarū's place. Her house was filled with fear as the girls waited anxiously for the violent wind and rain. To avoid having things blown and tossed about, Hyaaku helped the girls put everything inside the house. The sun had just set when the storm brought torrents of rain. As the doors of the house began rattling, the walls and beams trembled. After a time, the electricity went out, and candles were lit. Kamarū's face looked pale in the candlelight flickering through the gloom. When the doors started shaking violently, she hurried over next to Hyaaku, crying, "I wonder if we're safe here!" Outside, the gale howled and sent tiles flying off the roof to crash shattering against the stone wall in front of the house.

The violent storm continued for three days and three nights. Skipping a day of work, Hyaaku spent all of those nights with Kamarū. Amid the sounds of roaring wind and rain, they looked into each other's eyes and talked of many things, their mutual attachment growing stronger than ever. By now they could not bear the thought of being apart, even for a single day. Hyaaku proposed they live together but knew this was impossible, since he had no income other than his twenty-three-yen monthly salary. *How I wish I had money!* he thought, and understood for the first time why a man would commit a crime for a woman. He realized that *right now, if the opportunity came, even I . . .* and was frightened by his own thoughts.

· · ·

On the fourth day the wind and rain stopped, so Hyaaku left Kamarū's place around noon but didn't feel like going home. Instead, he walked aimlessly through a cemetery behind the pleasure quarters. Here and there on the wide hillcrest sat Ryukyuan-style tombs carved from sheets of rock lacquered white, making them look like stone huts. With the rain gone, the sky was clear, but in this deserted field of graves Hyaaku felt lonely.

With no destination in mind, he wandered among the graves, passing in front of a gabled tomb, when the shadow of something moving inside caught his eye. Peering in, Hyaaku saw it was a man. He rushed inside all at once and dragged him out. In that moment Hyaaku's languid mood vanished and he became the consummate policeman.

"Sir, I have not done anything wrong. I am just hiding here," the man said. Hyaaku forcibly searched the man's clothing and found one yen and fifty sen tucked into his waistband. He assumed the man had stolen the money. Though Hyaaku repeatedly asked the man his name and address, he wouldn't say a thing. "I will not do anything bad, sir," he said, as Hyaaku dragged him off to the police station for questioning. Hyaaku was filled with pride at having arrested his first criminal. He shoved the man roughly into the interrogation room, as if he'd been some stray dog, then went to give his report to the police inspector. Warm sweat dripped from Hyaaku's forehead onto his cheeks.

When the inspector heard Hyaaku's report, he smiled. "Well, now, this is your first real achievement. Good work. Hey, Chief Watanabe," he called, and ordered the patrol chief to interrogate the suspect. Officer Ukuma stood nearby and listened to the questioning. He admired the skill with which the chief conducted his interrogation, thinking how great it would be if the suspect really turned out to have committed a theft. On the other hand, if he hadn't, Hyaaku realized it would make him look inept, and waves of anxiety began rolling over him. But as the questioning progressed, it became clear that the man had indeed stolen the money, and eventually he confessed.

"I was a wealthy son in a certain town but got into business over my head, lost everything, and had to sell our rice fields and farm land. So you see, originally, I wasn't poor or a thief. Then, on top of my family's financial ruin, we had one poor crop after another, and it got so hard for us to make a living that I came to Naha on my way to Daitō Island. I was going there to find work as a migrant laborer but failed the physical because of some infectious disease and couldn't go." (Hyaaku thought it was probably tuberculosis, since even as he spoke, the man coughed frequently.)

"At that point all I could do was look for work in Naha, but before I could find some, I spent all the money I had and got thrown out of my rented room. I was walking around town when the storm hit, so I searched for shelter and found that open tomb. Staying inside there I was afraid I would starve. Fortunately, the rain let up this morning, so I left the tomb and headed for town. I went into a liquor store to ask for some water and saw some bills lying on top of a wine barrel. Before I knew what I was doing, I grabbed them. Then I got scared holding that money in my hand, and without looking back, I ran away again to the open tomb. So you see, originally, I was no thief. My younger sister has done quite well as a prostitute in Tsuji. If only I'd gone to her place I could have found a way out of my troubles, but with the awful state of my clothes I was afraid of what she'd think. Please forgive me. I'll never do anything like this again."

As the man told his story in a heavy Ryukyuan country accent, his voice gradually started to waver, and by the time he'd finished, tears were streaming down his cheeks. "Sir, please forgive me. Please." He bowed so low his head touched the floor.

Seeing this, the chief laughed loudly, obviously proud of his successful interrogation. "How about that, Officer Ukuma. It's just as you suspected. A true crime! Ha, ha, ha."

But Officer Ukuma was unable to laugh, and a lump of fear filled his chest and threatened to cut off his breathing.

"Well, what's your name?" the chief demanded.

The man did not answer, and now Officer Ukuma's face revealed the unbearable tension he felt as he stared at him. It might have been his imagination, but the man's face seemed to resemble that of Kamarū, whom he had left only a short time earlier.

Pressed relentlessly by the chief, the man finally spoke. "I'm Gima Tarū."

Now panic seized Officer Ukuma.

After revealing his name, the man took a deep breath and told the chief his age as well as the name, age, and address of his younger sister. Then, again he pleaded for forgiveness.

Officer Ukuma's hunch had been correct, and this man was none other than Kamarū's older brother. Painfully regretting his arrest, he raged and cursed at himself for having been so proud of dragging this man into the station only a short time ago. Now the chief turned toward him. "Hey, Officer Ukuma," he said, "since we have to question his younger sister as a witness, you go to her place and bring her in."

Officer Ukuma felt all the blood in his body rush to his head. For a time he could only stare blankly at the chief. Then his eyes began smoldering with the fear and rage of a wild beast fallen into a trap.

Subaltern Identity in Okinawa

DAVINDER L. BHOWMIK

A shift in political power from elder statesmen to party politics during the Taisho era (1912–1926), which fell between the long, chaotic Meiji period (1868–1912) that preceded it and the increasingly militaristic early Showa era (1926–1989) that followed, has led many historians to characterize these dozen odd years as a time of democracy and liberalism. Indeed, politician Yoshino Sakuzō popularized the idea of people-centrism (*minponshugi*) in the day's most prestigious journal, *Central Forum* (*Chūō kōron*), which functioned as the "dragon's gate" through which aspiring authors entered the literary establishment.[1] And, while people-centrism is still lauded as an indigenous liberal ideal that developed in Taisho Japan, this notion, and other era slogans such as "Taisho democracy," are undergoing scrutiny as revisionist historians seek to understand the period less as a heyday for democratic ideals than as a segue to the Pacific War.[2] To be sure, politicians heeded growing calls for popular representation in the domestic sphere, but the era also witnessed the expansion of the Japanese empire. The ink on colonial policies drafted in Korea, annexed in 1910, had already long dried when the nation embarked on a 70,000-troop expedition into Siberia in 1918, and subsequently made forays into former German territories in Manchuria, Inner Mongolia, and Micronesia.

In the late 1920s and early '30s Japan suffered from severe rural poverty and depression-induced unemployment in urban areas. Nowhere was rural poverty more acute than in newly incorporated Okinawa, where residents continued to bear the heaviest tax burden of the Japanese citizenry, as they had since the Meiji period.[3] Prior to the nation-state's absorption of Okinawa in 1879, it was the center of the Ryukyu Kingdom, which emerged in the fifteenth century and reigned until the nineteenth century. When the Shimazu clan from Satsuma in southwestern Japan invaded Ryukyu in 1609, the kingdom initially enjoyed a cultural efflorescence, benefiting from continued trade with China and Japan, countries to which it paid dual tribute. However, colonial rule by the Shimazu clan also foreshadowed a series of encroachments on Okinawa and its people made by the nation-state of Japan, soon after its formation in 1868. Soon after Okinawa attained prefectural status in 1879, it was plagued not only with inordinate taxes but also with natural disasters and social stigmas so relentless they effected large-scale emigration to the western Japanese region of Kansai, Hawai'i, South America, and a cluster of Pacific islands bordering the equator, collectively referred to as the South Seas (*Nanyō*). Weeks after the deaths of a third of the civilian population of Okinawa during the Battle of Okinawa that raged in spring 1945 when Japanese and American troops clashed in the bloodiest conflict of the Pacific War, Japan surrendered to the Allied forces, ceding Okinawa to the American occupiers. Whereas the occupation of Japan ended in 1952, Okinawa did not revert to Japanese sovereignty for another twenty years. On May 15, 1972, Okinawa regained its prefectural status, which it continues to hold today.

I focus in this essay on depictions of an ethnic minority in a work of Okinawan fiction from the Taisho period, underscoring relations of power to show who represents whom, and with what effects on the group's subjectivity. The reading of Ikemiyagi Sekihō's "Officer Ukuma" (*Ukuma junsa*, 1922) that follows is informed by contemporary theories of cultural hybridity, subalternity, and colonial mimicry, all of which permit me to consider the question of identity, the central theme of Okinawan fiction. As I will show, Ikemiyagi's representative story illuminates how we understand the very term "subaltern" and its various interpretations among postcolonial critics. In turn, the literary text I discuss shows how identity is fractured along lines of gender, ethnicity, and class, and confirms the heterogeneous nature of the subaltern.

"Officer Ukuma," authored by the nomadic poet and short-fiction writer Ikemiyagi Sekihō, is a quasi-canonical story that describes differing levels of discrimination an Okinawan policeman encounters during the fabled period of Taisho "democracy."[4] Ikemiyagi's story is brief, yet it speaks volumes on the difficulty with which Okinawans sought to construct a positive identity for themselves at the time. Following a sketch of the contours of Ikemiyagi's peripatetic life and an overview of the conditions that prevailed in Okinawa during the Taisho period I will analyze "Officer Ukuma," the crowning success of Ikemiyagi's many stories in which a police officer figures prominently. This work centers on a lowly officer from a disenfranchised segment of Okinawan society who yearns for sure footing and social acceptance despite his background. The figure of a policeman in a neocolonial locale makes it impossible to ignore the theoretical questions posed by Ikemiyagi's work. As we shall see, despite his outward success, the abject failure of the protagonist to escape his existential bind keeps him from rising above his socially prescribed station.

Wandering Poet, Drifting Ryukyuan

The question of identity, the central theme of Okinawan literature, is taken up by Ikemiyagi Sekihō in "Officer Ukuma," a representative work of Okinawan fiction from the Taisho era. The police officer, a character that offered Ikemiyagi the chance to reflect on issues of power, recurs frequently in the author's oeuvre, as does Kume, his birthplace. Known by many as a "wandering poet" (*hōrō no shijin*) or "drifting Ryukyuan" (*samayoeru Ryūkyūjin*), Ikemiyagi Sekihō was born in Kume, or Kuninda, as it is known locally, a historically noteworthy district in Naha, Okinawa's capital city, in 1893. In 1392, King Satto of Chūzan, the island's central kingdom, had designated Kume as the village in which Chinese immigrants would reside. Famous as a center of Chinese studies in the early years of the Ryukyu Kingdom, Kume later fell into decline and became "a lantern in the wind" when previously robust trade between it and China, particularly Fujian province, plummeted in the late 1500s.[5] The village's fortunes reversed in the seventeenth century, following the 1609 invasion when Shimazu rulers from Satsuma, insisting that Ryukyuans preserve their customs and traditions (*Ryūkyū hozon*), encouraged the study of Chinese since it proved essential for continued trade between Ryukyu and China, which fattened the clan's coffers.[6]

Once he graduated from the Prefectural Middle School in Okinawa, Ikemiyagi traveled to Tokyo to attend Waseda University, following the approved route to success for elites. When Ikemiyagi returned to Okinawa in January 1916, he assumed a position as journalist for the *Okinawa Morning Sun News* (*Okinawa asahi shinbun*). In March 1917, Ikemiyagi became a Japanese teacher at the Prefectural Second Middle School. He resumed his career as a reporter, this time for the *Okinawa Daily News* (*Okinawa nichinichi shinbun*), in 1920.[7] "Officer Ukuma," the fictional story that established Ikemiyagi's reputation as a writer, appeared in 1922 in *Liberation* (*Kaihō*), a major Japanese journal founded in 1919 by Yoshino Sakuzō, the very same politician who promoted the idea of a Taisho democracy. Essays and stories published in the journal display a clear socialist bent and reflect well the historical moment.[8] A habitual wanderer, Ikemiyagi traveled from areas in the extreme south such as Yonaguni, the Okinawan island closest to Taiwan, to the northern island of Hokkaido.[9] Though he is remembered today for his story "Officer Ukuma," Ikemiyagi was also known for his excellent short Japanese verse, or *tanka*, and a gift for languages that enabled him to translate works by writers as varied as Maupassant, Dostoyevsky, and Longfellow, for which he earned the much coveted praise of Kikuchi Kan, then dominant in Tokyo literary circles. In addition to publishing "Officer Ukuma" in 1922, in that year Ikemiyagi married fellow writer Arakaki Mitoko, with whom he had two sons.[10] Arakaki and Ikemiyagi later divorced; their first son, a draftee, died in the war, and the second disappeared in the chaos that followed. Ikemiyagi himself died accidentally in 1951; apparently intoxicated, he drowned while bathing.

A State of Ruins

In the Taisho period ethnologists such as Yanagita Kunio and Orikuchi Shinobu were drawn, as if to a magnet, to scrutinize Okinawa. Encouraged by the lead of Iha Fuyū, the father of Okinawan studies (*Okinawa-gaku no chichi*), Yanagita first visited the prefecture in 1920 and soon determined that without an intense examination of Okinawan cultural forms there could be no understanding of "ancient" Japan.[11] In the following year, Orikuchi went to Okinawa to conduct fieldwork on Japanese language and religion because of evidence of archaic Japanese words and extensive shamanism. From the mid- to late-Taisho period, scholars cast Okinawa into the limelight, eager to find commonalities between Okinawa and the mainland.

Ironically, during the same period that Okinawa was showered with long overdue attention, it was plagued by a series of famines and beset with a flagging economy. Owing to the intense gaze scholars focused on aspects of Okinawan culture that helped to reconstruct what they believed to be a shared ancient Japanese culture, the actual state of affairs in Okinawa during the Taisho period has, until late, been largely forgotten. In fact, during the late Taisho period, *if* Okinawa was mentioned in the mainland newspapers, it was referred to either as "The Sago Palm Hell" (*sotetsu jigoku*) or "A State of Ruins" (*bōkoku*).[12] The use of these terms relates to the severe economic distress that Okinawa experienced in the early 1920s when sugar prices plummeted worldwide. Since sugarcane was the mainstay of the island's economy, the drop in value was painfully significant. The weakened economy left many Okinawans unemployed, precipitating a wave of emigration to the mainland and beyond the nation's borders. Okinawans who remained in the prefecture were subject to abject poverty and a hunger so great they risked their lives to eat the fruit of the Sago palm, through a process that first required boiling the fruit to draw out its poison.

Richard Goldschmidt (1878–1958), a German-born geneticist, offers an insightful view of Okinawa during the Taisho period. While head of the Kaiser Wilhelm Biology Research Institute, Goldschmidt was invited to lecture at Tokyo Imperial University from 1924 to 1926. On his way back to Germany in 1927, Goldschmidt traveled to the Japanese territories of Taiwan, Okinawa, Ogasawara, Korea, and southern Manchuria. He recorded his impressions in a lengthy travelogue that included over two hundred photographs and was subsequently published in Berlin under the title *The New Japan* (*Neu Japan*, 1927).[13]

Among the numerous anecdotes cited in the book, two are particularly noteworthy. The first involves an encounter Goldschmidt had on a ship from Kagoshima bound for Okinawa. Striking up a conversation with several young Okinawans on their return from Brazil and Hawai'i, Goldschmidt is shocked to hear the islanders say proudly that were Japan and Germany to go to war, Japan would surely win.[14] Given the dire straits Okinawa was then in, not to mention the exploitation of Okinawa since the Satsuma invasion in 1609, the fierce patriotism the Okinawans revealed for Japan takes Goldschmidt by surprise.[15]

A second anecdote confirms how strongly the Okinawans Goldschmidt met during his travels wished to ally themselves with mainland Japan. While visiting Okinawa, Goldschmidt, wishing to see some local textiles, paid a visit to a wealthy merchant who had employees attire themselves in richly dyed (*bingata*) Japanese kimono for Goldschmidt to peruse.[16] Impressed by the beautiful, vibrant colors of the cloth, Goldschmidt asked permission to snap some photographs. The owner flatly refused, explaining that if outsiders saw photographs of Okinawans dressed in traditional kimono they would think that the islanders were an uncivilized people who still clung to ancient customs.[17] Again, Goldschmidt is taken aback by the extent to which so many Okinawans felt compelled to erase any perceived differences between themselves and mainland Japanese.

These two episodes succinctly capture Okinawans' desire for inclusion in the nation, and attest to Benedict Anderson's observation that, regardless of nationalism's "roots in fear and hatred of the Other, and its affinities with racism . . . nations inspire love, and often profoundly self-sacrificing love."[18] The situation in Okinawa is a textbook case. Despite rapid assimilation, which apparently the vast majority of Okinawans strove for in the Taisho period, objective factors such as an economy that had nearly ground to a halt, and subjective factors such as the pervasive fear of appearing to lag behind the times, thwarted the efforts of the Okinawans to identify them-selves as Japanese.[19] Alan Christy explains the crux of this dilemma: "The analysis of a weak, insufficiently modernized Okinawan economy discur-sively constructed an Okinawan identity, which was correspondingly weak and undeveloped, to serve as the origin of the economic problem."[20] Known only through negative images as the "Sago Palm Hell" or "A State in Ruins," and impossibly rooted in a perceived time lag by which Okinawa was denied contemporaneity with the rest of Japan, a condition Johannes Fabian calls "allochronism," Okinawans found it difficult to construct a positive identity in the Taisho period.[21] Ironically, Anderson's idea of "homogeneous empty time," a historical state in which there is no time lag, is one of the fundamen-tal philosophical assumptions upon which Anderson posits the possibility of national identity. This is quite opposite from the notion of "allochronism." Whereas Anderson's rosy view of nationalism promises unity among the masses, Fabian's argument against the coevalness of time suggests a harsher reality, one that is perhaps closer to that experienced by residents of Oki-nawa. That is, when bureaucrats, whether in government or education, pos-ited a time lag between Tokyo and Okinawa, they did so to justify their rule and legitimate existing social hierarchies.

The Winning Story

"Officer Ukuma," a work selected from among hundreds of manuscript submissions,[22] is the story of a young man named Ukuma Hyaaku who hails from a "special hamlet" (*tokushu buraku*)[23] on the outskirts of Naha. The setting is critical in this story of ambivalent identity. As the narrator explains, the inhabitants of the community descend from Chinese immi-grants who lived in the Ryukyus in prior times.[24] Shunned by Okinawans for their poverty and engagement in menial labor, the villagers eke out a living by hunting for frogs and carp to sell at the marketplace or by weav-ing straw sandals and plaiting caps. As a young boy, Hyaaku shows much promise in his studies and is encouraged by his family to do his best. As a teen, he excels to such a degree that his family allows him to avoid working in the fields so that he can concentrate on his schoolwork. The young man becomes so motivated he attempts to take an examination required for en-try to the police department. Not only does he sit for the exam, he passes, thereby becoming the first person from his marginalized community to at-tain a position in the police force.

Needless to say, Hyaaku is the pride of both his family and his village. A huge celebration is held to commemorate his success and soon afterward Hyaaku begins his work as a policeman. Each day, when he dons his uniform and cap and fastens his sword, Hyaaku grows increasingly accustomed to his new life outside the village. Two or three months of relative peace ensue, whereupon Hyaaku inexplicably becomes rankled by the squalid conditions in which his family lives. Displeased by the untidiness of his home, Hyaaku vents his anger upon his family. Gradually he finds himself irritated by the relaxed lifestyle of his fellow villagers. One day, during a festival that draws the villagers to gather at the central square, Hyaaku—appearing as though he had been waiting for such an opportunity—begins to address the assembled crowd.

Given that I am reading Ikemiyagi's work to shed light on the question of subaltern identity and the theoretical bind Gayatri Chakravorty Spivak introduces when she questions whether subaltern speech is possible, Hyaaku's utterances in this key passage are symbolic, perhaps even synecdochical. The crowd's anticipation is palpable. They listen, rapt, expecting their native son to deliver good news. Since Hyaaku has become a policeman despite his lowly background, they hope the bureau might provide them with conveniences that would improve their abysmal living conditions. Visions of conveniences such as reduced taxes, free health care, and road repair dance in their heads. Instead, Hyaaku lectures:

> From now on the sewers must be cleaned thoroughly every day. When it's hot in the summer, many of you go around without clothes. This is a crime punishable by law, so if a policeman sees you, expect to be fined. I'm a policeman, too, and from now on I won't let you get away with anything just because you say you're from this village. We public officials value nothing more than impartiality. So we can't look the other way even if a member of our own families or a relative does something wrong or vulgar.[25]

Startled by Hyaaku's decidedly imperious tone, the villagers slowly distance themselves from the man who has begun to view his own family and neighbors with contemptuous disdain.

As Hyaaku becomes estranged from his community, he begins to associate more frequently with his colleagues, the majority of whom are described as stalwart (*takumashii*) men from cities in southwest Japan that, incidentally, most officers, unhappily appointed to serve in Okinawa, called home. Disregarding the rules he himself enforces while on the job, Hyaaku invites his co-workers home at night, whiling away the hours in drink and song. Indifferent to the inconvenience his wild nights cause his family and neighbors, Hyaaku persists in his efforts to become a well-liked and respected member of the police force.

Okinawans, for their part, keenly resented the central government's practice, begun in the Meiji period, of placing outsiders in positions of local leadership. As the decades wore on, the quality of these Tokyo appointees declined, particularly at the lower rungs, where a large percentage of the police force and lower-level bureaucrats happened to be men from Kagoshima who were unable to find ready employment after the failed Satsuma Rebellion of 1877. Many Okinawans particularly despised these appointees for they represented a none-to-subtle continuation of Satsuma authority in the prefecture.

The story's ultimate irony is that Hyaaku's career success and "impure" heritage result in his exclusion from both his workplace and community. While his colleagues socialize with him, they never let Hyaaku forget that he is somehow different. The narrator states that his peers regard Hyaaku as a foreigner (*ikokujin*), and this cool reception leads Hyaaku, who has diligently endeavored to assimilate, to view his associates in the same manner.[26] Hyaaku's estrangement from the family and larger community to which he belongs deepens in accordance with the rise in his social status following his attainment of the coveted position of a police officer. In spite of the cruelty Hyaaku inflicts on his family and neighbors, Ikemiyagi manages, through concise and well-crafted descriptions of Hyaaku's mental state, to elicit the reader's sympathies for the young policeman as he struggles in vain to establish an identity for himself.

Lost in Transition

Not unlike fellow male protagonists in Japanese fiction, Hyaaku seeks refuge from his problems in the pleasure quarters. Ostracized by his colleagues and those in his community, Hyaaku spends his off-duty hours in Tsuji, a red light district in Naha.[27] There he meets a young woman, Kamarū, the daughter of a wealthy man who has died. The woman's older brother, having squandered the family money, had had no choice but to sell his sister into prostitution.[28] The story's two tragic characters, Hyaaku and Kamarū, fall in love, but have no chance of a life together as Hyaaku cannot afford to redeem her contract.

The Tsuji interlude is an important part of "Officer Ukuma" for it suggests the possibility of a gendered reading of the story. Tsuji, with its teahouses bedecked with painted scrolls and elegant fans and filled with the plaintive notes of the *jabisen* and *koto*, is eroticized. Amid these surroundings, Kamarū, a hapless victim, occupies a place lower in the social hierarchy than does Hyaaku. That she is an economic outcast endears her to Hyaaku, whose own feelings of loneliness and inferiority are somehow assuaged in her presence. Of their bond, Ikemiyagi writes: "Amid the sounds of roaring wind and rain, they looked into each other's eyes and talked of many things, their mutual attachment growing stronger than ever."[29] In Tsuji, Hyaaku experiences freedom, albeit briefly, and only in the arms of his lover, a prostitute similarly ostracized by the outer world. It may be futile to measure the degree to which Ikemiyagi's characters are oppressed, but one might consider Hyaaku and Kamarū as equals in that the former is an ethnic minority within Okinawa and the latter is both Okinawan and female. Hyaaku stands side by side with Kamarū in his shared lack of identification with mainland Japanese.

In one of the story's slight, but telling details, Ikemiyagi includes a scene in which Hyaaku changes out of his uniform and into street clothes before visiting his lover. The rush of power he experiences with his lover arises from his own masculinity, not that derived from his state-issued sword, cap, and uniform. In an early scene, the narrator describes Hyaaku looking "like some victorious general, wearing a uniform and cap and carrying a glistening sword."[30] Trapped and powerless, Kamarū serves as a convenient foil for Hyaaku, a man whose acute feelings of inferiority only disappear when in Tsuji. No longer constrained by his uniform, a symbol of the Japanese state and its authority, Hyaaku, the narrator tells us, reverts to his "true self."

This self, merging with the nation-state, is the very subject of Albert Memmi's writings on the nature of master/slave relations under conditions of colonialism.

> The first attempt of the colonized is to change his condition by changing his skin. There is a tempting model very close at hand—the colonizer. The latter suffers from none of his deficiencies, has all rights, enjoys every possession and benefits from every prestige. He is, moreover, the other part of the comparison, the one that crushes the colonized and keeps him in servitude. The first ambition of the colonized is to become equal to that splendid model and to resemble him to the point of disappearing into him.[31]

The critical attention Ikemiyagi pays to Hyaaku's change of clothes, and the liberating effect this act has on the protagonist, affirms Memmi's point that those who are oppressed simply change their skin.[32] In Ikemiyagi's story, Hyaaku's "true (native) self" is lost when he is in uniform, and resurfaces when he is clad in civilian wear. When one bears in mind Memmi's ideas of colonial transformation, Hyaaku's change of clothes takes on greater weight. A postcolonial critic, eager to find the slightest sign of resistance, might claim that Ukuma displays agency in this scene because he is effectively reversing, or negating Memmi's description of the process of colonial transformation. That is, Ukuma insistently removes the skin/uniform that makes him one with the nation, rather than allowing it to sublate him. However, this same critic would then, perforce, be confronted with the fallacy of an originary, true self.

One morning on his way home, brooding over his debauched love affair after having spent the preceding three days and nights with Kamarū in Tsuji, Hyaaku spies a suspicious movement in an abandoned tomb. Although he is out of uniform, Hyaaku dashes inside the tomb, discovers a man crouched in hiding, and drags him out. Ikemiyagi writes: "In that moment Hyaaku's languid mood vanished and he became the consummate policeman."[33] Nakahodo Masanori cites this passage in arguing that Hyaaku's transformation from a naive young village minority to a member of the police force is irreversible; however much he may try, Hyaaku cannot shed his "uniform."[34] Humorist and essayist Fujiki Hayato, whose contemporary performances in the central Okinawan castle town of Nakagusuku delve into the sacrifices Okinawans made for the nation in the prewar period, is careful to show that the soldiers who appear in his plays embrace militarism. Fujiki insists that an Okinawan subject is not simply overwritten by Japanese military discipline; rather, he experiences joy in the process of transformation. Fujiki's point is important to keep in mind here, for it is impossible to know whether Hyaaku's actions are selfish or selfless. In other words, is his self-cultivation motivated by a desire to improve himself or the nation to which he tenuously belongs?[35] In either case, the joy Hyaaku experiences upon being recognized as a police officer functions as a crucial tool for identification and self-consciousness.

Excited by his single-handed capture, Hyaaku takes the suspect to police headquarters and arrests him upon obtaining a confession to theft. The elation Hyaaku experiences after making his first arrest dissipates the instant he learns that the man is none other than his lover's older brother.

The story concludes as Hyaaku's chief commands him to escort Kamarū to police headquarters for interrogation. In the memorable concluding lines, Ikemiyagi describes Hyaaku's pained reaction: "Officer Ukuma felt all the blood in his body rush to his head. For a time he could only stare blankly at his chief. Then his eyes began smoldering with the fear and rage of a wild beast fallen into a trap."[36]

"Officer Ukuma" is the tragic story of a young man who exists in a state of limbo. As a second-class Japanese citizen of Chinese descent, Hyaaku achieves outward success only to become doubly estranged: his background prevents him from becoming a full-fledged member of the police force, and his authoritarian attitude ensures his ostracization from the villagers and family members who have encouraged him to succeed. Disillusioned, he escapes to Tsuji, a modern-day "floating world" where he finds temporary solace. Even the pipe dreams he has of ransoming his lover are in the end quashed as he realizes the full import of his constrained position. Not only does the identity Hyaaku strives for continue to elude him, but, as the story's final line reveals, he is reduced to a wild, frightened animal.

Officer Ukuma as Subaltern

As well as bringing to mind the alienated anti-hero of Japanese and Western modern literature, Ikemiyagi's portrait of a native police officer whose position of authority ironically leads to feelings of powerlessness corresponds to contemporary debates on subalternity that inform postcolonial theory. Okinawa's position as a neocolonial area of Japan makes it useful to go beyond a modern analysis of the story to an examination of it through a postcolonial frame. The main source of contention among theorists such as Gayatri Chakravorty Spivak and Homi Bhabha concerns agency and stems from the immense influence deconstruction has had on postcolonial theory. Because of the dissolution of the post-Enlightenment subject, it is difficult if not impossible to construct a speaking position for the subaltern.[37] While there is much disagreement about the theoretical legitimacy of the subaltern subject, postcolonial critics are united in their concern over how to effect agency for the (bracketed) subaltern subject.

One of the major problems that complicate the issue of subalternity is the unproblematic usage of the term "subaltern."[38] Notable exceptions to this practice occur in the writings of historians in the Subaltern Studies Collective as well as in essays by Spivak and Bhabha.[39] In the preface to *Selected*

Subaltern Studies, Ranajit Guha clearly states that the word "subaltern" in the work's title has the meaning given in *The Concise Oxford Dictionary*, namely, "of inferior rank."[40] He explains that the term will be used throughout the studies as "a name for the general attribute of subordination in South Asian society whether this is expressed in terms of class, caste, age, gender and office or in any other way."[41] For further clarity, Guha appends to the preface a note that specifically defines the terms "elite," "people," and "subaltern." Briefly stated, the term "elite" signifies dominant groups, both foreign and native, with the native group further divided into regional and national levels. The terms "people" and "subaltern class" are synonymous, and the category is said to represent the difference between the total Indian population and the elite. Guha concludes his note by stating that the task of the collective is "to investigate, identify, and measure the specific nature and degree of the deviation of these elements from the ideal and situate it historically."[42]

While cognizant of the point that both dominant and subaltern groups are heterogeneous, Guha's fastidiousness is such that even Spivak, always specific, voices alarm over what she perceives as an overly taxonomic and essentialist program. In her well-known essay "Can the Subaltern Speak?" Spivak argues that the critique of the subject, as engaged in by Michel Foucault and Gilles Deleuze, unwittingly gives rise to a subject, in their cases, that of Europe. She further reveals that in the epistemic violence that attends the disclosing of the oppressed colonial subject, or subaltern, as other, the intellectual remains transparent. Spivak concludes that, on the other side of the international division of labor, there is "no unrepresentable subaltern subject that can know and speak itself."[43] Spivak's negative response to the question of whether the subaltern can speak is not simply delivered. To support her views on the theoretical illegitimacy of any kind of authentic voice, or subaltern agency, Spivak painstakingly analyzes the discourse of Indian widow sacrifice (*sati*) to show how the gendered female subaltern is doubly shadowed by native patriarchy and foreign masculinist-imperialist ideology and thereby rendered historically mute.[44]

Spivak views the nature of the subaltern as "irretrievably heterogeneous" and cautions against regarding the relationship between colonizers and colonized as simply a binary or hierarchical one. Subaltern subjects, given the variegated types of colonial relationships in which they figure, cannot be homogenized. Although Spivak's complication of the term "subaltern" is necessary and productive, it makes the critic's task of recovering subaltern voices far more difficult. In the case of Ikemiyagi's story, neither Hyaaku nor

Kamarū can speak, precisely because their voices are always already lacking authority. This lack is due less to the dissolution of the Cartesian (bourgeois) subject than to the subaltern's specific position within a historical nexus in which power concentrates in an elite class, which oppresses the colonial subject.

Reading "Officer Ukuma" with Guha's definitions in mind, it is clear that Officer Ukuma is a character who occupies a place Spivak calls "the floating buffer zone of regional elite-subaltern."[45] Ukuma's position as a police officer marks him as a member of the regional elite, while his status as a second-class citizen from a discriminated village relegates him to the subaltern. The native police officer's authority is undermined precisely because of this ambiguity. Caught between the imperialist power structure, represented by the officer's Yamato or mainland Japanese colleagues and chief, and his emotions for the Tsuji prostitute, another member of the heterogeneous subaltern class that peoples Ikemiyagi's story, Ukuma stares vacantly, helpless as a trapped animal at the story's end. While his silence supports Spivak's thesis on subalternity, Ikemiyagi's depiction of the officer's mentality counters it.

Ikemiyagi's final description of Ukuma is not as negative and bleak as Spivak's portrait of the subaltern. The fact that the officer's eyes are smoldering with fear *and* indignation is critical since these contradictory elements are not only what constitute the subaltern, they are what make him a potential threat to dominant groups. Historian Gautam Bhadra singles out defiance and submissiveness as the two elements that together form the subaltern mentality.[46] He argues that the subaltern's collaboration with and resistance to the elite merge and coalesce to form a complex and contradictory consciousness.[47] Officer Ukuma cannot be reduced to an absolute negation for he is painfully cognizant of, and incensed by, his double bind. It is precisely the nature of the subaltern consciousness that makes the figure a compelling one. Just as the subaltern is complex and contradictory, so too is Okinawan fiction. That is, when read with an eye to its regional aspect, the fiction affirms the idea of Japan as a nation, of which Okinawa is but a part. And, when read with an eye on its alterity, whether linguistic, cultural, or historical, the fiction contests the notion of a seamless nation.

While Spivak's writings on the subaltern come readily to mind in establishing the police officer's significance in Ikemiyagi's story, Homi Bhabha is, finally, of greater use for he offers a more hopeful view of the subaltern than does Spivak. As a consequence of his own heavy debt to deconstruction, Bhabha sees in the nature of language and the sign a split that produces polyphony and ambivalence. Bhabha argues that "people," the term Guha uses interchangeably with the "subaltern," are both objects of national pedagogy and subjects of a process of signification. He relates this doubleness to the idea of hybridity, which is defined in part as "the perplexity of the living as it interrupts the representation of the fullness of life."[48] For Bhabha, national narratives are disrupted by the presence of the subaltern whose identity-in-difference provokes a fundamental crisis. He elaborates that the identity of true subalterns lies in their difference.[49] The processes by which colonizers groom native elites to serve as a buffer between them and the masses produce "a subject of difference that is almost the same, but not quite."[50] Hyaaku, a local policeman in the employ of the Japanese state, thoroughly indoctrinated by state apparatuses of power such as schools and the police force, performs the duty of surveillance. What makes his gaze threatening is its doubleness. Observing through the eyes of a colonial representative *and* disenfranchised minority, Hyaaku mimics the colonizer yet always retains his distance, precisely because of his identity-in-difference.

Because the mimic man, Hyaaku, is constructed around the ambivalence of being both native and elite, Ikemiyagi must reveal the police officer's difference in order to maximize his potential to disrupt colonial authority. Hence, words such as "foreigner" are used to refer to Hyaaku throughout the text. While the partial presence of the subaltern turns mimicry into menace, it does not signify that an essential identity, or "true" self, is anywhere concealed.[51] Hyaaku's predicament is due to the fact that he is neither an ordinary citizen nor a respected official; his hybrid nature accounts for his utterly despondent state.

In Ikemiyagi's "Officer Ukuma," Hyaaku is a subaltern who attempts to emulate his Yamato colleagues. The passage quoted above in which Hyaaku instructs his village on proper deportment is perfectly illustrative of the type of colonial mimicry described by Bhabha. Positioning himself as an impartial public official, Hyaaku addresses his neighbors in an imperious manner. The crowd's shock can be explained by the fact that they recognize in Hyaaku their native son, not the colonial mimic he has become. Hyaaku's transformation leads to his estrangement from the village and feelings of alienation. By the end of "Officer Ukuma" the protagonist's realization that he is powerless in both his civil and official capacities causes him to feel subhuman. Ikemiyagi's description of Hyaaku as a vacantly staring trapped animal would lead one to agree with Spivak's pronouncement that the subaltern, by definition, cannot speak. However, considering the contradictory and ambiguous nature of the subaltern consciousness, what cannot be said becomes important. If Hyaaku's fearful and indignant silence is measured, then the disturbing noise of the mimic insurgent is clearly audible.

Notes

1. Edward Mack, *Manufacturing Modern Japanese Literature* (Durham, NC: Duke University Press, 2010), 284n23.

2. See, for example, Jung-Sun N. Han, "Envisioning a Liberal Empire in East Asia: Yoshino Sakuzō in Taisho Japan," *Journal of Japanese Studies* 33, 2 (Summer 2007), and Peter Duus, "The Takeoff Point of Japanese Imperialism," in *Japan Examined: Perspectives on Modern Japanese History*, eds. Harry Wray and Hilary Conroy (Honolulu: University of Hawai'i Press, 1983), 153–57.

3. Gregory Smits, *Visions of Ryukyu* (Honolulu: University of Hawai'i Press, 1999), 149.

4. I use the term "quasi-canonical" as it is arguable whether literature from Okinawan is a part of the canon of Japanese letters. "Ukuma junsa" is as canonical as a work from Okinawa can be. In an essay that follows the collected works of Ikemiyagi, Nakahodo Masanori suggests that the writer, a renowned wanderer, whose alter ego appears in Ukuma, is emblematic of Okinawa itself. See Nakahodo's essay "'Chairudohuddo' no tama" (The Spirit of Childhood), in *Ikemiyagi Sekihō sakuhinshū* (Collected Works of Ikemiyagi Sekihō), eds. Nakahodo Masanori and Tsunori Setsuko (Naha: Niraisha, 1988), 192.

5. Smits, *Visions of Ryukyu*, 40.

6. Ibid.

7. *Okinawa kindai bungei sakuhinshū* (Collected Works of Modern Okinawan Literature) (Naha: Okinawa taimususha), 111. For further biographical information on Ikemiyagi, see also Nakahodo Masanori and Tsunori Setsuko, eds., *Ikemiyagi Sekihō sakuhinshū*.

8. "Officer Ukuma" was the second piece of Okinawan fiction to appear in a major Japanese magazine, the first being Yamagusuku Seichū's "Mandarin Oranges" (*Kunenbo*), which was published in the well-known haiku journal *Cuckoo* (*Hototogisu*).

9. For details regarding Ikemiyagi's years traveling throughout Japan, see Nakahodo Masanori's chapter "Hōrōsha no bungaku" (The Literature of a Wanderer) in his book *Shinseinentachi no bungaku* (The Literature of Youth) (Naha: Niraisha, 1994), 148–81.

10. Though divorced in life, Arakaki and Ikemiyagi remain united by the publication of their adjoining collections of literature, *Ikemiyagi Sekihō sakuhinshū* (The Collected Works of Ikemiyagi Sekihō) and *Arakaki Mitoko sakuhinshū* (The Collected Works of Arakaki Mitoko), ed. Miki Takeshi (Naha: Niraisha, 1988).

11. In his study *Nantō ideorogī no hassei* (The Birth of the Ideology of the Southern Islands), Murai Osamu argues that Yanagita's discovery of the southern islands

in the period was a direct result of the unease he felt about his involvement in the drafting of colonial policies on agriculture in Korea, where he served as a bureaucrat in the Ministry of Agriculture. Murai writes convincingly of Yanagita's longing for therapeutic relief from the distress of his involvement in the Korean affair. Resigning his governmental post in 1919, Yanagita quickly retreated to the Ryukyus, concealing his past by rapidly absorbing himself in southern manners. See Murai Osamu, *Nantō ideorogī no hassei: Yanagita Kunio to shokuminchishugi* (The Birth of the Ideology of the Southern Islands: Yanagita Kunio and Colonialism) (Tokyo: Fukutake shoten, 1992), 7–58. See also Murai's "Iha Fuyū to Yanagita Kunio" (Iha Fuyū and Yanagita Kunio), in *Okinawa kara mita Nihon* (Japan Seen From Okinawa) (Tokyo: Kazama shobō, 1995), 165–202. Of related interest is Kawamura Minato's chapter on the place of the South in modern Japanese literature, *Nanyō/Karafuto no Nihon bungaku* (The Literature of the South Seas/Sakhalin) (Tokyo: Chikuma shobō, 1994), 59–82.

12. See Nakahodo Masanori's commentary in Hirotsu Kazuo, *Samayoeru Ryūkyūjin* (The Wandering Ryukyuan) (Tokyo: Dōjidaisha, 1994), 74–82.

13. R. Goldschmidt, *Taishō jidai no Okinawa* (Okinawa in the Taisho period), trans. Taira Ken'ichi and Nakamura Tetsumasa (Naha: Ryūkyū shinpōsha, 1981), 1–7. This publication is a translation of the Okinawa section of Goldschmidt's travelogue. Goldschmidt uses the term "Ryukyu Island" rather than Okinawa prefecture. The former term suggests a premodern, colonized entity.

14. Ibid., 17–22.

15. Postwar writer Shimao Toshio devotes the "Amami—Nihon no nantō" (Amami—The Southern Islands of Japan) section of his series of essays on the southern islands, collectively titled *Theory of Yaponeshia* (*Yaponeshia ron*), to a fascinating and historically specific account of the Shimazu clan's economic exploitation of Amami Ōshima through forced sugarcane production from the beginning of the seventeenth century. The profits the clan garnered through colonial policies in the Ryukyus are convincingly related to its key role in the formation of the modern Japanese state. See "Amami—Nihon no nantō" (Amami—The Southern Islands of Japan), *Okinawa bungaku zenshū* 18 (The Collected Works of Okinawan Literature, Vol. 18), (Tokyo: Kokusho kankōkai, 1992), 273–76. The curious phenomenon of an oppressed group showing unflagging loyalty to its oppressors can also be seen in the case of Taiwanese aborigines, who displayed fervent loyalty to the Japanese, despite their position at the lowest rungs of the colonial hierarchy. See Leo Ching, "'Give Me Japan and Nothing Else!': Postcoloniality, Identity, and the Traces of Colonialism," *South Atlantic Quarterly* 99, 4 (Fall 2000): 781.

16. *Bingata* is a dyeing technique developed in Okinawa. Various indigo-based colors are inserted onto a sewing pattern resulting in a complex color tone. Flowers, birds, mountains, and rivers are used frequently in bingata designs. See *Daijirin* (15th ed.), ed. Matsumura Akira (Tokyo: Sanseidō, 1989), 2079.

17. Hirotsu Kazuo, *Samayoeru Ryūkyūjin*, 72–73. Nakahodo Masanori relates Goldschmidt's account in the extended commentary appended to Hirotsu's book.

18. Benedict Anderson, *Imagined Communities* (London: Verso Editions/NLB, 1983), 141.

19. Prior to Japan's success in the Sino-Japanese War (1894–1895), owing to a long history of Ryukyuan trade with China, there were segments of Okinawa's population that allied themselves with Qing China rather than with the Meiji government that had appropriated the Ryukyus in 1879. In light of the Japanese victory, loyalties quickly switched to Japan, the nation that was clearly emblematic of strength and modernity. The result of the Russo-Japanese War (1904–1905) only confirmed Japan's power, and by the Taisho period, Okinawans redoubled their efforts to align themselves with the Japanese. See Okamoto Keitoku, *Gendai Okinawa bungaku to shisō* (The Literature and Thought of Contemporary Okinawa) (Naha: Okinawa taimususha, 1981), 3–88.

20. Alan S. Christy, "The Making of Imperial Subjects in Okinawa," *positions: east asia critique* 1, 3 (Winter 1993): 614.

21. Johannes Fabian, *Time and the Other: How Anthropology Makes Its Object* (New York: Columbia University Press), 1983.

22. In response to a contest for literary submissions, *Liberation* received 445 manuscripts. Of these, seven or eight won awards. In October 1922, two stories, one of which was "Officer Ukuma," were published from this smaller group. Ikemiyagi's story was selected as the top story. See Tsunori Setsuko's unpublished manuscript, "Taishō kōki no sakuhin: shōsetsu 'Ukuma junsa' ni tsuite" (Concerning "Officer Ukuma": A Latter Taisho Period Work), 173.

23. Ikemiyagi's use of the term *tokushu buraku* indicates that the village in question is far from ordinary. Okinawan critics uniformly agree that the village Ukuma writes about is Kuninda, an area of Naha inhabited by many naturalized Japanese originally from China. See the roundtable discussion "Okinawa no kindai bungaku to sabetsu" (Modern Okinawan Literature and Discrimination) featuring Kuniyoshi Shintetsu, Okamoto Keitoku, and Ōshiro Tatsuhiro, *Aoi umi* (Blue-green Sea) 26 (Fall 1973): 88–99.

24. Although the story is no more specific about the group of Japanese of Chinese descent that live in certain quarters of Kume, critics have noted that the inhabitants of this special hamlet are people whose relations were once employed by the Chinese diplomats and traders who lived in the Ryukyus from the fourteenth century until the time of the Sino-Japanese War. After the defeat of the Chinese in 1895, Okinawans increasingly discriminated against these descendants from other villages. Having lost their means of income, they fell under the protection of Kume village, and because they owned no land, the group could not engage in agriculture and were therefore reduced to performing menial labor. See Horii Ken'ichi, "Densetsu kara jijitsu e: shōsetsu 'Ukuma junsa' no koto" (From Legend to Fact: The Story of "Officer Ukuma"), *Aoi umi* (Blue-Green Sea) 26 (Fall 1973): 100–102.

25. Ikemiyagi Sekihō, "Officer Ukuma," trans. Davinder Bhowmik, in *Southern Exposure*, eds. Michael Molasky and Steve Rabson (Honolulu: University of Hawai'i Press, 2000), 63.

26. Ibid., 68.

27. Tsuji, Okinawa's red light district, was constructed in 1672, expanded in 1908, and laid to waste by the October 10 air raid in 1944, 270 years after it came into being. See *Okinawa daihyakka jiten* (The Encyclopedia of Okinawa) (Naha: Okinawa taimususha, 1983) 2: 818.

28. Economic conditions being what they were at the time, many Okinawan families were forced to sell their daughters to brothels. See Nakahodo Masanori, *Shinseinentachi no bungaku*, 148–65.

29. Ikemiyagi Sekihō, "Officer Ukuma," 68.

30. Ibid, 64.

31. Albert Memmi, *The Colonizer and the Colonized* (Boston: Beacon, 1965), 120.

32. It would be remiss to leave unacknowledged Memmi's intellectual debt to Frantz Fanon, whose *Black Skin, White Masks* is perhaps the *locus classicus* in post-colonial writing for the idea that colonization effects changes in colonial subjects' very consciousness.

33. Ikemiyagi Sekihō, "Officer Ukuma," 69.

34. Nakahodo Masanori, *Shinseinentachi no bungaku*, 166–79.

35. See Christopher T. Nelson, "*Nuchi nu Sūji*: Comedy and Everyday Life in Postwar Okinawa," in *Japan and Okinawa: Structure and Subjectivity*, eds. Glenn D. Hook and Richard Siddle (London: Routledge, 2003), 218.

36. Ikemiyagi Sekihō, "Officer Ukuma," 71.

37. I do not mean to imply that there is no theoretical possibility for subaltern speech. Whether the story's protagonist Ukuma "speaks" or not, the author Ikemiyagi Sekihō, a subaltern Japanese writer and noted representative of Okinawan fiction, clearly has little problem expressing himself.

38. To cite just one egregious example, in his article "The Subaltern Speaks," Alan Wald precedes a lengthy analysis of the ways in which American writer Guy Endore succeeds in allowing Caribbean "others" to represent themselves in the 1934 novel *Babouk* with only the briefest mention of Gayatri Chakravorty Spivak's well-known essay "Can the Subaltern Speak?" Wald frames his own essay by stating that Spivak has questioned the ways Western scholars have given voice to "colonial subjects, the third world subalterns, of their first world societies" and asks whether there are techniques that would allow "subaltern subjects to represent themselves with maximum authenticity." Except for the apposition "colonial subjects" and the prefix "third world," nowhere does Wald define what he means by subaltern. See Alan Wald, "The Subaltern Speaks," *Monthly Review* 43, 11 (April 1992): 17.

39. Fredric Jameson is also scrupulous in his use of the term "subaltern." Influenced by Antonio Gramsci, Jameson refers to subalternity as "the feelings of mental inferiority and habits of subservience and obedience which necessarily and structurally develop in situations of domination—most dramatically in the experience of colonized peoples." See Fredric Jameson, "Third-World Literature in the Era of Multinational Capitalism," *Social Text* 15 (Fall 1986): 76. I should note, too, several critics have responded to Jameson's provocative essay. The most articulate of these remains Aijaz Ahmad, who notes that Jameson's "cognitive aesthetics" of

third-world literature rests upon "a suppression of the multiplicity of significant difference among and with both the advanced capitalist countries on the one hand and the imperialized formations on the other." See Ahmad, "Jameson's Rhetoric of Otherness and the 'National Allegory,'" *In Theory: Classes, Nations, Literatures* (London: Verso, 1992), 376. For a spirited defense of Jameson, see Imre Szeman, "Who's Afraid of National Allegory? Jameson, Literary Criticism, Globalization," *South Atlantic Quarterly* 100, 3 (Summer 2001): 803–27.

40. *Selected Subaltern Studies*, eds. Ranajit Guha and Gayatri Chakravorty Spivak (New York: Oxford University Press, 1988), 35.

41. Ibid.

42. Ibid., 44.

43. See Gayatri Spivak's "Can the Subaltern Speak?" in *Marxism and the Interpretation of Culture*, eds. Cary Nelson and Lawrence Grossberg (Urbana: University of Illinois Press, 1988), 285.

44. Ibid., 271–313.

45. Ibid., 285.

46. See Gautam Bhadra, "The Mentality of Subalternity: Kantanam or Rajdharma," in *Subaltern Studies VI*, ed. Ranajit Guha (Delhi: Oxford University Press, 1989), 54.

47. Ibid., 91.

48. See Homi K. Bhabha, "DissemiNation: Time, Narrative, and the Margins of the Modern Nation," in *Nation and Narration* (London: Routledge, 1990), 314.

49. Gayatri Spivak also identifies the true subaltern as one whose identity lies in difference. See "Can the Subaltern Speak?" 285.

50. Homi K. Bhabha, "Of Mimicry and Man," in *The Location of Culture* (London: Routledge, 1994), 86.

51. Ibid.

CHAPTER FOUR

TEXT
Demon Bird

SATŌ HARUO

CONTEXT
Taiwan

CRITIQUE
Violence, Borders, Identity: An Ethnographic Narrative Set in Colonial Taiwan

ROBERT TIERNEY

SATŌ HARUO (1892–1964) was a distinguished Japanese poet, novelist, and essayist and a leading figure on the literary scene of the first half of the twentieth century. Born in Shingū, Wakayama prefecture, he was the eldest son of a prosperous doctor. He studied at Keio University under the writer Nagai Kafū, but quit before graduating. He fell in love with and eventually married Ishikawa Chiyoko, the estranged wife of Tanizaki Jun'ichirō, creating a scandal that was sensationally reported in the press and treated in subsequent works by both writers.

Satō began his career as a romantic poet, but is best known today for his modernist fiction and his literary criticism from the Taisho and early Showa periods. His most famous works include "Beautiful Town" (*Utsukushii machi*, 1920), a story about an architect creating a utopian city, and *The Sick Rose* (*Den'en no yūutsu*, 1919), a novel that portrays an author who flees the bustle of Tokyo for a peaceful life in the countryside. He continued to write poetry and fiction throughout his life and was an active translator, publishing one of first translations of the modern Chinese writer Lu Xun.

In his "Demon Bird" (*Machō*, 1923), the narrator tells his civilized audience about a "superstition" in an unnamed "barbaric" society. The "barbarians" believe in a bird that causes all those who behold it to die immediately; they also subscribe to the belief that certain malevolent individuals possess supernatural powers to manipulate this bird to cause harm to others. When these bird manipulators are discovered, they and their families are targeted as scapegoats and massacred by other members of the community, particularly in times of crisis. After offering an interpretation of this custom, the narrator recounts a recent episode of persecution, which he learned about while he was traveling in an aboriginal region of Taiwan.

Demon Bird

SATŌ HARUO

TRANSLATION BY ROBERT TIERNEY

Preface

The story I am about to tell you is about a superstitious belief held by certain barbarians.

Naturally, barbarians believe in superstitions. On this point, they are not the slightest bit different from civilized people. If I were to venture a comparison, I would say that the superstitions of the civilized are complicated and overly cerebral, while those of the barbarians are more natural and beautiful.

Perhaps some people think that only barbarians believe in superstitions while the civilized do nothing of the sort, but they are completely off the mark. Just as civilized people discover many superstitions in the manners and customs of barbarians, barbarians would probably find an equal number of superstitions in the social constraints that govern life in civilized society. Indeed, I would go so far as to say that what we take for justice and morality are nothing but superstition in the eyes of the barbarians—just as we dismiss their morality and humanity as mere superstition.

Part 1

To tell this story in the proper order, I must first explain to you that a very mysterious bird is to be found among these barbarians and that it plays an important part in their life. They call this bird the *hafune*.

What kind of bird is the *hafune*? Well, it looks a bit like a dove, is white and has red feet—and that is about all one can say about it. Or rather, the only ones who could offer a fuller description of the bird are no longer in this world. To put it differently, no one who has actually seen the *hafune* has survived to tell about the experience. To be sure, some human beings can gaze at the bird without being fated to sudden death but they are extremely rare. These are the demon bird manipulators. People who can freely control the demon bird or *hafune* are called the *mahafune*. As a rule, when these barbarians attach a prefix beginning with the letter "m" to a noun, the new word is verbalized. And that verbalized noun takes on the meaning of the agent who performs an action. In reality, I am far from being an expert on the precise meaning of this word and since it has no bearing on the story I will tell you, I ask you to simply think of *hafune* and *mahafune* as "demon bird" and "demon bird manipulator" respectively. And one other thing: I will dispense with all proper names of persons or places in the rest of this story.

Part 2

The barbarians place a high value on human life. In this regard too, they hardly differ from people in civilized societies. Consequently, the members of this tribe fear nothing more than having to die after coming face to face with the demon bird. They also regard someone who can control this bird and use it to inflict harm on others as the bane of society and the scourge of the human race. And, in fact, their attitude makes perfect sense once you accept the premise, as they do, that the demon bird actually exists.

As a result, if the villagers discover a demon bird manipulator in their midst, they rush to put that individual to death; and they not only kill that one person but also systematically slaughter all the members of his/her family without exception. Since the abilities of the *mahafune* are said to be passed from one generation to the next, a family that has produced one such person is likely to give birth to another one at some future time if given the chance. In such a situation, if a member of the tribe helps or offers encouragement to the family of a *mahafune*—perhaps out of a sense of obligation for some past act of kindness—then that person, too, will be treated as a demon bird manipulator and massacred along with all the members of the family. For the barbarians, this is a matter of simple justice.

Part 3

In light of what I have said, the greatest evil in their society is to be a demon bird manipulator. Ordinary people are even more afraid of being mistaken for demon bird manipulators than of seeing the demon bird. If they see a demon bird, then they alone are condemned to die. However, in the case of the demon bird manipulator, all the members of their family must suffer a cruel death. And I should add here that this barbarian tribe cherishes the family above all else. Why would people knowingly choose to become a demon bird manipulator and court disaster for their entire family? I simply cannot comprehend the mind of such people. I often posed this question to barbarians when I was traveling through their lands. Generally, they responded as follows:

"We have no idea why because we are not demon bird manipulators. But perhaps *yakkai otsutofu* has taken possession of them."

Yakkai otsutofu literally means "evil spirit" and is the name of the malefactor among their ancestral spirits. The phrase "*yakkai otsutofu* has taken possession of them" sounds very childlike, but I cannot help but find something unexpectedly suggestive in this belief that evil must spring from an ancient and mysterious source. Suppose someone had a supernatural power and could exercise this power freely as he saw fit. In this case, wouldn't he be likely to forget the difference between right and wrong, sacrifice his highest moral values and yield to the temptation to make use of this wonderful gift? This is certainly conceivable. Such a disposition lurks in the hidden depths of all human beings and some people doubtless possess it to a much higher degree than others. When young children hear about the cloak of invisibility or the magical umbrella, aren't they drawn by the seductive power of such mysterious stories? Perhaps it is not such a mystery after all that certain human beings deliberately become demon bird manipulators.

Part 4

It goes without saying that the demon bird does not actually exist. In addition, there are no demon bird manipulators who have extraordinary abilities beyond those that nature grants to man. Nevertheless, the members of this tribe entertain no doubt about the existence of the demon bird; they think it perfectly natural to believe in something they have never seen with their own eyes. After all, no living person has seen the demon bird and lived to tell about it. In addition, when they are on the verge of death, it is likely that barbarians really do see this small bird with red feet and white wings that their ancestors, in the grip of their morbid hallucinations, described to them.

But what are we to make of the so-called demon bird manipulator? Who discovers the demon bird manipulator and how? This is also an interesting problem.

Part 5

Essentially, the members of the tribe end up manufacturing the demon bird manipulator and unanimously recognize him as such. Aside from that, there is no other proof that such a person actually exists. Nor could there be any such proof. What sort of person is taken for a demon bird manipulator? Chance seems to play its part. Someone who—for whatever reason—inspires uneasiness in his fellows, and does so more than once, and who appears to have caused harm to another person, may discover some day to his chagrin that he cannot escape from suspicions of being a *mahafune*.

For example, let us assume that there is a certain person. Suddenly his behavior exhibits a marked change from the usual. For reasons no one can fathom, he suddenly becomes misanthropic or depressed. People begin to notice him. They come out with comments such as, "he has a strange look in his eyes." People begin to pay even greater attention to the expression in his eyes. He is, needless to say, filled with terror when he realizes that others are starting to take him for a *mahafune*. He begins to avoid other people. His companions regard him with suspicion and he tries hard to measure the extent of the suspicion that they harbor. By now, both sides have passed the point of no return. Since they have lost the master key of trust and love, they are locked in total darkness; flames of suspicion shoot up and rage in the darkness of their minds. A villager happens to pass by the person who is thought of as a demon bird manipulator. He looks at him with intense hatred. The latter looks back with fear and loathing. Let us suppose that by pure coincidence the former becomes feverish after he returns home. On his sick bed, he ransacks his brain to find the cause of his sudden fever and recalls that a chill struck him only after he came into contact with a particular person. And he concludes: "Of course. I ran into *that* person. This fever started right afterward. He must be a demon bird manipulator."

Again, from pure chance, this fever turns out to be contagious and infects others. Villagers come to pay a visit to the invalid but leave having caught his fever. Then, they too begin to say: "A demon bird manipulator is truly a terrifying thing, is it not?"

One of the patients, weakened by illness, eventually dies. Then, the toll rises: three deaths, then five. Perhaps one of these victims—or more likely all of them—catch a glimpse of the demon bird just as he or she is about to die. At this point, the person who is said to be a demon bird manipulator has truly become one, and the people in the village can no longer let the matter rest without taking action.

In this fashion the *mahafune* ends up being *recognized* as such by his fellows after some chance event. Lying on their sickbeds, the villagers spend their every waking moment in dread anticipation that the demon bird will suddenly appear before their eyes. Even worse than the fate of the sick and dying, however is the terrifying state of the person suspected of being a demon bird manipulator.

Part 6

However, you must not think that they just pick someone out at random, label him a demon bird manipulator and begin to persecute him unfairly.

The type of person who arouses suspicion (and provides others with a reason for thinking he is a demon bird manipulator) is, in practically every case, as previously stated, someone who, over a long period of time wears a very worried and uneasy expression on his face for reasons that are totally incomprehensible to his fellows. On this point, I think that this barbaric superstition is pregnant with meaning.

Indeed, for these extremely simple-minded people who live such a primitive life, a psychological state of deep depression is all but unimaginable. They have no trouble understanding why someone might become depressed as a result of illness and physical pain. In addition, as members of a social community, they sometimes brood about friction with other tribes and other external problems. However, in these cases, all members of the tribe share the same predicament. Private, interior anguish is completely different in nature from these cases, and when a person is so wrapped up in his spiritual self that he cannot unburden himself and confide in others, others assume he is possessed by a spirit. According to their way of thinking, the fact of spirit possession is, in and of itself, sufficient proof that the person in question is guilty, no matter what the cause of the possession. In fact, their grounds for viewing the spirit of depression as an inherent evil are not entirely illogical. And perhaps they are right to try to eliminate every last trace of this dark shadow from the minds of the members of their tribe.

Leaving aside the pros and cons of the case, we can say that they wish to destroy someone who wears a different expression from the majority of their group. There may be some of you who think "what a lawless people they are!" And you would be right. I will not deny that they are lawless. However, I will call your attention to the fact that this lawlessness is not a feature unique only to barbarous societies; rather the same sort of thing also happens in so-called civilized societies.

During the same voyage, I witnessed the colony of a certain civilized country. The people of that civilized country did not go so far as to kill the natives, who possessed a high level of civilization, but they treated them as beasts for the simple reason that they had different customs and mores. This is a single example of the common tendency of civilized people to suppress those with a slightly different facial expression from themselves. In addition, I have also seen the government of a civilized country arrest, imprison and sometimes even put to death those with slightly different views than the common run of men—thinkers considered dangerous because they believe it is possible to increase the general sum of human happiness through their ideas.

The civilized resemble barbarians insofar as they arbitrarily deem evil everything they do not understand and strive to exterminate people who wear an incomprehensible facial expression. There are many among us civilized folk who are *identified* as *mahafune*. However I am not here to talk about civilized people. So let me return to my story about the barbarians. It seems that from ancient times there have been many cases of entire families being branded as demon bird manipulators in the manner described above and then physically wiped out. Even today such stories from the past are handed down by word of mouth. It would probably be worthwhile to investigate in each of these cases the process by which the members of these unfortunate families come to be identified as demon bird manipulators. However, I am not so interested in this topic to go that far. Instead, I will write down for your reference one particular tale that I overheard by accident during my voyage. In all likelihood, this is the most recent example of this custom.

Part 7

The greater part of this enormous island was referred to as the savage lands and, accordingly, there were many regions yet to be explored. In fact, one could even say that most of the mountainous terrain inhabited by the savages remains uncharted even today. Certain places are unknown not only to adventurers but even to the savages themselves.

In recent years, a certain explorer is reported to have stumbled upon spectacularly beautiful landscapes by accident; these were most likely situated in the savage lands. I think the main reason that this region has remained terra incognita up to the present is that it has such a treacherous topography even though the altitude of the highlands only occasionally exceeds 10,000 feet above sea level—and I would naturally add the fact that savages inhabit the land. Furthermore, these unusual dangers have only heightened the fame of this region in recent years. Until now, the western route was the only secure route a traveler could take to each region. Traveling from the east, one faces cliffs almost as steep as sheer precipices since they drop almost in a straight perpendicular from the mountains to the seas—consequently, if you stand on the top of this cliff and look down, you will see, spread out beneath your feet, a panorama of the sea under low-lying clouds. For that reason, it is absolutely impossible to travel from the east, and as for the northern and southern routes, they are fraught with perils and pass through innumerable savage villages along the way. Not only is the western route the easiest to travel, but one can also enjoy extraordinary vistas along the way and one passes through relatively few savage villages and their inhabitants are relatively subdued. Generally, the traveler has no reason to fear for his safety unless he happens to be traveling when there is an armed uprising among the savages. In addition, the savages living in this region have long been known for their mild customs and, at the time that I was traveling there, they were said to be favorably disposed toward the Japanese, which is why I decided to take in this landscape during my trip. Even if this region had not been well known for its striking views, it was the best place for a traveler who simply wanted to see what a savage village looks like. However, conditions in the savage frontier are volatile and hard to predict. As I am writing today, I have heard that the people in that region harbor an intense hatred for our fellow countrymen because of some minor miscalculation on the part of the authorities. If this is indeed the case, then I must have come to see the landscape at the right moment.

The evening before my departure, I slept at the police station in the savage village. To call it a "police station" is a bit of an understatement since it was a fort, albeit a small one. The fort was surrounded by two concentric breast-high walls built of aqueous rock that had been quarried in the region, while nearby, a separate storage hut for weapons was guarded by a dog and a watchman who was on lookout all the time. After spending the night there, I left in the early dawn and expected to reach a most romantic destination by noon if all went according to plan. Just as we had done the day before, we followed the course of the river and headed upstream. However, you must not get the impression that we were walking right along the river banks when I say that "we followed the course of the river." Rather, we could see the river flowing under our feet—and this was a very interesting sight—as we walked along a path that was extremely high and afforded a marvelous view in every direction. So we continued along our way, on the

lookout for savages who might appear suddenly out of nowhere, and enjoy-
ing the stunning scenery along this route, which, like most of those in this
savage land, was built at a very high elevation.

Two armed police officers protected me on my right and left. This is
common practice even when one is traveling through the most peaceful
parts of the savage lands. Walking right behind us, two completely assimilated savages served as our guides and porters. This tale I have been keeping
you waiting for was told in turns by these two porters as they were walking
along and then translated for me by one of the policemen in our party.

I believe it is the most recent case of the destruction of an entire family of
demon bird manipulators. However, there is a touch of the legendary about
this tale that passed through innumerable different lips before it reached my
ear. The narrative style is crude and unpolished but the story holds together.
Indeed, this tale recounts an event that I can scarcely conceive of and am
not in a position to verify. In spite of their simplicity, these savages have a
real talent for tying up the loose ends in a story in a suggestive way and may
have invented the entire tale.

Part 8

Pira is the daughter of Satsusan. Kōre is Pira's younger brother. I have heard
that Satsusan had other sons and daughters but they were all massacred.
Pira, the eldest, and Kōre, the youngest were the sole survivors at that time.

Pira is said to have been the cause of the trouble. She had reached the age
of eighteen, but she refused to tattoo herself. Since Pira was a very beautiful
girl, many eligible bachelors would have been happy to wed her. Among
these savages, however, no woman could be called "beautiful" if she did not
daub her forehead and cheeks with dark ink, no matter how gorgeous her
features were. The savages would have thought it disgraceful even to desire
such a woman, let alone to marry her. If a man were to live with her as husband and wife, the others in the village would look down on him and say
that he had bitten into an unripe fruit. Not only was Pira beautiful but she
had a great talent for weaving and sewing, and the fact that she had reached
the age of 18 without getting tattooed meant that even she thought of herself as an unripe fruit. That was the first incomprehensible thing. And then
there was the fact that, in Pira's family, all, starting with Satsusan, had the
habit of walking about looking down at the ground; they lifted their eyes
when they happened to pass by someone else, but then immediately averted

their glance. In their family, no one ever laughed, not even the children. It is not unreasonable that everyone started to think that the people in Satsusan's family might be demon bird manipulators. But that wasn't the only cause.

At that time a great misfortune befell the village. All of a sudden, a large detachment of troops from a civilized country marched right through their lands. The soldiers were so numerous that the savages had never before seen such a huge throng. They wondered in amazement whether such an enormous population inhabited the plains. What's more, this unimaginably large force from the plains treated them far worse than any plains people had done in the past. Without offering the slightest reason, they ordered the villagers, who had not lifted a hand against them or offered the least resistance, to surrender unconditionally. As a proof of their surrender, the village men were commanded to assemble inside a building and promised gifts. They were told: "All of you men must gather in this building. As soon as you have done so, we will assume that you have honestly surrendered to us and will distribute the different gifts that we have brought. Those that do not obey this order will be viewed as rebels and ruthlessly punished." The savages were astounded as they looked at this vast and well-armed force ranged against them. The men were confused how to respond to this incomprehensible command, but in the end they realized they had no choice but to comply. They gathered in the designated building, about eighty men in all. The doors were securely shut and then flames shot up from outside the building. All eighty men were burned to death. The army later claimed that the savages in this village were violent and evil creatures. Then they left that village and continued on their march.

The village where Satsusan lived was not the one that was burned down, but it was only a short distance away. In Satsusan's village, only about three or five people perished, far fewer than the 80 people killed nearby. Any village located along the path of the marauding army, no matter how small it was, lost at least three or five people. The savages believed that the disaster that struck their village could only be caused by the *mahafune*.

Villagers spread rumors that Pira had been trailing after the soldiers of this marauding army. At the time, she was only sixteen years of age. At first, no one lent much credence to these far-fetched rumors. However, everyone recalled them when they saw how Pira was behaving and observed how her family reacted. And no one could understand why a young girl would pine after the soldiers of this brutal army. However, some villagers claimed that Pira had been raped by one of the soldiers. According to them, Pira refused to tattoo her forehead and cheeks because she had been raped. Even if she were to tattoo herself, no man in the tribe would wed a woman who had had sexual intercourse with someone from a different tribe. Before she tattooed herself, she would have to make a clear and public confession of everything that had happened to her body up to the point of being tattooed. This was the iron rule that governed the tribe. A few villagers believed that this was what really happened to Pira, but the vast majority concluded that the girl and her family must be demon bird manipulators.

Part 9

They set fire to Satsusan's hut. Surrounding the hut on all sides, they rounded up members of the family as they fled to escape the flames. Then they stabbed them all to death. However, Pira and Kōre were not among those caught fleeing the hut. Pira must have managed to escape carrying her youngest brother Kōre on her back. However, it was still not clear where they went or how they managed to get away. But no one could dispute the fact that they had somehow managed to slip away.

Part 10

Pira carried her brother Kōre on her back and fled to a place that seemed far from any human settlement. However, three days later, Pira returned to her village bearing her brother on her back. She made a complete confession—and her confession was identical in content to the rumor first spread by one of the villagers. Because she made a full confession, Pira's life was spared. But she was banished by the villagers for having hidden her impurity for a long time and for having been the cause of a disturbance. To harbor such a woman in their midst would have been an unpardonable crime for the villagers.

Escaping from death by the skin of her teeth, Pira again picked up her brother and returned to the mountains. For many years, she tended her younger brother and lived with him in the mountains. Occasionally the members of her village on a distant hunting expedition would approach their hut—or rather the cave in which they lived—but they always passed it by, pretending not to have noticed.

Part 11

One day Pira said to her brother Kōre: "We are not demon bird manipulators. None of us were demon bird manipulators. Even though mother and father were killed, their *ottofu* has crossed the *hangō ottofu* and gone to *poken*. They are not in *yaajao*. A great misfortune has befallen us and I do not know who brought this misfortune upon us. Yet we must avenge ourselves on the people who have harmed us. Kōre, when the new moon rises in the west, you must always fire an arrow at it. If you don't do this, we will become spineless cowards and will be the targets of the wrath of *hangō ottofu*."

And then Pira broke off a tree branch and fashioned a bow-like weapon for Kōre. Kōre released an arrow at the new moon. The new moon kept moving westward and eventually shone above the village that had banished them.

Part 12

(The word *ottofu* refers to the spirit world. They also use this term to designate their own shadows and the pulsation of their blood. In this single word we can catch a glimpse of the entire philosophy of life of this savage tribe. *Hangō ottofu* means the bridge of spirits, which the *ottofu* cross to reach *poken* or paradise. The term *poken* also signifies foundation or roots as well as hometown. However, only good spirits—*barakku ottofu*—are permitted to reach *poken*, while evil spirits or *yakkai ottofu* are banished to *yaajao*. The bridge of spirits is like a rainbow, but when evil spirits attempt to cross it, the bridge vanishes in midair and they fall straight into *yaajao*. *Yaajao* means hell and a gigantic crab lives there and metes out punishment to the souls that have fallen into his kingdom.

In addition, these savages believe that revenge is an ethical duty. When the new moon appears in the sky, they customarily shoot an arrow toward the sacred new moon as a sign of the vows they have made to their ancestral spirits. Even when they are unable to carry out revenge, they must let the latter know that they have not lost the will to seek revenge.)

Part 13

The thirteen-year-old Kōre discovered a place to play in the middle of the mountains. One day, surprised by a violent squall, a common occurrence in this region, Kōre returned home from this playground to find that Pira was dead. A snake had bitten her fingertip and the venom had traveled along her arm and risen all the way to her throat. Kōre spent a long time weeping beside her corpse. Finally coming to himself, he looked up at the sky and saw that the squall had cleared up and a rainbow had appeared. What's more, the rainbow came straight out of the hut where they had been living. Kōre was absolutely certain that Pira was striding along the rainbow bridge on her way to *poken* for the rainbow lay etched clearly across the vast sky and did not dissipate.

Part 14

Kōre thought that his elder sister, who had raised him as a mother would, and his parents and other siblings, whose faces he could only dimly recall, must be standing at the end of the rainbow bridge that spanned the sky. Why did he not run to the end of the rainbow that remained in the sky the day he lost his sister? He had thrown away any chance to console himself for the misfortune of finding himself all alone. He wandered around aimlessly like a stray animal. He made no effort to return to the hut where he had lived before. There was nobody waiting for him even if he did go back and, besides, there was no food left.

By accident, Kōre came out onto a plateau that he had never seen before. White lilies in full bloom covered the whole field and they all bent in the direction the wind was blowing. According to the beliefs of the tribe, it was a favorable omen to see lilies moving in the wind. But Kōre continued to walk on alone, free of any hopes or desires. A *shiireku* bird was crying under the shade of the trees. The bird stood right in the middle of the path where Kōre was walking. What omen might this be? It was called *meraafu* and meant bad luck. But Kōre did not despair and kept on walking right ahead. Of course, the omen of the white lilies must be the correct one. Suddenly rain began to fall from the sky in big droplets. But there was nothing very unusual about that either. It was just an ordinary squall. Kōre squatted underneath the tallest tree. The storm passed, the sky cleared and a broad rainbow appeared in the heavens.

Kōre gave out a shout of joy and, staring up at the sky, he dashed off in the direction of the rainbow and ran as fast as his legs would carry him. I have no idea how far he ran but he eventually came out onto a mysterious place. From this point on it was impossible to advance any further. If one looked down, one could see low-lying clouds. The rainbow, which had settled beneath the clouds, was snuffed out in the bluish depth of the clouds. Kōre just stood there looking absent-mindedly off into the distance.

Part 15

Wearing rattan garments embroidered with red patterns, a group of savages were lurking in their hiding place in the forest and getting ready for the hunt. They had cornered a deer and waited for it to emerge from its hiding place. Suddenly, one of them noticed a small boy standing off in the distance with his back turned toward them. They crept up to him, trying not to make any noise. When they realized he was not a member of their tribe, one of them aimed his rifle at him and fired a shot. The boy fell to the ground. Crawling through the undergrowth, they came out into the clearing.

One of the hunters raised his hand to beckon the stragglers behind him. "Come quickly. Hey, you should cut off his head. Here is your chance to qualify for taking a bride."

A young man appeared, looked down at this boy whom he had never seen before in his life and lopped off his head with a broad-edged sword.

Part 16

Naked and headless, the small torso remained behind in this desolate and lonely place. Rising straight above it, a huge rainbow gradually faded away and disappeared. And evening approached from the depths of the sea that lay beneath the cliff. . . . As I listened to the story told by the savages, I imagined that we were traveling toward this extraordinary landscape where the young boy's corpse still lay. As we continued to move forward, I started to reflect about the many superstitions that exist in barbarian society as well of the superstitions of the civilized—just as I have written in the first half of this story.

Violence, Borders, Identity:
An Ethnographic Narrative
Set in Colonial Taiwan

ROBERT TIERNEY

> . . . of all learned discourses, the ethnological seems to
> come closest to a fiction.
>
> Roland Barthes

In the summer of 1920, the writer Satō Haruo (1892–1964), a respected figure in the Japanese literary establishment, spent three months traveling in
Taiwan, which had become a Japanese colony in 1895. Satō's trip to Taiwan
took place during the high imperial period, a time of political democratiza-
tion in Japan, which was commonly referred to as Taisho liberalism, and of
aggressive assimilation reforms in the colonies. The trip proved extremely
fruitful in terms of the writer's later literary production. Based on his experiences there, he went on to write a series of essays, children's tales, travel
memoirs, and stories, including a handful set in aboriginal Taiwan.[1]

In recent years, scholars of Japanese colonial literature have singled out
Satō's stories about aboriginal Taiwan as among the few prewar literary works
that are highly critical of Japanese colonial policies and discourses. Fujii
Shōzō writes in the epilogue to a recent reprint of the travelogue *Musha*,
published by Satō Haruo in 1925, that "Satō hints at the unhappiness of the
aborigines assimilated into the Japanese empire and indirectly criticizes the
repressive policies of the colonial government by his cool, clearheaded observations."[2] Writing about Satō's story "Demon Bird" (*Machō*, 1923), Faye
Yuan Kleeman notes that he fashions "a critical discourse on Japan's internal
and external colonial conditions during the 1920s."[3] When these scholars
praise Satō's works, they employ a vocabulary that is not ordinarily used
to describe literary writers or to characterize purely literary works. Indeed,
these words are more commonly employed to depict an ideal ethnographer
in the field, this "cool, clear-headed" observer of another society who brings
a critical perspective to bear on those he studies but nevertheless feels em-
pathy toward them. Curiously, however, these scholars have overlooked the
author's engagement with the point of view of the ethnographer and with

ethnographic discourse. Yet this engagement is central to his Taiwan works and to his critique of Japan's colonialism.

Through a close reading of Satō's "Demon Bird," a short story published in the October 1923 issue of the journal *Central Forum* (*Chūō kōron*), I will highlight the centrality of ethnographic content and narrative style to the author's critique of Japan's colonialism. In the first half of "Demon Bird," a first-person narrator discusses a superstitious belief shared by the members of an unnamed "barbarian" society. In the second, he tells of an episode of persecution that he heard about while he was traveling in aboriginal regions of Taiwan. As we will see, the narrator of this story adopts the perspective of an ethnographer toward the society he describes and his style recalls the writings of Japanese ethnographers who had begun to study the different aboriginal societies of Taiwan shortly after it became a Japanese colony.[4] Indeed, Satō borrowed the central motif of the story, the superstition of the "demon bird" (*hafune*), from a single passage in an ethnography of the Atayal aborigines by Mori Ushinosuke (1877–1926), an ethnographer who spent decades studying the Taiwanese tribes. The two men met during Satō's 1920 trip to Taiwan and Mori helped to arrange the traveling writer's itinerary for his excursion to the aboriginal lands.

In this essay, I will argue that Satō engages with the discourse and viewpoint of ethnography in "Demon Bird" in order to criticize Japanese imperialism. As a work critical of Japanese imperialism, his story exemplifies the anti-imperial critique during the Taisho period (1912–1926), when Japan's colonial policies were challenged by liberal reformists in Japan and by pro-independence movements in the colonies. At the same time that he uses ethnography to criticize Japanese colonial policy, Satō implicitly deconstructs colonial ethnography itself as a form of knowledge complicit with the structures of colonial domination. In his mise-en-scène of an ethnographic encounter in Taiwan, he shows that the ethnographer owes his position as cool-headed and critical observer to a colonial apparatus that facilitates his encounter with the natives and that the violent subjugation of the latter is the condition that enables his "objective" knowledge. Before turning to the intricacies of "Demon Bird," I will first address the early history of Japanese anthropology and the career trajectory of Mori Ushinosuke, who came to exercise such an important influence on Satō, in order to situate his works within this historical moment.

Ethnographers and the Colonial Project of Knowledge

Along with steamships and conscript armies, the discipline of anthropology entered Japan during the late nineteenth century. Western scholars hired by the Meiji government to teach in the nation's new educational institutions were the first to bring this science of "savage" peoples to Japan. Just as Japanese scholars would later investigate the origins of the people they colonized, these Western academics initiated research into the origins of the Japanese. Edward Morse, a professor of zoology at Tokyo University, conducted Japan's first archeological excavations of shell mounds in Ōmori in 1879 and speculated that Japan's earliest inhabitants were Stone Age cannibals who were later conquered by more "advanced" invaders from Asia. Stimulated by his speculations, a group of intellectuals centered on Tsuboi Shōgorō (1868–1913), a scholar credited with founding Japanese anthropology and a professor at Tokyo University, began to use the conceptual apparatus of Western anthropology to launch their own studies of the origins of the Japanese. In the course of their investigations, they came to pay close attention to the Ainu people living on the northern frontier of the nation, who were incorporated into the Japanese nation in 1869. These "domestic" foreigners were thought to hold important clues as to the origins of the Japanese people, a mystery that truly baffled early anthropologists.[5]

In addition, these early pioneers of Japanese anthropology also sought to reclaim from Westerners the task of searching for the roots of the nation and to establish their own national branch of the discipline. During this period, anthropology encompassed disparate fields such as archeology, physical anthropology, ethnography, and linguistics, and in this essay, I will use the terms "ethnography" and "anthropology" interchangeably. In contrast to Western ethnographers, who tended to investigate "savage" others living in colonies, Tsuboi and his contemporaries first turned their attention to the prehistory of the society to which they belonged. Their first object of study was not the colonized other in the *gaichi* (outer colonial territories), but rather the different ethnic groups that had been incorporated into Japan's empire in the early Meiji era (1868–1912), notably the previously mentioned Ainu and the Okinawans. In later years, the ethnic origins of the Japanese remained a central concern to Japanese anthropologists, notably to Yanagita Kunio (1875–1962), the founder of Japanese folklore studies. Unlike these early scientists, Yanagita tended to search for ancient traces of the Japanese not on the northern periphery of the nation, but rather in Okinawa, which he viewed as a "museum" of ancient Japanese culture.

After defeating the Qing empire in the Sino-Japanese War (1894–1895), Japan emerged triumphantly as an imperialist power in East Asia and acquired its first formal colony, Taiwan.[6] While Japanese anthropologists had not previously ventured far from the home islands to conduct fieldwork, they now went to Taiwan to study the "savage" other. The aboriginal territories of the island became the first overseas field in which they operated. Within one year of the victory over China, three ethnographer-pioneers traveled to Taiwan to inform their countrymen about the exotic peoples newly placed under the protection of the Japanese emperor: Torii Ryūzō (1870–1953), Inō Kanori (1867–1925) and, most importantly for this essay, Mori Ushinosuke.

The colonization of Taiwan not only provided ethnographic pioneers with a new field in which to work, but it also gave them a new object to study: the Taiwan aborigines became Japan's very own "savages." Torii Ryūzō noted that these "savage" tribes provided scientists with an object of genuine intellectual interest. Believing that the aborigines had remained isolated from any outside contact and unchanged in their way of life throughout history, Torii regarded them as specimens of primitive humanity preserved in a test tube.

> In the rich, beautiful Japanese colony of Taiwan . . . several savage tribes can be found who have completely turned their backs on civilization. . . . They are a matter of astonishment to all travelers. From the point of view of civilization and human solidarity, they are unhappy creatures who merit our pity; but for the anthropologist they constitute a marvelous field of studies. To what race do these populations belong? What are their customs, their diet, their way of life and their social institutions? For science, all of these matters are of the highest interest.[7]

Besides gaining an object of study, Torii also staked out a privileged position for himself within this new field. As a scientific observer, he was separated from his object of study by a sharp epistemological boundary that overlapped with other boundaries: those dividing the civilized and savage, the colonizer and colonized. At the same time, however, he distinguished himself from his civilized countrymen by his purported "objectivity" and his freedom from "prejudices." As a matter of principle, it was claimed that the anthropologist left his preconceptions behind when he stepped into the society of the aborigines. For him, their society could be objectified and rendered intelligible: his job was to decipher this rational "text" and to translate it into terms the layperson could understand.

The first item of business for these early ethnographers was to devise a system to classify the different aboriginal groups in Taiwan and to draw clear borders between their distinct territories. From the late seventeenth century, Chinese writers had divided all of the aborigines into the "raw barbarians" (*shengfan* or *seiban*) and "cultivated barbarians" (*shufan* or *jukuban*), according to their proximity to Chinese cultural norms and their submission to Qing government control.[8] To the Japanese ethnographers, this nomenclature was "nothing more than ancient Chinese tradition" and was "completely lacking in any scholarly value."[9] The ethnographers sought to free themselves from the Sino-centric taxonomy of Taiwan's former ruler and replace it with an ostensibly modern, scientific system that grouped aborigines according to physical or cultural markers of differences. They conceived of these aboriginal groups as internally homogeneous entities that occupied externally distinct and bounded territories. Believing that these aboriginal subgroups were static and coherent entities, they developed "colorful images of the interior of Taiwan that aggregated the myriad villages into geographically contiguous but distinct 'culture areas' or 'tribes' according to perceived similarities in village social organization, architectural styles, religion, forms of personal adornment, language, physique and economic life."[10]

For the colonial government, Taiwan's "savage frontier" was essentially terra incognita for at least the first decade of Japanese rule. Only after the regime completed its military conquest of the aborigines in 1914 did it dispatch surveyors to make accurate maps of their territories.[11] Many years before these surveyors arrived to chart the central highlands of Taiwan, however, ethnographers had already mapped out the area. Geographies of the mind rather than of space, these ethnic maps manifested a subordination of the tribes to Japanese intellectual power. This mapping did not merely reproduce a preexisting reality but rather projected onto space an imaginative production of the ethnographer's mind. Just as new states in the postcolonial period continued to inhabit the same territories the colonial power previously ruled, these ethnic borders proved durable and were perpetuated after the colonial ethnographers had left Taiwan. Indeed, the categories conceived by colonial ethnographers later became the basis for aboriginal self-identifications. The writer Satō Haruo was able to make strategic use of ethnography in his "Demon Bird" in large part because both ethnography and literature were imaginative projections onto aboriginal society.

The Meeting of Ethnographer and Writer

Mori Ushinosuke first came to Taiwan in 1895 at the end of the Sino-Japanese War during which he had served as a Chinese language interpreter attached to the Japanese army. In his later memoirs, Mori recalled that he had been motivated to travel to Taiwan by his long-standing fascination with the savages of the South Seas: "As a child I remembered having heard tales of tropical islands and of ogre-like savages living in Taiwan. Now that Taiwan had become part of our territory and we Japanese could travel there, I suddenly felt a strong urge to go there and see for myself."[12] A self-described "adventurer" who studied the aborigines primarily "to amuse himself," Mori conducted fieldwork over most of the next two decades, published widely on the Taiwan aboriginal groups and established a taxonomy of the tribes that was adopted by the colonial state in 1913.

Significantly, Mori was the only ethnographer of note to remain active on the "savage frontier" during the brutal military conquest of aboriginal lands in the second decade of the twentieth century. In 1909, Sakuma Samata (1844–1915), the sixth governor-general of Taiwan, launched the "Five Year Plan to Conquer the Northern Tribes," a centrally coordinated campaign to put an end to resistance by the tribes by force and to accelerate the development of mineral and timber resources in aboriginal lands.[13] To continue with his research, Mori reluctantly joined the paramilitary Survey Section of the Bureau for the Control of Aborigines in 1909 and remained until the bureau was disbanded in 1913. In a speech given in Taipei, Mori argued that the ethnographer could serve the state by increasing understanding of the ethnic nature of the tribes. "I was confident that by promoting mutual understanding and smooth communication between us and them, I would be able to reduce (even slightly) the sacrifices needed to reach the goals of extending the guard-line, building roads, developing the aboriginal lands and confiscating weapons. The way to do this was to survey and thoroughly research their customs and their ethnic mentality, their feelings and thoughts." However, he frankly acknowledged that ethnography provided essential knowledge of the enemy, a necessity in any war: "If we are to subjugate the aborigines, we must of course know them."[14]

In Mori's view, the ethnographer should be an intermediary between indigenous societies and the Japanese state. However, Mori proposed to mediate when the space for mediation had been virtually eliminated by the government's very policies of military conquest. Accordingly, he faced a

problem encountered by any anthropologist who puts his cultural expertise at the disposal of one of the parties to a war. Even though he hoped to
use his knowledge to avert conflict and promote cultural understanding, he
risked becoming a mere accomplice to the military and his knowledge simply another weapon by which to destroy the enemy. Mori's statement betrays
personal regret that Japanese colonial officials neither took him up on his
offer to put his expertise at the disposal of the state nor accepted his good offices as a neutral go-between. Indeed, Japanese officials made little use of the
knowledge of Japanese ethnographers when they crafted concrete policies
toward the aborigines and relied instead on the time-tested policies of "savage control" implemented by the police, who continued to rule the savage
zones as "special administrative districts" during most of the colonial period.

In his later years, Mori assailed Japan's colonial policies on the grounds
that they were eliminating the object that he sought to study.

> [Opening up the savage territory] entails very rapid and severe changes in
> the aborigines' particular cultures, if not their outright destruction. Further-
> more, their oral traditions are being forgotten, while their precious heir-
> looms and material artifacts are destroyed in fires. Hit by the waves of civili-
> zation, the aborigines may become mere shells of their former selves and lose
> the lofty and noble qualities that arise from their ethnic character.[15]

Since the object of study was vanishing before his very eyes, Mori saw his
role as that of a "salvage" ethnographer who would "investigate and record
their social customs and traditions today, since in the future there will be
no way to study their history."[16] Besides writing about aboriginal customs
and beliefs, Mori collected aboriginal artifacts and donated most of them to
the Taiwan Museum, which was established in 1915 to exhibit articles from
Taiwan, southern China, and the South Seas.

Indeed, when Satō Haruo traveled to Taiwan in 1920, Mori was the deputy director of the Taiwan Museum. Mori befriended the writer, drew up a
travel plan for him and introduced him to Taiwan colonial officials, including Shimomura Hiroshi, the chief of civil administration of Taiwan, who
arranged for him to obtain permits to travel into aboriginal lands. Due to
sporadic uprisings against the Japanese authorities, the aboriginal lands were
normally off-limits to travelers and anyone wishing to visit them needed first
to obtain a special permit from the police administration. Traveling with a
police escort, Satō set out for the aboriginal areas shortly after the outbreak
of a rebellion against Japanese rule in the village of Slamao, in which 19 Japa-

nese policemen were killed. By the time Satō reached Musha, the principal administrative town in the highlands, the colonial authorities were organizing a punitive expedition to put down the uprising. After visiting Musha, he returned to Taipei, where he was a guest at Mori's house for two weeks.

In the final section of the travelogue *Musha*, the narrator cites the views of an ethnographer referred to as M (a clear reference to Mori) and records his criticisms of Japanese colonial policies. He describes M as a scholar who has "a deep knowledge of aboriginal societies" and as an adventurous fieldworker who never "carried an arm to defend himself during his fieldwork." Regarding the Slamao uprising that coincided with Satō's visit, he cites M's opinion that "the savages (*banjin*) have been provoked to anger by the fact that Japanese authorities have completely disregarded the customs of their society." M also laments the destruction the Japanese have inflicted on the aborigines' culture, claiming "handicrafts are in danger of disappearing before long because their traditional methods are completely disregarded by the authorities and receive no official encouragement."[17]

However, the narrator of *Musha* does more than merely cite the authoritative words of this eminent ethnographer. Mori's views inform his own descriptions of aboriginal society, which are imbued with the same "imperial nostalgia" toward traditional aboriginal culture that Mori adopted toward the end of his career. Renato Rosaldo describes this nostalgia as follows:

> Curiously enough, agents of colonialism often display nostalgia for the colonized culture as it was "traditionally" (that is, when they first encountered it). The peculiarity of their longing, of course, is that agents of colonialism long for the very forms of life they intentionally altered and destroyed. Nostalgia is a particularly appropriate emotion to invoke in attempting to establish one's innocence and at the same time talk about what one has destroyed.[18]

Rosaldo argues that imperial nostalgia helps these agents to establish their innocence and to deny their complicity in the destruction of the lost cultures whose passing they mourn. As I have shown, Japan's conquest of Taiwan was the condition that made it possible for Japanese ethnographers like Mori to discover aboriginal cultures. By the same token, Mori did not intervene on behalf of the threatened aborigines to prevent their cultural extinction, but rather sought to record their cultures in the short period remaining before they disappeared for good

When he visits the different colonial institutions that Japan has created, the narrator of *Musha* displays a similar imperial nostalgia when he notes the destructive impact Japanese colonialism has on aboriginal culture. Encountering a group of aboriginal porters on the road to Musha, he describes a man suffering from venereal disease. The man wore "a military cap that resembled the kind porters wear in Japan and had his hair cut short. But it was not just in his taste in appearance and costume that he seemed to have caught the disease of civilization. The bridge of his nose had fallen and his ugly nostrils sprawled in the center of his face. In this savage land, and among these savage people, I was shocked to find a man ravaged by syphilis."[19] Promoted by the Japanese state as the cure for backwardness of the "savages," civilization is here depicted as "syphilization." The narrator finds traces of ruin wherever he looks: in the trading posts the Japanese set up in the villages "where there was almost nothing for sale except the most inferior goods from Japan," in the spread of prostitution, in the abandonment of aboriginal women by Japanese men who marry them, in the schools that teach students "concepts they can scarcely imagine in their own world."[20] In general, for the narrator, the Japanese are the carriers of the "disease of civilization" in aboriginal Taiwan and the aborigines are their passive victims.

Deconstructing Colonial Ethnography

Satō Haruo's short story "Demon Bird" represents his deepest engagement with ethnography and his most radical critique of Japanese imperialism. Based on an aboriginal legend, the story is told by an ethnographic narrator and imitates the style of an ethnographic report. Satō was apparently inspired to write "Demon Bird" by the following passage from Mori's *Ethnography of the Taiwan Savages* (*Taiwan banzokushi*).[21]

> According to aboriginal legend, there is a magical bird called the *hafune*. It looks like a dove, with white feathers and red feet. The savages believe the bird has supernatural powers and that anyone who sees it is certain to die. Certain savages called the *mahafune* have the ability to manipulate this bird. If a man is suspected of being a *mahafune*, he and all the members of his family will be massacred. In addition, if a village is rumored to harbor a man who is a *mahafune*, other villages will be terrified and avoid all contact with it.[22]

The narrator of "Demon Bird" does more than simply reference this passage of Mori's ethnography. This aboriginal "legend" is the kernel for the entire plot of "Demon Bird" and inspires the narrator to propose his own ethnographic theories on aboriginal culture. The narrator fleshes out his narrative and buttresses his hypotheses by paraphrasing from Mori's interpretations of aboriginal beliefs and invoking his commentary on aboriginal customs.[23] As a result, Mori's study informs both Satō's detailed descriptions of the fine points of aboriginal culture and society and the overall narrative frame of "Demon Bird."

More importantly, the narrator attempts to carve out an authorial point of view that stands aloof from both the native culture and his own society. He starts his story about the "superstitious belief held by certain barbarians" by drawing a boundary between the civilized (which implicitly includes both the ethnographer and his readers) and the barbarians. Then he establishes his own authority as an ethnographer by asserting his distance from his "civilized" audience. He writes, "Just as civilized people discover many superstitions in the manners and customs of barbarians, barbarians would probably find an equivalent number of superstitions in the social constraints that govern life in civilized society. Indeed, I would go so far as to say that what we take for justice and morality are nothing but superstition in the eyes of the barbarians."[24] Here the narrator not only simulates the ethnographer's attitude of cool detachment and his cultural relativism, but he also simulates his position as a fieldworker. As readers, we see him out in the field asking his native informants how they interpret their own customs and make sense of their own experience.[25]

Even though the narrator of "Demon Bird" impersonates an ethnographer, his story is not literally an ethnographic report but rather a mock-ethnography. I use this term advisedly because the narrator occasionally undercuts his own position and drops his mask. For instance, "In reality, I am far from being an expert on the precise meaning of this word [*mahafune*] and since it has no bearing on the story . . ."[26] In effect, the narrator both imitates and distances himself from the ethnographer. From this ambiguous and double position, he is able both to pastiche and to deconstruct colonial ethnographic discourse. I have already noted that Satō had an enormous regard for Mori, but in "Demon Bird" he treats the language and the praxis of colonial ethnography in a highly critical manner.

Like the ethnographic report that it imitates, "Demon Bird" mixes speculation about another culture with transcriptions of indigenous oral legend. In the first part of the story, the narrator speaks implicitly to a civilized listener about an aboriginal belief in a demon bird. This superstition is used metonymically to illuminate the construction of social borders by members of a primitive community. In the same way that the ethnographers estab-

lished the borders dividing different aboriginal groups and proposed tax-
onomies of the tribes, the narrator of "Demon Bird" concerns himself with
how primitive communities define and manage the boundaries that separate
them from others. According to the narrator, the "savages" believe that certain individuals in the community—called the *mahafune*—possess supernatural powers to manipulate an imaginary bird (*hafune*), a harbinger of
death. When a natural catastrophe strikes the community, members of the
group blame their misfortunes on this individual and massacre his or her
entire family. After asking the barbarians how they can identify the nefari-
ous *mahafune*, the narrator notes that they invariably "destroy someone who
wears a different expression from the majority of their group."[27] Although
villagers and *mahafune* share the same geographical space, they are divided
by an impalpable boundary and an invisible difference. By recognizing the
mahafune, his or her fellow villagers exercise a social power to police their
borders and determine group membership.

Moving on from the first half of "Demon Bird," which explains the
scapegoat mechanism, the second half features a legend that gives a concrete
example of this mechanism in action. The narrator had hitherto addressed
the reader from an undisclosed location, but he now situates himself in
aboriginal Taiwan.[28] In addition to being set in Taiwan's aboriginal interior, the legend contains other new elements that, paradoxically, complicate
rather than confirm the narrator's theories about the *mahafune* set forth in
the first part of the story. Unlike the expert on "barbarian superstitions"
who holds forth authoritatively in part one of "Demon Bird," the narrator undermines his own theory by his indiscreet revelations. In the first
place, he puts colonial violence, which the ethnographer eliminates from
his speculations by positing a traditional aboriginal culture, at the very center of the legend. In the second, the narrator places his ethnographer right
in the middle of a colonial apparatus when he tells how he happened to
hear the legend. The legend thus forces the reader to rethink his theory of
the *mahafune* and to reconsider the position of the ethnographer toward
the object of his knowledge.

If the narrator of the first part isolates the custom of the *mahafune* as a
tradition internal to the aboriginal community, then the story of Pira shows
that foreign invasion and colonial conquest play a key role in triggering the
hunt for a scapegoat. The legend recounts the destruction of the family of a
young woman called Pira. Villagers mistake the members of Pira's family for
demon bird manipulators because Pira refuses to tattoo herself and because

her family exhibits unusual behavior. Rumors start to circulate when villagers witness the young Pira trailing after the soldiers of a "civilized country" who have recently invaded their village.

> A large detachment of soldiers from a civilized country suddenly marched through their lands . . . [and] ordered the villagers . . . to surrender unconditionally. As a proof of their surrender, the village men were commanded to assemble inside a building and promised gifts . . . The men were confused how to respond to this incomprehensible order, but in the end they realized they had no choice but to comply. They gathered in the designated building, about eighty men in all. The doors were securely shut and then flames shot up from outside the building. All eighty men were burned to death. The army later spread the word that the savages in this village were violent and evil creatures . . . The savages believed that the disaster that struck their village could only be caused by the *mahafune*.[29]

Indeed, as we learn later, Pira "is said to have been the cause of the trouble" because she refuses to tattoo herself and her refusal attracts the suspicion of the villagers. The reason for Pira's refusal, we later learn, is that a soldier from the "civilized" army has raped her. The rape of Pira prefigures in graphic form the Japanese violation of the boundaries of the aboriginal community and foreshadows later armed invasion of aboriginal lands. While I have found no evidence that the violent scene described above is based on a real historical event, historians of this period have shown that the Japanese army systematically terrorized the indigenous peoples into submission and carried out public executions of warriors in aboriginal villagers. According to a recent deposition to a UN working group on aboriginal affairs, over 10,000 Atayals (the largest northern tribe) are believed to have perished during Sakuma's five-year campaign.[30]

Not only do Pira and her family come to be seen as *mahafune* after the colonial army invades their lands, but crucially their persecution is depicted as a response to this invasion. Unable to strike back against the invading army, the villagers vent their rage onto a vulnerable and proximate member of their own community. Pira and her family are substitute victims sacrificed in lieu of the Japanese army beyond the reach of reprisal. Moreover, the persecution of the *mahafune* is also an imitation of colonial violence. When the villagers attack Pira and her family, they employ the very tactics the colonial army had used against the male villagers: like the army, the villagers round up all members of Pira's family, lock them in a hut, and set it on fire. The custom of the *mahafune* may predate the Japanese intrusion into aboriginal society, but in this scene it is fundamentally inflected by and repeats the colonial conquest. Satō's strategic mirroring of the violence points readers to the parallels between the punitive acts that ultimately justify his critique of the Japanese colonial project in Taiwan.

Besides complicating the theory of the scapegoat, the narrator also discloses the colonial conditions under which the ethnographer comes into contact with the story of Pira.

> Two armed police officers protected me on my right and left . . . Walking right behind us, two completely assimilated savages served as our guides and porters. This tale I have been keeping you waiting for was told in turns by these two porters as they were walking and then translated for me by one of the policemen in our party.
>
> I believe it is the most recent case of the destruction of an entire family of demon bird manipulators. However, there is a touch of the legendary about this tale that passed through innumerable different lips before it reached my ear. The narrative style is crude and unpolished but the story holds together. Indeed, this tale recounts an event that I can scarcely conceive of and am not in a position to verify. In spite of their simplicity, these savages have a real talent for tying up the loose ends in a story in a suggestive way and may have invented the entire tale.[31]

If the narrator in the first part of "Demon Bird" addresses his readers from the privacy of his study, then he is in this scene located squarely in what Mary Louise Pratt refers to as the contact zone: "social spaces where different cultures meet, clash and grapple with each other often in highly asymmetrical relations of domination and subordination."[32] Peopled by a variety of colonial actors—guards, porters, police escorts, translators—who occupy asymmetrical positions, the contact zone mediates the encounter between ethnographer and indigenous legend. In the first place, the narrator is beholden to "assimilated savages" who are removed from their native village and employed by the police; these "native informants" are associated with the network of routes crisscrossing the aboriginal lands and are hired to provide indispensable services as guides. But he also depends on the protection of armed Japanese police to traverse a largely hostile territory. In calling attention to the circumstances surrounding the transmission of the tale, the narrator offers us a mise-en-scène of the ethnographic encounter and shows us that this encounter is deeply indebted to colonial structures of domination.

By the same token, he also calls into question the status of the legend as a transparent sign of a traditional aboriginal culture. The legend had to "[pass] through innumerable different lips" before it reached the narrator's ear. The porters carry the legend through the countryside just as they transport the narrator's baggage—their status as "assimilated savages" makes them the ideal intermediaries. A policeman who overhears this conversation by accident translates it into Japanese for the narrator. After passing through the voices of the porters and the translation of the policeman, the legend reaches us—the readers—only after the ethnographer/narrator records it in writing, leaving some margin for the tricks of ethnographic memory. Filtered through these different mediations, the legend becomes an opaque, enigmatic cultural artifact with an indeterminate meaning.

Besides allowing for errors in transmission, the narrator acknowledges the agency of the porter narrators who are the first in the line of messengers who transmit it. As Pratt notes, the "contact zone" is a zone of unequal exchange, in which subordinated groups rework the materials transmitted to them by the dominant culture by a process of auto-ethnography. The porter narrators who recount the story are in that sense the first real "ethnographers," who interpret the society they are describing from a detached position. They bring to light the violent intrusion of the Japanese military into aboriginal society but they also fashion this tale into a narrative, tie up "the loose ends in a story in a suggestive way" and perhaps "invented the entire tale." When they tell each other this tale, they do not address themselves to the Japanese directly and the latter only come to overhear the legend by chance. The ethnographer-narrator of "Demon Bird" thus stands at the end of a long and involved process of violence, fabrication, hearsay, and translation. He never comes into direct contact with the isolated "primitive" society that he had evoked in his theory of the scapegoat but only with a society as it has been transformed by the imposition of colonial rule and by the response of local subjects to that rule.

In his story "Demon Bird," Satō experiments with the perspective of the anthropologist to report to Japanese readers on a superstition in aboriginal Taiwan. Like the anthropologists who first classified the aborigines into distinct groups and mapped the borders of the aboriginal tribes, he is concerned with the definition of social boundaries and the construction of cultural identities. Just as the colonial border-making in Taiwan was accompanied by state-initiated massacres of recalcitrant tribes, the bordering in the aboriginal village involves persecution and violence against those who challenge its boundaries. In "Demon Bird," Satō discloses the terrible destruction that the establishment of colonial borders entails in an aboriginal village of Taiwan.

He also engages in a critical way with anthropology's project to make aboriginal Taiwan an object of colonial knowledge. Although colonial ethnographers had relatively little impact on government policies toward the aborigines, they owed their field of study and their position in that field as scientific observers to the fact of Japanese colonization and to the subjugation of the aboriginal territories. When Satō places the narrator of "Demon Bird" within an apparatus of colonial institutions, he makes visible the location from which the ethnographer speaks. He also sows doubt in the reader's mind about the truth of the legend he reports by tracing the complicated mode of transmission by which the story of Pira is passed along to the narrator. Furthermore, he shows that the members of the violated aboriginal village reconstruct the borders of their community after colonial invasion by a displacement of violence onto the *mahafune* and an imitation of colonial violence.

At the time that Satō Haruo wrote "Demon Bird," Japan was a well-established empire that had ruled Taiwan for more than twenty-five years. The reader of "Demon Bird" finds himself/herself in the topography of Japan in the high imperial period, with its well-defined boundaries between colony and metropole and its stable hierarchical relationship of "civilized" Japan and "primitive" Taiwan. Yet, in the course of the story, these boundaries blur and even threaten to disappear. When Satō shows us that the superstitions of the "aborigines" are actually a repetition of colonial violence, he destabilizes the "civilizing mission" of the metropolis. When he undermines the grounds upon which the ethnographer bases his understanding of aboriginal society, he exposes the hollow pretensions of the colonizer to an authoritative knowledge of the colonized. Published during the heyday of Taisho liberalism, "Demon Bird" is in many ways an oppositional and radical work. It is also an isolated work in the archives of Japan's colonial literature and an exception in the work of Satō Haruo, a road not taken in the literary history of the period.[33]

Notes

1. In this chapter, I will be concerned primarily with the 1923 "Demon Bird," but I also mention the 1925 travel piece *Musha*, an account of Satō's visit to the aboriginal highlands first published in the journal *Kaizō* in March 1925 and the 1928 "Kidan" (Strange Tale)—later retitled "Nisshōki no shita" (Under the Japanese

Flag). Both of these latter works were included in an anthology of the author's Taiwan stories that first appeared in 1936 under the general title *Musha*.

2. Fujii Shōzō, "Atogaki" (Afterword) to Satō Haruo's *Musha* (Tokyo: Yumani Press, 2000), 5.

3. Faye Yuan Kleeman, *Under an Imperial Sun: Japanese Colonial Literature of Taiwan and the South* (Honolulu: University of Hawai'i Press, 2003), 39.

4. The multiethnic population of Taiwan is composed of Han Chinese, who make up the vast majority, and more than ten distinct Indo-Polynesian groups, who collectively comprise about two percent of the population.

5. Shimizu Akitoshi, "Colonialism and the Development of Modern Anthropology in Japan," in *Anthropology and Colonialism in Asia and Oceania*, eds. Jan van Bremen and Akitoshi Shimizu (London: Curzon, 1999), 115–26.

6. The Meiji regime incorporated Hokkaido and Okinawa into the Japanese nation-state in 1869 and 1879, respectively. The policies adopted by the Meiji regime toward the people of Okinawa and toward the Ainu offered precedents for later government policies toward the colonized when Japan acquired a formal empire.

7. Torii Ryūzō, "Taiwan no genjūmin joron" (Introduction to the Study of Taiwan Aborigines), *Torii Ryūzō zenshū* 5 (Complete Works of Torii Ryūzō, Volume 5) (Tokyo: Asahi shinbunsha, 1976), 4–5.

8. Emma Teng argues that these categorizations were first invented to distinguish friendly from hostile aborigines and that their meanings shifted over time. Indeed, the "raw savages" later became "the symbols of cultural difference, in both the positive and negative sense" for Qing travel writers, prefiguring and anticipating some of the tendencies of Japanese colonial discourse. Emma Teng, "Taiwan as a Living Museum: Tropes of Anachronism in Late Imperial Chinese Travel Writing," *Harvard Journal of Asiatic Studies* 59, 2 (1999): 460.

9. Sakano Tōru, *Teikoku Nihon to jinruigakusha 1884–1952* (Anthropologists and Imperial Japan, 1884–1952) (Tokyo: Keisō shobō, 2006), 236.

10. Paul Barclay, "'They Have for the Coast Dwellers a Traditional Hatred': Governing Igorots in Northern Luzon and Central Taiwan, 1895–1915," in *The American Colonial State in the Philippines*, eds. Julian Go and Anne L. Foster (Durham, NC: Duke University Press, 2003), 220–21.

11. Kojima Reiitsu, "Nihon teikokushugi no Taiwan sanchi shihai" (Mountain Rule in Taiwan under Japanese Imperialism), in *Taiwan Musha hōki jiken kenkyū to shiryō* (Research and Documents on the Musha Rebellion Incident in Taiwan), ed. Tai Kuo-Hui (Tokyo: Shakaishisōsha, 1981), 56–62.

12. Mori Ushinosuke, "Seiban angya" (Pilgrimages among the Savages), in *Taiwan jihō* (Taiwan Newsletter) (Taipei: Taiwan Sōtokufu, 1924) 55: 106–7.

13. From 1895 to 1902, the Japanese authorities pursued a policy of alliance with the aborigines in order to combat a Han Chinese insurrection. After crushing the Han guerrillas in 1902, they sought to develop the timber resources—notably camphor— of the aboriginal areas in order to rebuild the depleted coffers of the colonial state.

14. Mori Ushinosuke, "Taiwan banzoku ni tsuite" (Regarding the Taiwan Aborigines) (1913) preface to *Taiwan banzokushi* (History of the Taiwan Aborigines)

(Taipei: Taiwan Sōtokufu, 1917), 4–5. In his ethnography (*Taiwan banzokushi*), Mori studied the Atayal, the largest of the northern tribes.

15. Mori, "Taiwan banzoku ni tsuite," 18–19.

16. Ibid.

17. Satō Haruo, *Musha* (Tokyo: Yumani Press, 2000), 137.

18. Renato Rosaldo, *Culture and Truth* (Boston: Beacon, 1989), 69–70.

19. Satō, *Musha*, 142.

20. Ibid., 145–46, 147, 150.

21. Satō had Mori's book at hand during his travels. In one scene of his travelogue *Musha*, he describes the aboriginal maid in an inn who is looking at the pictures of aborigines in Mori's book and laughing at them in the company of a friend. Ibid., 148–49.

22. Mori, *Taiwan banzokushi*, 274.

23. For example, Part 12 of "Demon Bird," which is enclosed in parentheses, is essentially a footnote to the preceding chapter, which explains aboriginal beliefs in the afterworld. Satō paraphrases Mori's descriptions of the Atayal culture in "Beliefs and the Spiritual Conditions" (*Shinkō oyobi seishinteki jōtai*), ibid., 279–81.

24. Satō Haruo, "Machō" (Demon Bird), in *Satō Haruo zenshū* 7 (The Collected Works of Satō Haruo, Vol. 7) (Tokyo: Rinkawa shoten, 1998), 373.

25. For example, he asks aboriginal villagers why someone would choose to become a demon bird manipulator. Ibid., 374.

26. Ibid., 373.

27. Ibid., 376.

28. In Part 7, the narrator writes: "The greater part of this enormous island was referred to as *banchi* (savage land)." Whereas he has hitherto employed a general graph used to signify barbarian (*ban*), he uses a graph that refers specifically to the "savages" of Taiwan. Ibid., 379.

29. Ibid.

30. Alliance of Taiwan Aborigines, I. Chang, and Lava Kau, "Report on the Human Rights Situation of Taiwan's Indigenous Peoples," in *Indigenous Peoples of Asia*, eds. R. H. Barnes et al. (Ann Arbor, MI: Association of Asian Studies, 1995), 360.

31. Satō, "Machō," 378.

32. Mary Louise Pratt, *Imperial Eyes: Travel Writing and Transculturation* (London: Routledge, 1992), 4.

33. While Satō's story is a critique of Japanese colonialism, it also illustrates the weaknesses of the Japanese liberal humanist criticism of colonialism, which was never addressed to the victims of Japan's imperialism. The author's refusal to address the Other in dialogue also marks the limits of Taisho liberal critique, a point I discuss in greater detail in Robert Tierney, "Ethnography, Borders, and Violence: Reading Between the Lines in Satō Haruo's *Demon Bird*," *Japan Forum* 19, 1 (2007): 89–110.

CHAPTER FIVE

The Manual of Home Cuisine

THE WOMEN'S DIVISION
OF THE GREEN FLAG ASSOCIATION

CONTEXT

Korea

CRITIQUE

Eating for the Emperor: The Nationalization of Settler Homes and Bodies in the Kōminka Era

HELEN J. S. LEE

T HE GREEN FLAG ASSOCIATION (Ryokki renmei) was a
civilian Japanese settler organization based in the capital of colonial
Korea, Keijō. Founded in 1925, this group devoted itself to a wide range of
activities that largely aimed at the cultivation of personal spirit, betterment
of living conditions, and wartime fundraising. Some of the organization's
primary activities included providing public lectures, publications, and education, as well as initiating collaborative projects with Koreans. The Green
Flag Association was established by Tsuda Sakae, professor at Keijō Imperial
University, and contributors included men and women who hailed from the
elite educated class of Japan and Korea.

The Manual of Home Cuisine (*Katei shokuji tokuhon*, 1941) is the work
of the women's section of the Green Flag Association, which was headed
by Tsuda Sakae's wife, Tsuda Setsuko. The number of readers is undocu-
mented; however, the energy behind the project is evident in the revision of
its first edition (1939), which was produced in 1941 through Kōa Publishing,
the central venue for all Green Flag publications.

The passages, charts, and advertisements from *The Manual of Home Cuisine* translated below provide a satisfying taste of the work's six sections, which address topics such as proper meals for wartime, staples, side dishes, mealtime etiquette, and diet and disciplinary measures for children. Based on the nutritional science of the time and survey results, this ambitious cookbook presents readers with up-to-date information on ingredients and practical recipes that maximize nutritional intake, accompanied by numerous tables and hand-drawn illustrations. The recommendations are delivered in a gentle but firm voice that attempts to choreograph the daily practices of cooking and dining in settler homes.

The Manual of Home Cuisine[1]

THE WOMEN'S DIVISION
OF THE GREEN FLAG ASSOCIATION

TRANSLATION BY HELEN J. S. LEE

Preface

Japan is on the eve of making a great leap onto the world stage. What Japan needs is the collective effort of people who have healthy minds and bodies. We, the women's division of the Green Flag Association, believe that healthy children are the key to Japan's prosperous future and, therefore, have devoted ourselves to raising healthy children and maintaining the health of the nation. If young mothers cannot raise children with healthy minds and bodies, then who else can bear the burden of such work?

Not just the children's health but also the health of the entire family can only be attained through the hands of mothers who protect the home. Among many determining factors, meals in the home have a tremendous effect on health. Correct and appropriate meals result in the enhancement of health, while inappropriate meals cause harm. Whether the meals of one million Japanese comply with national policies is critical to the management of the entire nation and can even determine its rise and fall.

The women's division of the Green Flag Association has researched how we can comply with national policies in the home and studied the ways to improve our health.

We compiled our studies and published *The Manual of Home Cuisine* in October 1939, receiving encouragement from many readers. We are pleased to announce that we have included additional research results in this expanded edition.

Ōhashi Toshiko, researcher of the Japanese Culture Research Institute of the Green Flag Association, was in charge of this edition and helped define the dietary objectives in accordance with the Green Flag Association's spirit; new sections on ways to conserve rice based on scientific research, the national diet, wild greens cuisine, and meals for guests and the ill have also been added. Additional recipes for ceremonial offerings in accordance with national policies have been introduced as well.

We live in an era of serious political upheaval and food shortages; we hope that this volume can aid everyone in their daily endeavors to eat the right meals.

The Women's Division of the Green Flag Association, April 1941

Chapter One: Meals for the Future

OUR LIFE

We must embrace life, learn from it, and transcend it. Our body and mind, plus our living conditions, constitute life. Not one of these three elements can be missing.

Aside from these, no additional element is needed for living.

In order to improve the quality of our living, we must improve our bodies, minds, and environment (nation, society, and home). These three elements are inseparable. For example, if one only works to strengthen one's body, to accumulate wealth, to nourish one's mind, or occupy oneself with societal issues, one still cannot attain a good life. One can only achieve the ultimate goal in life when one focuses on accomplishing all three elements.

OUR HEALTH

To be healthy is everyone's wish, but the kind of health that we have aspired to thus far stems from a modest line of thinking that holds that sickness causes pain, financial burden, and inconvenience to others. This kind of "health," of course, is more valuable than "sickness" but it is the lowest form of health. The kind of health that we wish to acquire from now on, as we mentioned above, has to accompany a noble, healthy body and mind that aim to achieve one goal, namely to build a sacred, cooperative, communal body that accords with His Majesty's benevolent heart.

Nowadays the population problem is at the heart of social debates, and this is all because Japan's ideal future requires a larger population. We will realize our ideal future when physical and cultural power, as well as national defense and production, are generated with full vigor.

Let us recognize that the health of each and every person must serve a greater cause and maintain our health for Japan and the world.

As mentioned in the preceding section, our health will improve as we adopt an outlook on life as articulated above and live and work in earnest.

TEN MANTRAS FOR HEALTH
(MINISTRY OF HEALTH AND WELFARE GUIDELINES)

1. To protect the country of the rising sun, health, first health.

2. During winter, ventilate air even during sleep! Open the windows!

3. Sleep tight at night for tomorrow!

4. Chew well, eat well, digest well. Eat nutritious food in the right amount.

5. Comply with the rules at all times. Breaking the rules will harm your body.

6. If your body and mind are inseparable, your heart will rejoice and your body will be pure.

7. Do everything to keep your health! Keep your circulation in good shape and do not be lazy with calisthenics.

8. Prevent illness. Have physical examinations.

9. Do not beautifully bundle up inside the home. Get outside under the big sky.

10. To complete the noble mission, do your best at work.

OUR MEALS

Our meals play a key role in nourishing healthy bodies and maintaining healthy lives. In the East and West, much research on nutrition has emerged, but the Western study of nutrition is just a study of food that does not consider the larger picture of human life. In the Eastern study of nutrition, the spiritual is connected to all things, and certain foods can cure sickness and nourish a healthy body. The Eastern study of nutrition requires faith prior to thinking about the body itself, and its emphasis on both the body and mind is considered to be within the parameters of the field of study of human nutrition. All of this is centered on the individual. Additionally, former director of the National Research Institute of Nutrition, Dr. Saeki Tan, argues that the study of nutrition should begin by seeking a means to unify three essential elements: individual health, national production, and societal morals. This argument was a new development in the study of nutrition, and we understand it exerted a tremendous influence on foreign countries even more than on our own.

When we think of the foundation of life, the notions "individual," "nation," and "society" represent three aspects, but one's life cannot be divided into "individual," "nation," and "society." Issues concerning these three aspects ultimately permeate all facets of life. This premise is the foundation of our study of nutrition.

From this stance on nutrition and life, in other words when all things—such as research on foodstuffs, the creation of menus, cooking methods, and ways of dining—are included, then the study of nutrition is one that corresponds to the heart of the Emperor. This is the true study of nutrition, indeed.

We now reflect on our meals to reassess our situation from this position and to continue to strive for better meals.

Chapter Two: Staples

RICE

The National Policy to Abolish the Consumption of White Rice

The history of rice reveals to us that white rice consumption and beriberi are closely connected. Since the Meiji Restoration the consumption of white rice has become widespread, and despite efforts to popularize a rice-grain mixture, patients with beriberi have increased. The mortality rate from beriberi is as follows:

Year	Deaths
1899	9,034
1910	15,085
1918	22,632
1923	26,796

Research results have indicated that beriberi is caused by a deficiency of vitamin B, which is plentiful in rice bran husks, and researchers have collectively urged a reform in the staples of our diet. However, the general public has not modified its daily meals, through which one can most effectively prevent beriberi; some contract beriberi and belatedly start substituting white rice with mixed grains with barley, while others drink vitamin B supplements and then forget entirely once they have recovered from the disease.

The Ministry of Health was established as a measure to respond to problems of the deterioration of national health, such as the decline in physical strength and the rise in infant mortality. In an effort to improve the national health, an encompassing investigation was conducted in all sectors of society as well. Since the outbreak of the Manchurian Incident, the entire citizenry has become concerned with nutrition and has begun to think seriously about developing strong bodies.

In Korea, the Government-General's ordinance of November 1, 1939, required the use of multigrains with seventy percent refined, un-rinsed white rice that contains no sand. This multigrain rice refers to polished rice that does not contain powder (acidic white-soil limestone) or coating (diatomaceous earth and boushu sand).

One of the primary reasons for this was to use less polished white rice, which can relieve the shortages arising from damage caused by drought. There is a saying that one can only learn from one's own mistakes, and the rice problem of recent years has led to correcting the consumption of rice. At any rate, it could not please us more that staples have now been clearly defined in Korea and are being implemented.

Let us address the significance of the newly instituted seventy percent refined, un-rinsed white rice as a main staple.

About Foreign-Imported Rice

Since 1940, especially in the main islands, foreign rice has been in wide use. Most of the foreign rice is made up of Thai, Rangoon, and Saigon rice, all of which are imported as white rice. Importing white rice serves to reduce transport costs, given that the polished grains are smaller than those with the rice bran still intact, and white rice is more durable in storage. However, this white rice is often mixed with sand and has the same drawbacks as the white rice in the main islands. As is addressed in the previous section, white rice does not contain even the slightest bit of the essential vitamin B, so it is important to prepare it with cooking methods that can supply vitamin B, such as boiling it with rice bran or other supplements such as barley and beans or noodles. Also, one of the drawbacks of foreign rice is that it is high in fine fiber and less tasteful to Japanese. Stir-frying the rice in oil or cooking it with beans or sticky rice can raise the temperature and help glutenize the starch. Eating the rice with potatoes and sticky rice, which are easily digestible, can also make the rice more palatable.

To compare the composition of the foreign rice to the Japanese ricegrain mixture, see the results in Table 5.1. Foreign rice is as good as if not better than Japanese rice, showing no inferiority in any of its nutritional composition. People say it is low in fat, making it distasteful, or it lacks moisture, but neither is proven scientifically. Further, being delicious or not

TABLE 5.1
Nutritional Comparison between Japanese White Rice and Foreign Rice

White Rice Nutrition	Water	Protein	Fat	Carbo-hydrates	Fiber	Minerals	Calories
Japanese rice-grain mixture	13.25	6.93	0.34	77.56	0.27	0.71	350
Thai rice	13.10	7.88	0.81	78.30	0.70	0.68	361
Saigon rice	13.16	7.34	0.15	79.47	0.75	0.44	357
Rangoon rice	13.64	7.61	0.67	78.75	0.67	0.62	360

SOURCE: Released by Dr. Saeki Tan, July 1940.

delicious depends on personal preferences, and the people in Thailand and India speak disapprovingly of Japanese rice.

As a nation-state with advanced defense forces we aspire to become self-sufficient in food, but today we are trying to establish the East Asia Co-Prosperity Sphere, and we inevitably have to import foreign and white rice-grain mixtures. Therefore, we should recognize the purpose of eating foreign rice, supplement its deficiency, and get rid of our complaints when we eat it. In order to do so, we also have to make sure to produce seventy percent germinated rice, which is rich in vitamin B.

Chapter Three: Side Dishes

Let us pick wild greens from the fields!

Until now, the people in mainland Japan have not widely used wild greens. Thanks to the benevolence of the Emperor, we have been able to maintain a politically peaceful era in which we were taught to till the land, plant seeds, apply manure, and grow vegetables as if raising our children. Wild plants have been incorporated into our diet on festive occasions—for example, we eat Seven Spring Herbs during New Years and make mugwort rice cakes and offer it to the deities of Ohina—reflecting our deep appreciation for and intimacy with nature.

Our people have not historically eaten wild greens. But people on the peninsula, even those of nobility, make delicious dishes with wild greens and eat them daily. It is disheartening to think of the pretty wild flowers merely as a source of food. So let us make sure that we do not lose our appreciation for nature.

During spring and autumn, let us use our Sundays as health days and go out to the fields and mountains. We will be able to breathe in the clean air and harvest wild plants! The wild plants that families pick together under the shinning sun, however modest the quantity might be, will make our meals richer and more enjoyable!

EXAMPLES OF WILD-GREENS DISHES:

Itadori
Family: *Polygonum*. Young sprouts can be eaten raw or steamed. They can be dried and mixed with miso paste. Soft stems can be stir-fried and then steeped in water to extract the sour taste. Then they can be added to miso soup. Young leaves are also edible.

Boke
Family: Wild Rose. Seeds can be used to brew sake.

Noibara
Family: Wild Rose. If peeled, young sprouts can be eaten raw. They can also be steamed or stewed.

Nazuna (Penpen grass)
Family: Cross Plants. A kind of Seven Spring Herbs. The shoots can be steamed or stewed. Can also be pickled. Can be added to rice porridge or rice dumplings. The roots are also edible.

Yomena
Family: Chrysanthemum. Young shoots can be picked and stir-fried. They can be seasoned with soy sauce or miso paste.

Tabirako
Family: Chrysanthemum. One of the Seven Spring Herbs. They look similar to the minty plant, Henbit. Blanch and stir-fry in oil and season.

Tanpopo
Family: Chrysanthemum. Young leaves and roots can be stir-fried or stewed. They can also be pickled. The roots can be chopped thinly and cooked with rice. In Germany, they use the minced roots as a substitute for coffee.

Noazami
Family: Chrysanthemum. Pick young shoots and leaves and blanch. Stir-fry in oil and season.

Aburana
Family: Cross Plants. Before the flowers bloom, pick leaves and stems and eliminate the overgrown parts. Stew and eat, or pickle them with salt.

Sumire
Family: Violet. Leaves and stems can be steamed and eaten. They can also be pickled. Boil the roots and chop them thinly and mix with rice.

Momiji
Family: Maple. Boil young sprouts until they turn yellow. Stir-fry them with oil and season with salt.

Fuji
Family: Legume. Boil young sprouts and leaves and eat them. Flowers can be boiled or stewed. Mix the young leaves with rice or barley to make Fuji.

Hageitō
Family: Portulaca. Pick shoots and leaves and wash thoroughly. Blanch, stir-fry, and season.

Keitō
Family: Portulaca. Leaves, particularly young leaves, are edible. In the past, shade-dried flowers were used to add red color to rice cakes.

Hohozuki
Family: Eggplant. Boil and soak shoots thoroughly and eat. Dry old leaves and make into powder. Fruits can be eaten raw.

Hōsenka
Family: Balsam. Soak shoots and leaves in order to blanch. Stir-fry with oil and season.

Gibōshi
Family: White Lily. Eat young leaves.

Kuanzō
Family: White Lily. Pick young shoots and flowers. Boil thoroughly and season with soy sauce.

Yabukanzō
Family: White Lily. Season young leaves with vinegared miso paste. Stew flowers and eat. In China, they call it *henge* and eat the baby sprouts, which they pull up from the ground.

Nobiru
Family: White Lily. Same as *wakegi* and *asatsuki*—roots and leaves are edible.

Nokogiriso
Family: Chrysanthemum. Boil leaves and stems. They are also good in clear soup.

Chōsen'azami
Family: Chrysanthemum. Pick when flower buds mature. Boil or deep-fry and eat. They are delicious summer vegetables.

Himeshion
Family: Chrysanthemum. Pick young leaves and blanch in water. Stir-fry in oil and season.

Tsuriganeninjin (Totokininjin)
Family: Chrysanthemum. Boil shoots and eat. The roots can be eaten boiled or raw.

Torachi
Family: Chinese Bellflower. Dig up the roots in the spring and season with mixed spices and make pickled vegetables. Deep-fry them with meat or chives. Boil the shoots and add them to stews or soup. Dry the mature leaves and make them into powder.

Chapter Four: How to Receive Meals

Even if the person who prepares food pours out her heart and soul and provides food with the utmost of care, food becomes meaningless if it is mechanically consumed to fill an empty stomach.

ALWAYS EAT WITH A THANKFUL HEART

Because of the blessings from His Majesty, we are able to afford modest yet enjoyable meals everyday without any distress and are able to work for our nation and the world. Every bit of our food is produced through the labor of people in our society before it comes to our table. We have so much to be thankful for. To think that money and power can bring us food is unacceptable.

We cannot forget nature, which supports us. We can easily forget the blessings of nature, but to receive meals with thankful hearts will guarantee a happy and healthy family life.

In order to reciprocate the efforts of the hands that prepare the food with the utmost of care, the party that receives the meal should also have a thankful heart to the Emperor for the meal, try to attain a healthy body, and not leave food on the plate. This is because our health is not for our own sake, but for that of our nation and the world.

We, the members of the women's division of the Green Flag Association, wish to remind ourselves of this at all times, and have made a rule to recite the following words before each meal:

> We are truly thankful that we are blessed with such meals everyday. Even a drop of water can nurture our universe, and even a grain of rice is indebted to the efforts of many. We wish to reflect on your generosity as we chew our food and live a stronger and more exemplary life. Thank you for our meals.

These words reflect our heartfelt thanks for our food and express a loyal oath that we will live lives that correspond to the utmost care that we receive from the Emperor. Each time we recite these words, every morning and every night before meals, we will know that we are offering all our lives to His Majesty.

Chapter Five: Disciplinary Measures for Children's Meals

Children are valuable, junior citizens who will lead Japan in the next generation. Unless we raise our precious children with healthy bodies and minds our country cannot fulfill its important mission. In order to do so, fathers and mothers must cooperate and raise happy, strong, well-mannered, and healthy children.

However, the infant mortality rate of Japan is high compared to other countries, and most deaths are due to pneumonia and diarrheatic enteritis. Moreover, the rise in the number of sickly and weak children has become noticeable. Looking at these statistical records, one can feel acutely how critical the nutrition of children is.

MEALS IN THE HOME
Serving Sizes in Accordance with Age

Let us adjust the amount of ingredients and serving sizes for children in accordance with the standard chart indicated in the section on staples and side dishes. In particular, let us make sure children intake sufficient amounts of protein from meat and various vitamins. It is cumbersome to keep separate portions of daily vegetables for children and adults, so use the same ingredients but simply adjust the volume. For example, for a *sukiyaki* meal give more meat and tofu to children.

Avoid Pungent Spices

Avoid the excessive use of pungent spices such as red chili pepper, black pepper, *wasabi* horseradish, ginger, and other spices. For those dishes that require such spices, cook the children's dishes separately. For example, do not add curry powder to children's curry rice. Instead, just stir in some wheat flour to add some color.

Discipline for Eating Meals

Even the meals prepared with a mother's heartfelt loving care can only be translated into healthy bodies in children when they are also accompanied by good disciplinary measures.

Good disciplinary measures in general, not exclusive to mealtime, are not those that only mimic form. Preserving the form of discipline is important, but what is equally important is spirit. That is to say, we need to teach fundamental character values to our children, an education that can only be done in the home, with a profound respect for the fact that our children are subjects of the Emperor as well as our own children. This is the essence of "Educating Children as Imperial Citizens" with which we must ready our hearts as we implement disciplinary measures in the home.

Having a Thankful Heart

It is essential to guide children so that they have an appreciation from the bottom of their hearts for the meals they eat. It would be ideal if they can give thanks to the Emperor for being born in peaceful Japan and able to eat their meals. They should thank their parents as well as helpers, and also be grateful for the delicious food on the table that transforms into healthy bodies. As mentioned in the chapter "How to Receive Meals," let us recite the words of thanks at the table before eating. When mothers and fathers practice the recitation at mealtimes, children will learn those words from early on. And from the ages of four or five they will be able to begin attempting those words, though only one word or two at first, and eventually memorize it in full.

Sitting at the Table Calmly

Disciplinary measures should be implemented from the time of breastfeeding. A mother's emotional changes are transmitted to her children, so a breastfeeding mother ought to maintain a gentle heart. In addition, from the age of three or four, children should become accustomed to coming to the table in a calm manner. Also, children should gargle and wash their hands before snacking or eating a meal.

Assign Children Bowls and Plates

When a child begins eating food, though it might be bothersome, designate a small bowl or a plate for him or her and distinguish it from those of adults. Frequently, overcome by adoration for children, adults feed children with their own chopsticks during mealtime. This has to stop. If you assign a child his or her own dishware, even after the child reaches the age of three or four, he or she will not ask for those foods intended for adults only. Also, when adults eat foods that are not appropriate for children, adults can say "you can have this when you grow up," and children will look forward to having it once they grow up and will not want it. This, in turn, rids adults of the necessity of eating in secret from children and will create a stress-free environment for child-reading.

All Things Should Be Distributed in Order of Seniority

Distributing all kinds of food among children—whether it is a second bowl of rice at mealtime or handing out snacks—should be strictly conducted in order of seniority by birth, and this order should not be compromised at any time. Then, no child will say "me first" and everyone will wait for his or her turn in a calm manner. This will teach children how to respect older people, and since the order is not determined by sex, it will not generate a male child's contempt for a female child.

Enjoyable Meals

We all wish for you to have enjoyable meals at the table through conversations among mother, father, and children, discussing topics such as what happened that day at school or what games they played. But one should not be engrossed in babbling, nor should anyone gossip about other people or bring up inappropriate subjects at the table.

Good Etiquette

Mothers ought to teach children the proper posture for sitting at the table, the correct way of holding chopsticks, and the right way to eat foods without spilling. If you eat while making loud sounds, you will give a bad impression of your character, and if you hold up a soup bowl with the same hand holding chopsticks, you will offend others. We ought to teach children that they should not pick up their chopsticks until everyone is seated, not stack their plates and bowls after the completion of a meal, and not leave any food on the plate. Habits from childhood persist, so let us pay special attention to boys while they are under the care of mothers and discipline them while they are under our care.

Eliminating Likes and Dislikes

Do children's likes and dislikes of food stem from a lack of their appreciation or adults' unnecessary comments during mealtime? Statistics indicate that children tend to dislike those food items that their mothers dislike, and we adults need to reevaluate ourselves. See Table 5.2.

For example, if any adult or older person says he or she finds today's dishes distasteful or dislikes them, a child can mimic the response even before eating, saying "me too," and end up not even trying them.

If children have a deep appreciation for food—a subject mentioned at the beginning of this work—they should not be self-indulgent with things such as likes and dislikes.

TABLE 5.2
Likes and Dislikes of Children and Mothers

Food item	Number of children who dislike it	Number of mothers and children who both dislike it	The ratio between the two columns
Fermented beans	268	183	0.68
Rice crackers	33	20	0.61
Eel	139	69	0.50
Sausage	227	100	0.44
Ham	210	90	0.43
Milk	140	54	0.39
Lettuce	327	96	0.29
Tomatoes	146	42	0.29
Buns	100	28	0.28
Mackerel	209	52	0.25
Sweet bean jelly	165	41	0.25
Buckwheat noodles	249	61	0.25
Carrots	551	133	0.24
Pork	336	89	0.24
Tofu	181	42	0.24
Rice cake	55	11	0.20
Beef	163	31	0.19
Soybean paste	241	40	0.17
Soybean paste soup	182	18	0.10
Onions	304	21	0.07
Scallions	433	29	0.07
Daikon radish	206	13	0.06

*Numbers below 10 in the column "both mothers and children dislike" have been omitted.

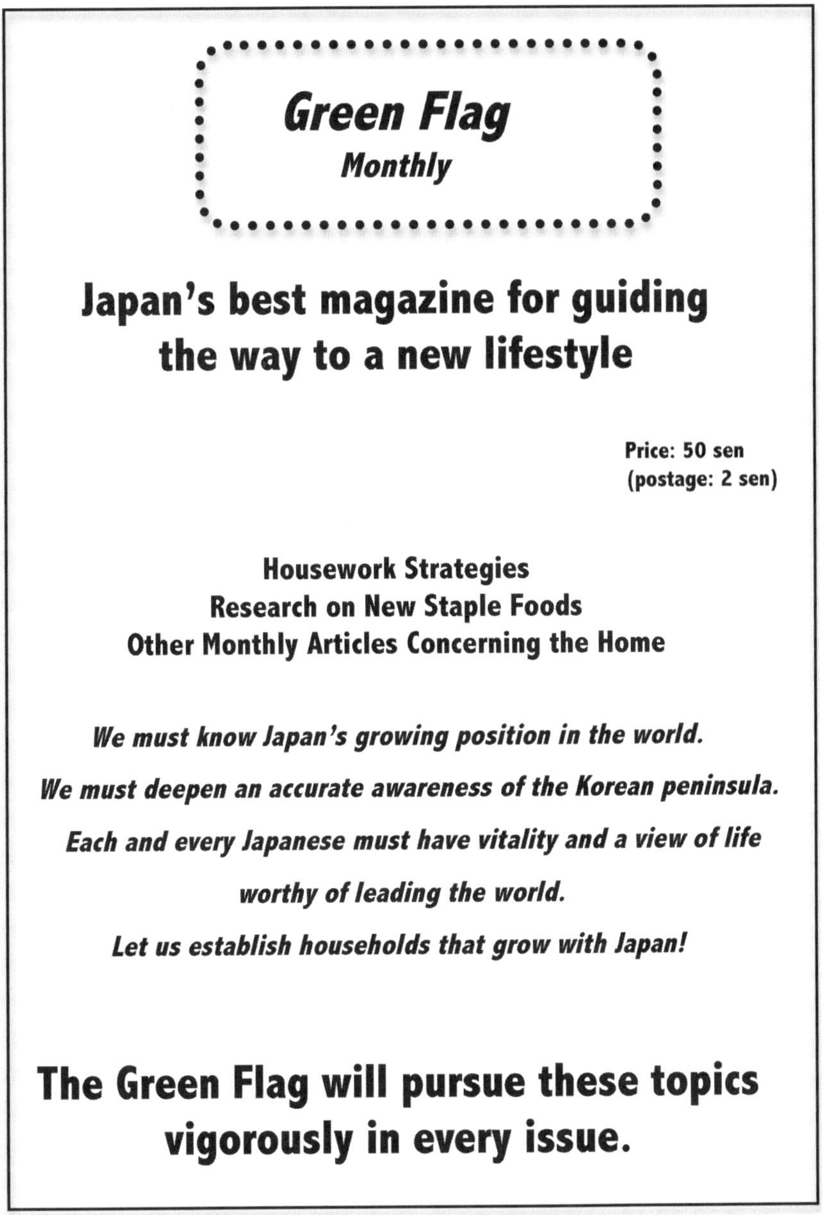

FIGURE 5.1   Ad for the *Green Flag* monthly

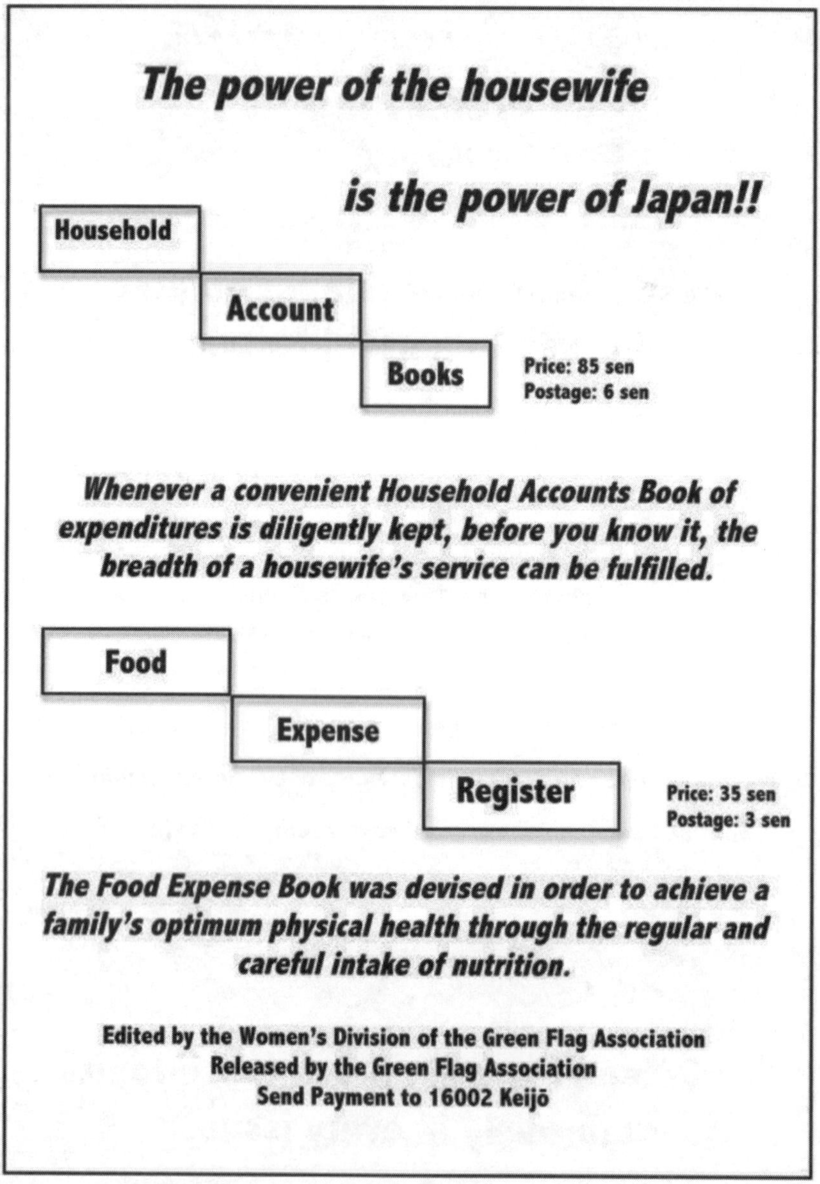

The power of the housewife

is the power of Japan!!

Household

Account

Books

Price: 85 sen
Postage: 6 sen

Whenever a convenient Household Accounts Book of expenditures is diligently kept, before you know it, the breadth of a housewife's service can be fulfilled.

Food

Expense

Register

Price: 35 sen
Postage: 3 sen

The Food Expense Book was devised in order to achieve a family's optimum physical health through the regular and careful intake of nutrition.

Edited by the Women's Division of the Green Flag Association
Released by the Green Flag Association
Send Payment to 16002 Keijō

FIGURE 5.2   Ad for Household Record-Keeping Supplies

Eating for the Emperor:
The Nationalization of Settler Homes
and Bodies in the Kōminka Era

HELEN J. S. LEE

Total Mobilization and the Politics of Food

Known as the "total war" period, the final years of the Japanese empire saw unrivaled state control over people and resources in support of the war effort. Mounting restrictions and bans on things ranging from foodstuffs and clothing to theater performances drastically reconfigured the patterns of everyday life. Japanese citizens throughout the empire were called upon to make "willing" sacrifices and to comply with greater regimentation of the most mundane aspects of their lives for the imperial cause. To cite just one telling example, a wartime citizen's uniform was introduced for men in 1940, which, in case of an emergency, could easily be used as a military uniform in combat. The female counterpart of the citizen's uniform was finalized by the Ministry of Health in 1942, of which the tapered pants called *monpe*, ubiquitous in photographs from the era, were widely disseminated.[2]

The "total mobilization" in colonial territories was no less intense than it was in the main islands (*naichi*). In fact, the phrase "the *kōminka* era" (1937–1945) has arisen to describe the particularities of the last phase of Japan's colonial governance. The literal meaning of *kōminka* is to "transform [colonial subjects] into imperial subjects," in other words to "imperialize" colonial subjects, and both the term and the panoply of policies instituted in those final years reveal the imperial state's ambition to mobilize all available human resources for the escalating war effort.[3] Spanning the years from 1937 to 1945, kōminka campaigns and regulations demanded concrete and imposing changes in the social landscape throughout the empire. This included efforts to eradicate indigenous cultures and uproot the cultural identities of the colonized in order to inculcate loyalty to Japan. In view of the ultimate goal of kōminka—thoroughly incorporting the colonized subjects into the empire—this movement should be understood as an attempt to "draft" the colonized to serve their ruler's mission in both body and spirit.

The most palpable features of the kōminka policies involved the reordering of daily activities. Colonial subjects were instructed to join Japanese imperial subjects in paying mandatory visits to newly constructed local Shinto shrines and proclaiming "Long Live the Emperor." Children would have noticed modifications in the school curriculum that ever more vigorously attempted to hone emperor-centered bodies and minds.[4] Compulsory name changes and Japanese language use was implemented in a wide variety of settings, while campaigns encouraging a voluntary soldier system and emphasizing healthy bodies and women's reproduction became more and more prevalent.

For ethnic Japanese colonial settlers, who, by definition, were not the target of the kōminka policies, total mobilization often translated into various forms of state intervention into their lives calculated to foster nationalistic norms and sentiment. Living among the colonized, Japanese in the colonies likely felt far greater pressure to exhibit the state-prescribed ideals and behaviors than their compatriots in the home islands. While all aspects of their daily routine were subject to wartime state control, food, one of the most fundamental components of everyday life, was a site where the colonial apparatus, especially at the close of Japan's exhausting Asia-Pacific War (1931–1945), unambiguously intervened. For Japanese settlers in colonial Korea the dwindling availability of Japanese foodstuffs presented both material and symbolic challenges. In addition to the difficulties of finding familiar ingredients with which to prepare meals, the expedient strategy of using traditional Korean foodstuffs threatened to blur the lines between colonizer and colonized. Even as kōminka policies professed to make colonial subjects full-fledged imperial citizens, Japanese, high and low, were called upon to remain vigilant in maintaining boundaries between the two. In this context, rituals of displaying Japanese cultural membership in the motherland at the family dining table took on a greater importance.

Drawing on numerous publications of the Green Flag Association (Ryokki renmei), including the journals *Green Flag* (*Ryokki*) and *New Women* (*Shinjosei*) and *The Manual of Home Cuisine* (*Katei shokuji tokuhon*, 1941), this essay investigates how Japanese settlers conceptualized the changing roles and significance of food, the home, and motherhood in the kōminka era.[5] The Green Flag Association, a Keijō-based official organ of the Japanese settler community, was founded in 1925 by Tsuda Sakae, professor of chemistry and mathematics at the Keijō Imperial University.[6] Although launched as a Buddhist study group that aimed at self-enrichment, there is evidence that this organization became dependent on government funding and was possibly co-opted by the government to propagate state ideology.[7] While an assessment of this claim is beyond the scope of this essay, the organization characterized its core activities—coordinating public lectures and study meetings and publishing official journals—as improving the quality of life in the colonial settlements. By 1940, the organization grew to list 2,000 active members, of which 600 were Korean.[8] Green Flag articles and editorials, penned by both men and women, illuminate the ways the Japanese settler community endeavored to muster mothers to nurture a "Japanese" cultural identity by way of "national cuisine" (*kokuminshoku*) as they negotiated overwhelming modifications in food supplies in colonial Korea. The project of managing food on the colonial frontline was facilitated by an ideological framework provided in Green Flag Association periodicals, which exhort ethnic Japanese to preserve their cultural and moral ties to the homeland, to envision their health maintenance as dutiful service to the emperor, and to dedicate activities in their homes to the growth of the empire.

Working in tandem with the periodicals, *The Manual of Home Cuisine* targets Japanese mothers, stressing their role as custodians of the home and family who protect and promote the "Japanese spirit."[9] Nationalistic and didactic in tone, the six main chapters address a wide variety of topics concerning the management of the home: ideal meals for the era, staples, dinning etiquette, and children's meals and their proper discipline during mealtime. In addition to stipulating how to find alternative ingredients, *The Manual of Home Cuisine* also details how much money to spend on food, how much to eat, and how and what to serve to guests. With recipe suggestions, nutrition charts, and practical cooking advice, the text provides the contents one would expect in a culinary guide. Yet, it ventures far beyond the confines of the kitchen and home as it attempts to attenuate the hardships of wartime privations through a rhetoric that positions quotidian domestic practices within Japan's lofty imperial project. No matter the subject, the central mission of *The Manual of Home Cuisine*, which must be understood as much more than a mere cookbook, was to promote the appropriate way for Japanese to perform their cultural membership in the motherland, loyalty to the emperor, and commitment to Japan's civilizing mission in Asia.

Intensifying material shortages, especially of staple foods, however, did not permit a wide range of viable options for expressing Japanese culture in settler homes. These texts reveal the gap between imperial demands and dire material realities in the colonies even as they attest to the attempts of some to mobilize an imperial-centered culture of food and promote eating for nationalistic purposes. While Kikkoman soy sauce and Ajinomoto spices, together with Japanese green tea, had been among the most popular products in the groceries serving settler communities, in the final years of the kōminka era these Japanese imports became highly scarce, if not non-existent. In other words, the channels through which settlers signified their cultural affinity with and fidelity to the homeland were not only disappearing but realistic alternatives on the horizon—those of the "natives"—posed new threats: losing Japanese identity altogether. *The Manual of Home Cuisine* indexes such potent anxieties of the Japanese settlers, some of whom endorsed and popularized civilian initiatives for radical modifications of culinary creations and customs in the home.

Nutrition and National Defense in Colonial Korea: From Rice to Wild Greens

During a time of material crunch such as the kōminka era, food often emerges as one of the most invested and critical mediums through which national ideology and domesticity intersect.[10] Katarzyna J. Cwiertka's work sheds light on gastronomic national identification during the kōminka era by showing how distinctively Western-style cuisine high in calories was first introduced to the Japanese military in the 1920s and later disseminated in the homes as the "national cuisine" throughout the 1930s and 1940s.[11] As the war intensified, the imperial state extracted material resources, especially various metals, for the war cause that inevitably resulted in the deprivation of the civilian population. Ingredients that Japanese had long relied on for cooking were affected as well, and mothers were assigned the daunting task of working with shrinking food supplies while maintaining nutritional standards for their children.

Just as the "national cuisine" became a natural feature of Japanese life—with its signature recipes regularly advertised, taught, and brought to dining tables throughout the empire—the necessary ingredients became especially difficult to find in colonial Korea. The imperial exhortation to mothers in the section of *The Manual of Home Cuisine* entitled "National Diet" stresses the importance of correct dietary norms that should be observed on a national scale in the same way that national clothing became standardized from Karafuto and Taiwan to Korea.[12] A mother's responsibility was to conform to the cost-effective criteria of a national diet that also demanded maximizing nutrition. The first step toward the optimal extraction of nutrients had to do with the handling of ingredients. In order to preserve nutritional value, for example, the text advises the quick rinsing of vegetables. Furthermore, minimization of waste, it was suggested, could be achieved by deep-frying small fish bones and the thorough use of vegetable skins.[13]

Among the many regulated staple foods, rice was to see some of the most severe restrictions and modifications under the kōminka policies. The Japanese government's legal control over rice distribution was implemented in the mainland in 1939 and was followed by the Food Control Act (*Shokuryō kanrihō*) of 1942 through which the government assumed far-reaching authority over almost all food items.[14] One concrete measure promulgated in 1939 in colonial Korea restricted white, polished rice consumption. To compensate, the use of a rice-grain mixture with no more than seventy percent refined white rice was championed.

A short column entitled "Current Affairs" (*Jikyoku kaisetsu*) in the 1944 issue of the *New Women* testifies to the tightened government control over rice distribution and the heightened expectations imposed on women as the providers of meals at home. Directed at housewives and unmarried young women living in the colonial cities, who are deemed to know little about the severe restrictions of the time, the male columnist Yamawaki Hideo insists, "The rice we eat today is no different from the rice we used to eat prior to the war, but our hearts must change. When we truly understand how valuable one grain of rice or one grain of millet is, won't our commitment in the kitchen be fully recognized and our efforts strengthen Japan's military power?"[15] Yamawaki goes on to aver that because rice is *the* essential source of energy needed to fight the war, the government has understandably taken over its purchase and distribution in colonial Korea.[16] Rice in this context refers to the favored polished, white rice that was to be sent to soldiers on the war front, whose victory in the war would eventually ensure white rice for all Japanese.

Given that polished Japanese white rice had come to be associated with status and affluence and was generally preferred over the more nutritious unpolished, brown rice (*genmai*) and foreign varieties, a deliberate ideological operation was undertaken to defend the necessary but unpopular alternatives. The emerging field of nutritional science was enthusiastically mobilized to promote kōminka-era diet reforms regarding rice. The Green Flag's cookbook features a chapter on staples, which elaborates on how insufficient intake of vitamin B had resulted in an increased death toll from beriberi since 1899. Scientific studies of nutrition and easy-to-comprehend diagrams in the text demonstrate that vitamin B is found in abundance in rice bran, or the outer shell of rice, and that harmful vitamin B deficiency could be attributed to the excessive polishing of rice. Ideally, it is asserted, nutritious rice is mixed with multigrains with no more than seventy percent un-rinsed, refined white rice that contains no sand.

Moreover, *The Manual of Home Cuisine*'s passage on "How to Cope with Foreign Rice" betrays the urgency in rice shortages and the need for the rulers to mitigate the Japanese population's unwelcoming responses to substitutes. It acknowledges that even the main islands have become increasingly dependent on foreign rice (*gaimai*) from Thailand and Vietnam since 1939 and urges settlers to quietly bear the circumstances. Since, unlike "mainland rice" (*naichimai*), such varieties lack vitamin B, combining "foreign rice" with barley or beans, or even noodles, is suggested. The high fiber content of imported rice, the authors claim, makes it difficult to chew and digest for Japanese, and innovative methods of cooking it are also recommended. These include stir-frying the imported rice in oil or adding beans, potatoes, or sweet rice, in order to aid the gelatinization of starch. Further, the text highlights the comparable nutritious quality of imported rice by including a nutrition composition table comparing foreign imported rice to Japanese white rice in seven categories: water, protein, fat, fiber, and others. It then admonishes those who complain about the imported rice: "[Japanese] people say it is low in fat, making it distasteful, or it lacks moisture, but neither is proven scientifically. Further, being delicious or not delicious depends on personal preferences, and the people in Thailand and India speak disapprovingly of Japanese rice."[17]

Moving beyond scientific logic, the section closes by appealing to nationalistic sentiment and urging continued sacrifice, situating rice and food consumption within the greater causes of the empire. "As a nation-state with advanced defense forces we aspire to become self-sufficient in food, but today we are trying to establish the East Asia Co-Prosperity Sphere, and we inevitably have to import foreign and white rice-grain mixtures. Therefore, we should recognize the purpose of eating foreign rice, supplement its deficiency, and get rid of our complaints when we eat it."[18] Echoing the state's campaigns to rally the Japanese public behind imperial gastronomic goals, *The Manual of Home Cuisine* directly links diet reforms to the fate of the national defense. Here, the authors call on Japanese citizens to shoulder the noble responsibility of realizing the East Asia Co-Prosperity Sphere by stoically accepting the alimentary strictures and conforming to the newly proclaimed fundamentals of a healthy diet.

Another striking instance of the extreme measures taken to nourish the dwindling empire was expressed in an injunction calling for a thorough use of one "food" that remained available, namely wild greens (*nogusa*). In the chapter titled "Introduction of Wild Greens," the authors go so far as to urge Japanese families in colonial Korea to adopt the Korean "tradition" of gathering and eating wild plants as a means to secure substitute foods.

> Our people have not historically eaten wild greens. But people on the peninsula, even those of nobility, make delicious dishes with wild greens and eat them daily. It is disheartening to think of the pretty wild flowers merely as a source of food. So let us make sure that we do not lose our appreciation for nature.
>
> During spring and autumn, let us use our Sundays as health days and go out to the fields and mountains. We will be able to breathe in the clean air and harvest wild plants! The wild plants that families pick together under the shinning sun, however modest the quantity might be, will make our meals richer and more enjoyable![19]

To entice Japanese families to introduce Korean wild plants in their diet, the cookbook invokes the notions of elitism and family values. That is, in order to rationalize the wild greens cuisine among Japanese settlers, the text downplays the humiliating act of searching in the wild for foodstuffs in order to survive and depicts it as a picnic-like field trip to the countryside, a practice, it is proclaimed, even the Korean nobility embraces. Then it carefully charts out the names of more than thirty "edible" wild greens and lists various ways to incorporate them in daily meals, using Japanese recipes.[20] The existence of this section suggests that espousing such radical measures was necessary even at the risk of obscuring the cultural demarcation between the colonizer and the colonized. In order to temper the potential threat the acceptance of such extremes posed, the proposition is delivered within a rhetorical framework that accentuates family-centered outings and an appreciation of nature, underscoring a romantic vision of a dignified "native" practice rather than a pragmatic compromise of one's "Japanese" essence.

It is, thus, against the backdrop of growing militarism that the Green Flag Association's cookbook amplified its message of the centrality of the home and the responsibility of Japanese mothers in colonial Korea. At their posts in the kitchen, they were to valiantly carry out the daunting task of minimizing waste and maximizing nutrition despite dire food shortages. Mothers would wield the tools of their trade in order to implement cooking procedures based on scientific findings. Their vocation was to negotiate constraining material reality and ideological demands within the nationalized sphere of the home and raise healthy children for the empire.

Beyond Nutrition: Imperial Rituals at the Dining Table

Certainly a primary aim of the publication of *The Manual of Home Cuisine* was the institutionalization of new standards in cooking. Yet the cookbook operates more as a prescriptive text than a recipe book, as it stipulates injunctions and behavioral norms. In addition to pragmatic sections about food preparation and substitutes, the text also effectively underscores the ways in which manners, behaviors, and rituals associated with eating are indispensible for harnessing "Japanese-ness" in the nationalized site of settler homes. Beneath realistic concerns about food shortages, there was another, underlying apprehension about the ethnic identity of Japanese citizens living in the colonies. It was feared that Japanese citizens adopting the native diet of the colonies would lose their cultural connection to the motherland.

Gathering at the table, therefore, took on symbolic meaning for many Japanese settlers in direct correlation with the increasing difficulties. In the face of having to modify the "Japanese" diet, mealtime took on significance not simply as a means of providing nutritional sustenance, but rather as a ritual through which to exact and affirm one's loyalty to the emperor. An instructive chapter in *The Manual of Home Cuisine* on proper dining etiquette, entitled "How to Receive Meals" (*shokuji no itadakikata*), proclaims that food becomes meaningless if it is mechanically consumed to fill empty stomachs.

> In order to reciprocate the efforts of the hands that prepare the food with the utmost of care, the party that receives the meal should also have a thankful heart to the Emperor for the meal, try to attain a healthy body, and not leave food on the plate. This is because our health is not for our own sake, but for that of our nation and the world.

A prayer to the emperor, composed by the Green Flag Women's Division, is proffered for regular recitation. It reads: "We are truly thankful that we are blessed with such meals everyday. Even a drop of water can nurture our universe, and even a grain of rice is indebted to the efforts of many. We wish to reflect on your generosity as we chew our food and live a stronger and more exemplary life. Thank you for our meals." Aside from an assumed religiosity, the rhetoric itself generates, or forcefully demands, unconditional and uncritical loyalty to the emperor.

Throughout, *The Manual of Home Cuisine* re-conceptualizes the home as a national site by subordinating the parent-child bond to the greater tie between the emperor and his beloved subjects. The chapter entitled "Disciplinary Measures for Children's Meals" calls for the cooperation of mothers and fathers in rearing healthy children. In addition to detailing suitable home meals and ideal lunch boxes and snack menus, the text defines parents as "caretakers" of their children, who ultimately belong to the emperor. "Our children are not only ours, but also the beloved subjects of the Emperor. Thus, we should respect them and provide them with guidance in the home to build their basic human qualities. We shall raise our children as citizens of the empire and practice our disciplinary measures accordingly."[21]

Parents are instructed to execute ideal disciplinary measures in order to inculcate "spirit" as well as proper etiquette. The first essential step in raising children as imperial citizens is instilling a sense of gratitude in their heart. This can be achieved by earnestly intoning the prayer crafted by the Green Flag Association at the table. If parents recite it daily, children will be able to memorize it from an early age. This assertion of devotion during mealtime accompanied a comparable set of disciplinary measures intended for children. For example, children should stay calm during mealtime, use the same, designated rice bowl every time, and converse with parents on topics that are befitting the dining experience. It is important that children should know basic conventions, such as holding the soup bowl with both hands, using chopsticks correctly, and refraining from stacking up bowls and plates at the end of meals. Focusing on proper table manners in the Japanese home, this section attempts to choreograph children's gestures in order to keep the empire moving in unison. Such micromanaging was at the heart of producing national identity. In other words, the enactment of nationally defined cultural cues meant performing a "Japanese" identity. In this prescriptive cookbook, then, both spiritual sustenance and behavioral propriety emerge as requisite criteria for raising ideal imperial children.

The promotion of emperor-mindedness also took the form of warnings against adopting indigenous customs in Japanese homes on the peninsula. The text criticizes "people" (a thinly veiled reference to Koreans) who do not use individual serving plates and cautions that this practice can result in an imbalanced intake of food, as well as contamination. The "contamination" alluded to here derives from the mistaken belief that Korean "family style" dining was unhygienic. While this claim is ostensibly grounded in science, the section reveals an anxiety directed at Japanese settlers going "native." To counter this threat, *The Manual of Home Cuisine* emphasizes the importance of proper seating posture at the dining table, how to distribute food at the table, and what kinds of plates to use. Collectively illustrated in this chapter is the wartime propaganda that tried to harness proper "Japanese mannerisms" by stressing behavioral norms and attitudes in Japanese citizens to "guard them" against the material compromises they were facing in the colonies.

The Colonial Home: A Gendered Space for the Empire

As was the case in European imperial discourse, the home and motherhood were central vehicles for the building and management of the Japanese empire. The home provided not only a spatially insulated shelter in the colonies, but more importantly a cultural site that fostered what was deemed "Japanese" character through coaching appropriate mannerisms and inculcating moral values. Mothers were bestowed with the auspicious responsibility of serving as stewards of the home, guarding the private quarters of the empire. By the late 1930s the home and motherhood constituted the most essential means of physically and spiritually nourishing the imperial citizens who would carry out the Japanese expansionist mission. To borrow Ann Stoler's term from another colonial context, the home was the prototype of "domains of the intimate" through which colonial policies were imagined, implemented, and evaluated.[22] That is to say, as private as the home was in settler communities, it was nevertheless a public matter, an imperial concern, because it was decidedly critical in manufacturing cultural authenticity and ensuring membership in the motherland.

In fact, the settler communities in colonial Korea had long been under public scrutiny for their perceived inadequate observance of "Japanese tradition" and overall morally lax mode of life. Put at risk because of their distance from the metropolitan moral center and proximity to the colonized, Japanese settlers were frequently described as promiscuous, deviant, and "Korean-bred" (*Sensan*). Concerned community leaders and colonial officers turned to the home in an effort to salvage the Japanese expatriates from their decadent lifestyle.

The Green Flag Association's concern about the domestic sphere as it related to the supposed lack of Japanese identity among the settlers was repeatedly and overtly articulated in their publications. In an essay in the April 1937 issue of *Green Flag* entitled "The Problems of Japanese in the Colonial Territories," Suekichi Tsukuru, a resident in colonial Korea and a member of the East Asian Development University (Tōyō takushoku daigaku), identifies a primary problem in the settler communities as a dearth of "character building" (*hinsei*) in second-generation Japanese.[23] According to Suekichi, second-generation Japanese in colonial territories (including Taiwan and Manchuria) are not competitive in the corporate and marriage markets compared to young men and women born and raised in the *naichi* (mainland/homeland). He identifies the root of this problem in their weak adherence to Japanese tradition and a licentious lifestyle in the colonies.

Reform in the colonial home, Suekichi asserts, is the only remedy for the ills of settler communities. Therefore, he calls upon mothers to revamp home life by eliminating servants and instilling self-sufficiency, which can also result in efficient home management and significant savings. Suekichi's argument suggests that the main concern of women should be the scientific management of the home in three central facets of domestic life: nutritional meals, childrearing, and clothing.[24] Given their distance from the cultural and moral hub of the empire, mothers must compensate by maintaining strict discipline within the colonial home in order to assure the successful assimilation of their children to the reigning doctrine of Japanese-ness.

In another essay, in the January 1937 issue of the same journal, Tsuda Setsuko, the wife of the founder of the Green Flag Association and an influential educator herself, argues that members of the home must have the same vision as the national polity (*kokutai*). She calls for "the home that grows with Japan" (*Nihon to tomo ni nobiru katei*) and declares the home a nationalized site of "growth" manifested through daily practices. Tsuda exclaims in delight, "Grow, grow, to the extent of the sky, grow! If asked how much, I would respond immediately 'as much as Japan grows!'"[25] "The home that can grow with Japan," she explains, "is the home that embraces Japan's ideals and embodies the founding spirit of the Japanese nation-state."[26] In Tsuda's essay the home emerges as a politicized sphere through which the individual and nation become intertwined.

The emphasis on the home in connection with the nation and empire voiced by Suekichi Tsukuru and Tsuda Setsuko would be reiterated over and over in a variety of print media channels, including newspapers and magazines, into the later years of the kōminka era. To raise loyal Japanese imperial citizens emerged as the foremost noble task for women. Women's place within the empire was valorized through their role as mothers, and their education, health, and purpose in life was overwhelmingly defined in terms of their service to the empire as *mothers*.

Creating the National Body

One is struck by the prevalence of both the corporeal metaphors describing the "national body" and imperial demands on material bodies during the kōminka era. By the late 1930s and the early 1940s, Japanese bodies were subjected to tightened measures of the state's regulatory regime. Men, women, and children were asked to view the maintenance of their own health as a national duty, a means to keep the "national body" strong and vigorous. Discussions of the national body date back to the late nineteenth century and were part of a much larger debate and social movements pertinent to what Sabine Frühstück calls a "modern health regime." Frühstück discusses how during the Meiji period (1868–1912) children emerged as a central category of national concern out of which scientific surveys and data collection were administered and campaigns for hygiene implemented.[27] Children's "body building," by way of hygiene and health, was conceived as a prerequisite for and a means of empire-building, and their bodies fell under direct state protection and instruction; boys' bodies, in particular, were directly linked to the fate of military might.[28]

The legacies of the Meiji commitment to building a healthy national body would manifest in concrete terms in the kōminka era with more pronounced and overbearing government policies that were to be executed by newly minted institutions. The establishment of the Ministry of Health and Welfare in 1938 in Tokyo underscored the state's concern with national health. Three years later, the Ministry of Health and Welfare was added to the Government-General of colonial Korea and charged with the mission of overseeing the health of Japanese citizens as well as Korean subjects. The promotion of the healthy body under an auspicious Healthy Body Movement (*kenmin undō*) was launched in colonial Korea in 1942, duplicating the same features of a home campaign. Calisthenics were implemented in the school curriculum and sports and healthy baby competitions were widely promoted.[29] The slogan "An Iron Body Is the Foundation of East Asian Prosperity" sums up the aspirations of the underlying kōminka ideology that accentuated the importance of Japanese national body/bodies in a broadened sphere of East Asia.

In keeping with the general ideology that the bodies of Japanese citizens and subjects belonged to the emperor, in the 1940s, women's bodies became the focus of campaigns for public duty. Women's health was no longer a personal matter; it was an issue of national policy and duty. A growing emphasis on healthy bodies resulted in a modification of the discourse regarding the "ideal mother" popular since the Meiji period—the *ryōsai kembo*, the good wife, the wise mother. The "ideal mother" in the 1940s included a homonym of the earlier phrase "the wise mother" (*kembo*). With the alteration of just one character, the new term meant "healthy mother" and specifically indicated a woman who was capable of giving birth to healthy children.

Mothers were called on to devote their entire bodies to their families and nation. This entailed (re)producing, rearing, and nurturing the next generation of loyal subjects for the empire.[30] More Japanese men were required to keep up with the commercial and military demands of the imperial state; more soldiers to battle in the colonial frontiers, more police to govern the colonized subjects, and more colonial officers to oversee and extract the resources of the colonial territories. Motherhood was articulated as a national service, a mother's womb was considered a national resource, and a mother's childrearing duty was viewed as indispensable for molding imperial citizens with Japan's superior national spirit and ideals.

Despite a notable reduction in advertisements for women's vanity items in the print media, the marketing of products related to women's reproductive health actually persisted with great vigor throughout the early 1940s. A wide range of woman's products and services, ranging from ointments for scarred nipples and supplements intended to prevent miscarriages to recruitment announcements for midwives, emblazoned newspapers, magazines, and flyers. For example, a vitamin E supplement called Yubera was promoted in the magazine *New Women* as a medicine to prevent miscarriages and premature births.[31] The third issue of *New Women* echoes the urgency for procreation in an advertisement that takes up almost an entire page. To the right the text reads:

> The vast sky is filled with enemy planes!
> Our soldiers fighting in the South said this and let out a sigh.
> To this voice, how can we respond?
> We have to send our planes with the Japanese national flag as soon as
>   possible.
> We have to raise as many children capable of flying planes as possible.

Is there any piece of metal you have not donated?
Is there anyone living a lifestyle that hinders strengthening military might?
Increase (Re)productivity! Forward Military!
Now is the time to mobilize a hundred million soldiers!

On the same page, to the left of this bombastic declaration, the Wakamoto Pharmaceutical Company plugs a medicine that enhances the growth of the fetus. The copy on the bottom reads, "A healthy nation and strong military begin with healthy mothers (kembo)," constructing motherhood as the locus of national and military might. When viewed together side by side, the pharmaceutical ad visually answers the urgent call on the right by asserting its product's immediate and direct impact on the improvement of reproductive health.

Although women were called upon to perform all sorts of private bodily tasks in the name of the empire, all imperial subjects were asked to outwardly exhibit loyalty with their bodies. The extent to which some went to choreograph Japanese identity is illustrated in the January issue of the 1942 *New Women*, which features six instructive photographs that demonstrate step by step the proper conduct for shrine visits. Having a pious heart is said to be the foremost preparation.[32] However, the column also prescribes carefully ordered mannerisms in the minutest detail, including the angle at which one should bow, how to wash one's hands, the exact number of claps and steps. Not inclined to leave anything to the imagination, it even coaches that when clapping, one must hold one's hands eight or nine inches away from one's chest and hold the hands with fingers turned slightly upward. Though seemingly mundane and repetitive, implementation of the "proper" Japanese mannerisms through such rites meant disciplinary programming of bodies—ones that would be sufficiently conditioned to carry out the emperor-centered ideology uncritically and tirelessly.

The state policy of embodying such gestures as a confirmation of Japanese identity is amplified in a fictional story that surprisingly offers a colonial subject as a model for Japanese citizens. Serialized from January to April in 1942 in *New Women*, Tateno Nobuyuki's *A Girl with a Flower* is narrated by a teacher at a girls' school in the main islands. The story details the blossoming of a Korean student, Kanemura Hanae, into a remarkable imperial subject. When the narrator first encounters Kanemura her coloniality is marked by her body; her "improper" Korean behavior, such as sitting with her legs crossed and poor Japanese speaking skills. Over the course of her education, however, Kanemura emerges as a model imperial subject, the result of her earnest attempts to adapt to the customs and mannerisms of the Japanese. Kanemura's exemplary success in the final episode is used not only to compliment her physical internalization of Japanese-ness, but also to reprimand her Japanese classmates, who are found to be insufficiently devoted to the preservation of the health of their bodies for the nation. The narrator-teacher therefore gives a lengthy speech alerting the Japanese pupils that their Japan-born status does not automatically qualify them as daughters of Japan. In order to earn that status, the narrator-teacher continues:

> You are in the wrong if you think your body is yours and you can therefore treat it the way you like! Your body is not yours, but something you received from your parents. On a grander scale your body is the body of the Japanese nation, a body that has been entrusted to you by the Emperor. When you realize the significance of your body you cannot possibly mistreat it. Everyone should look at Kanemura Hanae as a model to emulate and do your utmost to become Japanese women![33]

Intriguingly, the success of this Korean student is used to critique the complacency of Japanese students. In this piece of propaganda, which reiterates the kōminka ideology, the healthy body is also the Japanized body. As Kanemura's successful Japanization was confirmed by, for instance, her changed seating posture, her corporeal display of Japanese customs was the prerequisite for not only maintaining good health but also embodying Japanese identity.

Conclusion

An upsurge of hostilities coupled with an unraveling of the economic and social order in the Japanese empire demanded unprecedented action in the last years of the Asia-Pacific War. Within the larger context of escalating warfare and oppressive colonial expansion, food and domesticity hardly seem to warrant attention. Yet, the articles, advertisements, and cookbook published by the Green Flag Association attest to the all-encompassing nature of empire during the kōminka era. No arena, imperial subject, or resource was too insignificant to be overlooked by the Japanese state, which increasingly endeavored to choreograph the participation of all of its subjects, including women, children, and the colonized peoples of its empire. The reach of the state was facilitated in myriad, crucial ways by civilians, who attempted to address day-to-day concerns that had direct implications for their lives. The Green Flag texts, which buttressed official policy and ideology, represent efforts of ordinary Japanese settlers—men and women—to respond to the daunting task of survival brought on by worsening conditions in Korea.

The hardships of colonial life were not limited to the prosaic search for basic necessities. Assimilationist policies, employed to force the colonized to participate in their own subjugation, may have paid lip-service to the "equality" of all of the emperor's subjects, but they also engendered considerable anxiety among Japanese in the settler communities whose identities were predicated on the assumption of their inherent superiority. For Japanese colonists the boundary between authentic "Japanese-ness" and the colonial Other had to be fastidiously and tenaciously guarded. If, as we saw above, in rare cases a colonized girl could be singled out in the homeland to admonish complacent citizens, in the colonies, Japanese women were routinely called upon to marshal, manifest, and model Japanese preeminence for the edification of the next generation of Japanese and colonized subjects.

Nationalization of the settler homes operated on multiple levels. First, the state incorporated the private sphere in a tightened regulatory regime by directly linking the execution of quotidian behaviors to the rise and fall of the empire. Thus, trivial actions of home management, such as rinsing vegetables or cooking fish bones, were given new meaning and significance and glorified as fulfilling a national mission. A basic feature of everyday life—eating—was reconceptualized as a reified act of imperial devoutness that trumped the actual consumption of what little food, increasingly distasteful and unfamiliar, was available. Food, in this sense, no longer simply nourished the body; it nourished loyalty and devotion to the emperor.

The significance of *The Manual of Home Cuisine*'s prescriptive function, then, lies beyond its pragmatic nutritional advice, and food no longer simply belongs to the domain of material practice, but to that of the spiritual, symbolic, and ritualistic. The primary objective of the Green Flag publications, namely to prove and preserve "Japanese-ness," rested on the injunctions and exhortations directed at the immaterial realm, for example, table manners, praying postures, and the reiteration of imperial allegiance. It is this vital nonmaterialistic dimension of food that was instrumentalized as a state apparatus in wartime discourse to inscribe Japanese sentiments in individual imperial bodies and sustain Japanese supremacy in the national body.

Notes

I would like to express my gratitude to my coeditor and friend Michele Mason for her tireless support and encouragement during the writing of this chapter. This project would not have been possible without her uncompromising commitment and hard work. The title of this chapter, "Eating for the Emperor," came up during a conversation with Jim Fujii whom I would like to thank for his mentoring over the past two decades. This work was supported by the National Research Foundation of Korea, a grant funded by the Korean government (S-2009-A0004-00048).

1. Green Flag Women's Division, *The Manual of Home Cuisine* (Keijō: Kōa bunka shuppan kabushikikaisha, 1941). Page number references: Preface, 1–3; Chapter One: Meals for the Future, 1–6; Chapter Two: Staples, 7–9, 17–19; Chapter Three: Side Dishes, 53, 93–97; Chapter Four: How to Receive Meals, 98; Chapter Five: Disciplinary Measures for Children's Meals, 103, 129–33.

2. Ahn Taeyoon, "Iljemal Jŏnsi chejegi yŏsŏnge daehan pokjang tongje" (Wartime Japan and Control over Women's Clothing), *Sahoe wa yŏksa* (Society and History) 74 (2007): 5–33.

3. Wayyao Chou, "The Kominka Movement in Taiwan and Korea: Comparisons and Interpretations," in *The Japanese Wartime Empire, 1931–1945*, ed. Peter Duus et al. (Princeton, NJ: Princeton University Press, 1996), 40–69.

4. Leo T. S. Ching, *Becoming "Japanese": Colonial Taiwan and the Politics of Identity Formation* (Berkeley: University of California Press, 2001), 89–132.

5. *Green Flag (Ryokki)* was a monthly journal that began publication in 1936. Beginning in 1944, its name was changed to *Prosperous Asian Culture (Kōa bunka)*. *New Women (Shinjosei)* was published from August 1942 to the end of the Pacific War. The only remaining copies are from 1944.

6. Keijō is the Japanese reading of the capital city of colonial Korea, known in Korean as Kyŏngsŏng.

7. Hiroki Nagashima investigates the assumptions made about the Green Flag's political alliance with the Government-General through a detailed mapping of the genealogy of the organization and its members. See his doctoral dissertation, "Nihon tōchiki no Chōsen ni okeru 'shintaisei' no shiteki kenkyū" (Historical Survey of the "New Governmental System" in Korea under Japanese Colonial Governance) (Kyushu University, 2007).

8. Yi Kwangsu, who is best known as the "father of modern Korean literature," became a member of this association among many other educated Korean men and women.

9. It is possible that some Korean women might have read this text, and that the women's division targeted upper-class Korean women. There was a publication by the Green Flag Association that specifically targeted Korean women, *Improvement of Modern Korean Life: Lectures on Korean's Current Problems*.

10. For example, Katarzyna Cwiertka's work reveals how the distinctively non-Japaese national cuisine that emerged in the 1920s in the military later became disseminated throughout homes in the 1930s and 1940s. See Katarzyna J. Cwiertka,

"Popularizing a Military Diet in Wartime and Postwar Japan," *Asian Anthropology* 1 (2002): 1–30.

11. Katarzyna J. Cwiertka, *Modern Japanese Cuisine: Food, Power and National Identity* (London: Reaktion, 2006).

12. *The Manual of Home Cuisine*, 60–61.

13. Ibid., 62.

14. Ibid., 16.

15. *Shinjosei* 3, 2 (1944): 20–21.

16. The essay explains that a government agency, Chōsen shokuryō eidan, has overseen the purchase and distribution of rice in colonial Korea since the fall of the preceding year. For a book-length study of the centrality of rice in Japanese cultural identity, see Emiko Ohnuki-Tierney, *Rice as Self: Japanese Identities through Time* (Princeton, NJ: Princeton University Press, 1993).

17. *The Manual of Home Cuisine*, 18.

18. Ibid., 18–19.

19. Ibid., 53.

20. Adopting new staple foods in the colonies was not unique to those living in colonial Korea. In the 1943 Manchuria issue of the magazine *Shufu no tomo* (Housewife's Friend), a cooking column entitled "How to Make 14 Nutritious Dishes in Manchurian Homes" provides a variety of wartime recipes. The most intriguing new recipes are the pheasant meat dishes. The column encourages Japanese housewives to readily incorporate the unfamiliar poultry in home meals. From hotpot and soup to Korean-style barbequed pheasant, Japanese housewives writing from different parts of Manchuria submitted creative recipes and claimed they had found a cheap and tasty substitute for chicken. In this case, the pheasant meat is not even cooked in the Japanese style.

21. *The Manual of Home Cuisine*, 129.

22. Ann Laura Stoler, *Carnal Knowledge and Imperial Power: Race and the Intimate in Colonial Rule* (Berkeley: University of California Press, 2002), 1–21.

23. *Green Flag*, April (1937): 56–61.

24. For a study on the topic of gendering of the home in modern Japan and the emergence of household management as an institutionalized discipline, see Jordan Sand, *House and Home in Modern Japan: Architecture, Domestic Space, and Bourgeois Culture, 1890–1930* (Cambridge, MA: Harvard University Press, 2005).

25. *Green Flag*, January (1937): 14.

26. Ibid.

27. Sabine Frühstück, *Colonizing Sex: Sexology and Social Control in Modern Japan* (Berkeley: University of California Press, 2003), 21–20.

28. Ibid., 49–51.

29. Keun Sik Jung, "Shokuminchi shihai, shintai kiritsu, 'kenkō'" (Colonial Governance, Disciplining the Body, "Health"), in *Seikatsu no naka no shokuminchishugi* (Colonialism in Everyday Life), ed. Mizuno Naoki (Kyoto: Jimbun shoin, 2004), 61–102.

30. State interest in the healthy body was initially manifested with the prom-

ulgation of military conscription in the year 1873, when Japan's first physical ex-aminations of male bodies were conducted. This procedure involved such basic tasks as measuring height and weight, checking for illness, and assessing physical strength. During this time there were no standards available in Japan to function as a yardstick to classify and rank bodies. When first surveyed, the average height of Japanese men was determined to be 5.025 feet (154 cm). See Früstrück, *Colonizing Sex*, 17–54.

31. *Shinjosei* 3, 2 (1944): 1.
32. *Shinjosei* 3, 1 (1944): 17.
33. *Shinjosei* 3, 4 (1944): 22.

CHAPTER SIX

TEXT

Wolf Forest, Basket Forest, and Thief Forest

MIYAZAWA KENJI

CONTEXT

The Metropole

CRITIQUE

A Little Story of Settler Colonialism: Imperialist Consciousness and Children's Literature in the 1920s

KOTA INOUE

KNOWN MOSTLY as a poet and writer of children's tales today, Miyazawa Kenji (1896–1933) was not widely read during his short life. Miyazawa was born into a relatively wealthy family that ran a pawnshop in the northeastern city of Hanamaki, Iwate prefecture. He began writing around 1918, and this would be his passion throughout his life, together with his work with farmers to improve agricultural production and the Hokke sect of Buddhism. Miyazawa's intellectual interests were expansive, including geology, meteorology, astrology, chemistry, botany, art, Western musical instruments, history, Buddhism, and Esperanto, and his vast knowledge is incorporated into many of his stories. In 1924, Miyazawa published a collection of poems, *Spring and Ashura* (*Haru to shura*) and a collection of children's tales, *The Restaurant of Many Orders* (*Chūmon no ōi ryōriten*). They would be his only published books while he was alive. He died of acute pneumonia at the age of 39.

Since his death, Miyazawa's status has been elevated to a considerable level, his poems and stories becoming staples in school textbooks. Countless academic and popular books have been written on his work and life, commonly making Miyazawa into either a poet with an admirable human-istic moral vision or a nature-loving fantasy writer for children and adults alike who tragically died young of an illness. However, since the 1990s some scholars have begun reading his works with a critical eye, underscoring and analyzing the unsettling sense of Otherness in his works that defies the de-politicized and romanticized image of Miyazawa.

"Wolf Forest, Basket Forest, and Thief Forest" (*Oinomori to zarumori, nusutomori*), included in *The Restaurant of Many Orders* and believed to have been written in 1921, follows farmer families who settle in a clearing near four forests. Employing narrative techniques common in children's lit-erature—anthropomorphized animals and non-sentient beings, as well as rhythmic, stylized repetitions of events and expressions—the story relates how the families come to know their nonhuman neighbors through surprise encounters.

Wolf Forest, Basket Forest, and Thief Forest

MIYAZAWA KENJI

TRANSLATION BY KOTA INOUE

Four forests of black pine sit just north of Koiwai Farm. The southernmost one is called Wolf Forest, the next one Basket Forest, the next Black Hill Forest, and the northernmost one Thief Forest.

When and how the forests came to be, and why they got those odd names—the only one who knows all about it is me, bragged the giant rock in the middle of the Black Hill Forest one day; and he told me this story.

Long, long ago, Mount Iwate erupted many times. The surrounding area was completely buried in ashes. The giant black rock said he was flung away from the mountain at that time and fell onto the present location.

After a long while, the eruptions finally stopped. Soon, grasses—some with tufts and others without—began growing in the southern area and gradually covered all the flat lands and hills. Then, oak, pine, and other trees followed. And, eventually, the present four forests came into being. But without a name yet, each forest simply existed unconcerned about anyone else, thinking to himself, "I am just 'I.'" Then came an autumn day one year when a translucent wind as cold as water rustled the dry oak leaves and the crisp black shadows of the clouds were seen on the silver top of Mount Iwate.

Four farmers wearing simple armor and carrying all kinds of weapons of the mountain and field tightly tied to their bodies—machetes, three-pronged hoes, Chinese hoes, and so forth—came walking heavily across the angular flint of the mountain in the east and into a small clearing surrounded by the forests. If you looked closer, you would've also noticed the large swords they carried.

The farmer who was leading the group pointed in various directions into the lantern-like scenery, and said,

"How do you like it? Isn't it a good place? It would be easy to convert the grassland into vegetable fields, it's close to the forest, and there is a clear brook. We get plenty of sun, too. What do you say? I decided a long time ago this would be the place."

"But I wonder how good the soil is," said one of the farmers as he bent down to pull out a stalk of silver *susuki* grass and shook off some dirt from its roots onto his palm. After pressing the dirt this way and that way into his palm with his fingers for a while, and even licking it a bit, he said,

"Hmm. The soil isn't too great, but not too poor, either."

"Well, shall we finally settle down here, then?" said another, surveying the surroundings with a look of nostalgia.

"All right, this is our place," announced the last farmer, who had been quietly standing by until then.

Pleased with the decision, the four put their loads down on the ground with a thud. They then turned around to face the direction from which they had come and called out loudly,

"Hallo, hallo. This is the place! Come quick, come quick!"

Three wives with red faces from the large bundles on their backs emerged from the *susuki* grass bush in the distance. With them came nine children, all under five or six, boisterously scampering along.

The four men turned in different directions and cried out in one voice,

"Can we make vegetable fields here?"

"Yes, you can!" replied the forests in unison.

The men yelled out again,

"Is it OK to build houses here?"

"It's all right!" replied the forests all at once.

The men asked once again in one voice,

"Can we build a fire here?"

"Yes, you can!" replied the forests all at once.

The men yelled out once more,

"Is it OK to collect some firewood?"

"It's all right!" replied the forests in unison.

The men clapped their hands in joy, and the women and the children, who had been quiet and nervous, suddenly perked up and became animated. The children even started a fight in their uncontainable glee, and the women had to give them a hearty smacking.

By that evening, a small cabin with a thatched roof had already been erected. The children jumped up and down around it in delight. From the following day on, the forests watched the men and women working frantically. The men all worked in the field turning over the grassy land, their plow blades glistening rhythmically. The women busied themselves collecting walnuts that hadn't yet been carried away by the squirrels and wild mice, as well as making firewood from the pine trees they cut down. And soon snow arrived and blanketed the entire area.

During the winter, the forests worked hard to shield the families from the north wind. Still, sensitive to the cold, the small children often cried, "I'm so cold! I'm so cold!" pressing their frostbitten little hands on their throats.

Next spring, another cabin was added.

And it appeared that buckwheat and barnyard grass were planted. White flowers bloomed from the buckwheat, and black ears formed on the barnyard grass. That fall, when the plants bore grain, new fields were added, and another cabin was built, everyone, even the adults, pranced around joyfully. But one cold morning, when the earth froze hard, it was discovered that the smallest four of the nine children had magically disappeared overnight.

Everyone went out and searched frantically for the children, but no trace of them was to be found.

So they turned in different directions and cried out together,

"Does anyone know where the children are?"

"I have no idea," replied the forests in unison.

"Then we're gonna come search you!" everyone shouted again.

"Be my guest!" replied the forests in unison.

So they went to the nearest, the Wolf Forest, carrying an assortment of farm tools. As soon as they entered, a cold damp wind and the smell of dead leaves and humus suddenly assailed them.

The group advanced into the forest without hesitation.

Soon they heard a crackling noise coming from the back of the forest.

They hurried toward the noise and found a blazing bonfire with translucent rose-colored flames, and nine wolves trotting around it, dancing feverishly.

As the farmers slowly approached the fire, they saw the four missing children, who were all seated facing the fire and eating roasted walnuts and mushrooms.

The wolves were all singing and scampering around the bonfire—which was like a summer lantern—-creating dancing shadows.

In the middle of the Wolf Forest
The fire roars, click-clack
The fire roars, click-clack
The walnuts roll, click-clack
The walnuts roll, click-clack

At that point, the farmers hollered all together,

"Kindly, wolves, please give us back our kids!"

Surprised, all at once the wolves stopped singing, twisted their mouths, and turned toward the farmers.

The fire went out, and suddenly the surrounding area became quiet, like the color blue. So the children near the bonfire started to wail.

The wolves looked nervously around for a while, as if they didn't know what to do, but finally they all ran away together further back into the forest.

Holding the children's hands, everyone then proceeded to head for home. As they walked out of the forest, they heard the wolves shout out from the back of the forest,

"Don't think ill of us. We treated them to lots of walnuts, mushrooms, and more!"

After returning home, the men made millet cakes and left them in the Wolf Forest as a thank you gift.

Spring came. There were eleven children now. Two horses were brought in. Since the men augmented the field with grass cuttings and decomposed leaves, together with horse droppings, the millet and barnyard grass grew tall and green.

And the harvest was plentiful. The people were beyond happy at the end of fall.

But then came a cold morning when frost formed little columns in the ground.

The families were about to go to work, turning over the grassland to make more fields like the preceding year, when they realized that all the farming tools—machetes, three-pronged hoes, Chinese hoes, and all—had vanished from the cabins.

Everyone searched everywhere, high and low, but they just couldn't find them. Having exhausted every possibility, they turned in various directions and called out together,

"Do you know where my tools are?"

"I don't know," replied the forests all at once.

"We're gonna come search you!" cried everyone.

"Be my guest!" replied the forests in unison.

The families walked toward the forests in a drove, this time without tools. They first went to the closest forest, the Wolf Forest.

Upon their arrival, nine wolves came out right away with serious expressions, and, waving their hands briskly, said,

"No, no. We don't have them, we swear. Come back if nothing turns up elsewhere."

Everyone thought what the wolves said made sense, so they proceeded to the Basket Forest to the west. As they walked deep into the woods, they found a large basket made of boughs placed upside down under an old oak tree.

"This is definitely suspicious. You might think it's just natural to find a basket in the Basket Forest, but we don't know what's inside. Let's lift it and see what's in it." When they raised the basket, they found all the nine missing tools.

Not only that, in the middle of the tools a mountain man with a red face and golden eyes sat cross-legged. When he saw everyone, he opened his big mouth and said, "BOO!"

The children screamed and were about to run away, but the adults, standing unfazed, addressed the mountain man in one voice.

"Mountain man, please stop pulling a prank on us. We sincerely implore you. Please stop pulling our leg."

The mountain man stood there scratching his head as if in a gesture of contrition. Everyone picked up their tools and proceeded to leave the forest.

Just then, the mountain man cried out from the woods,

"Bring me millet cakes, too!" He turned around, and with his head in his hands, ran further back into the forest.

Everyone laughed heartily and walked back home. They made millet cakes again, carried them to the Wolf Forest and the Basket Forest, and left them there.

Next summer, the flat parts of the area were now all vegetable fields. Some houses had wooden shacks or large barns.

Also, they now had three horses. The fall harvest that year was a major celebration for everyone.

They felt that finally they could make as many millet cakes as they wanted without worrying about their food supply and seed stock.

Once again, something strange happened in the fall.

One frosty morning, it was discovered that all the millet in the barns had disappeared. Anxious and worried, everyone ran around in search of the millet, but they couldn't find even a single grain anywhere.

Disappointed, they turned in different directions and called out,

"Do you know where my millet is?"

"I have no idea!" replied the forests all at once.

"We're coming to search you!" cried everyone.

"Be my guest!" replied the forests in unison.

With their weapons of choice in their hands, everyone went to the nearby Wolf Forest first.

The nine wolves were already waiting at the edge of the forest. Upon seeing the families, they gave a little chuckle and said,

"The millet cakes again. There's no millet here, we swear. Come back here if nothing turns up elsewhere."

Everyone thought that made sense, left the place, then went to the Basket Forest.

The red-faced mountain man had already come out to the entrance to the forest and said with a grin,

"Here come the millet cakes, millet cakes. I didn't steal nothing. If you want to look for your millet, you should go further north."

Everyone thought that made sense and went to the entrance to the Black Hill Forest to the north, that is, the forest that told me this story.

"Please give us back the millet. Give us back the millet."

Without showing its form, the Black Hill Forest answered by calling out,

"At dawn today I saw big black feet flying in the sky to the north. Go further north." I was told that the forest said nothing about millet cakes. And I wholeheartedly think that was indeed the case. Because, after hearing this story from the forest, I gathered all my copper coins—7 *sen* in all—and gave them to him as my thank you gift; but he would not accept them. That's how upright this forest was.

Well, everyone thought what the Black Hill Forest said made sense, so they walked further north.

There they found none other than the Thief Forest, with pines that were pitch black. So the families entered the forest, saying,

"The name already smells," and yelled out, "Give us back the millet now! Give it back!"

An enormous dark man with long arms came out of the forest and said in a ripping voice,

"What? You call me a thief? I'm gonna squash anyone who says that! What in the devil is your proof?"

"We have a witness. We have a witness," said everyone.

"Who is that? Damn it, who says such a thing?" roared the Thief Forest

"The Black Hill Forest!" everyone shouted back, standing firm.

"You can never, never, never, ever, trust what he says, damn it!" yelled the Thief Forest.

Everyone thought that made sense; and they also felt scared. They looked at each other and were about to bolt.

Then, all of a sudden, came a clear, solemn voice from the sky.

"No, no. This will not do."

When everyone looked up, it was Mount Iwate, wearing a silver crown. The black giant from the Thief Forest covered his head with his hands and fell to the ground.

Mount Iwate said quietly,

"The thief was definitely the Thief Forest. I clearly saw him this dawn in the light from the east and the moonlight from the west. But perhaps everyone should go home now. I'll surely make him return the millet. So don't hold a grudge against him. After all, the Thief Forest just wanted so much to make millet cakes himself. That's why he stole the millet. Ha, ha, ha!"

Then Mount Iwate turned his gaze into the sky again as if nothing had happened. The black giant was nowhere to be seen.

When the stunned families returned home, talking nosily among themselves, they found all the millet returned to their barns. They smiled, made millet cakes, and brought them over to the four forests.

They gave the Thief Forest the most. I heard that there was a little bit of sand in them, but it probably couldn't be helped.

After that, the four forests were all good friends with the farmers. And they got millet cakes from the farmers at the beginning of winter every year without fail.

Those millet cakes have become much smaller these days. But this, too, can't be helped, said the giant black rock in the middle of the Black Hill Forest at the end of his story.

A Little Story of Settler Colonialism: Imperialist Consciousness and Children's Literature in the 1920s

KOTA INOUE

Colonialism, as a political and economic system of domination and exploitation, functions through a certain set of state and non-state apparatuses—treaties, legal codes, education, taxes, the military, militias, settler-farmers, and so forth—but its asymmetrical power relationships are also enabled and reinforced by cultural practices and discourses, particularly those around subjectivity and the notion of the Other. The prevailing logic of colonialism finds ways into cultural representations within the metropole, sometimes overtly promoting itself in the most unequivocal, supremacist terms, and other times serving only as an unarticulated assumption or forming the horizon of expectation about what can be presented and how. In other cases, however, its manifestations are questioned and challenged, resulting in a destabilized narrative. The textual readings in this volume, for the most part, reveal complex and sometimes even contradictory cultural and ideological systems of domination that governed the relationship between, and the very definitions of, the colonizer and the colonized in modern Japanese history. While "colonialism" may conjure images of brutality and violence in occupied territories, colonial administration, with all its ambiguities and contradictions, would not be possible without justifications, explicit or subtle, woven into the everyday consciousness of the imperial homeland through cultural practices.

For this reason, the culture of the metropole is an integral part of colonial practices, even when it does not directly refer to oppressive acts in the colony. Since Edward Said's *Orientalism* (1978), a number of penetrating studies on the deep-rooted relationship between colonialism and the culture of the metropole have been produced, particularly in regard to the British and French empires. Academic focus has largely shifted from the high politics and economics of colonialism to the impact of imperialism on the culture and society of the metropolis, and historians now regularly study European metropolitan cultures in relation to imperialism.[1] Some studies of pre–World War II Japan, beginning in the early 1990s, have recast metropolitan culture, both highbrow and popular, in the light of Japan's imperialism and colonialism.[2] Scholars of modern Japanese literature have opened up new paths of inquiry by shedding light on works by ethnically non-Japanese writers, by critically engaging the works produced by Japanese artists in the colonies, and by examining the representations of the colonial Other. Kawamura Minato opens his well-known essay "Popular Oriental-ism and Japanese Views of Asia" (1992)—one of the pioneering works on colonialism and Japanese culture (included in this volume in translation)—with an analysis of a serialized, illustrated story, which appeared in a juve-nile magazine in the 1930s, about a Japanese boy's adventures on an exotic South Seas island. Pointing out the ways in which the Japanese protagonist and the South Pacific islanders are visually distinguished, Kawamura argues that this wildly popular story subscribes to the colonialist dichotomy of civ-ilization vs. barbarism operating in the cultural milieu of Japan at the time.

While Kawamura's analysis perceptively brings out the colonialist logic of the adventure story, it also highlights the pervasiveness and potency of colo-nial discourse in the prewar Japanese homeland by demonstrating the dis-quieting connection between colonialism and children's stories. By the 1920s, a distinctive nationwide culture of schoolchildren existed that was largely shaped by the growing mass media. Japan's overt, aggressive expansionist pol-icies since the Manchurian Incident of 1931, which would continue until 1945 in the prolonged military conflict with China and the Allied nations known as the Asia-Pacific War, undoubtedly played a role in shaping this children's culture during wartime, particularly in regard to the concepts of masculinity and patriotism. But even before 1931, Japan was already a full-fledged empire with sizeable overseas colonies, and it is reasonable to suspect that conscious-ness about colonialism, whether accommodating or critical, would be dis-cernible in many areas of domestic culture, including children's literature.

In considering the relevance of colonialism to the culture of the metropole, I take a close look at a story in this genre from the 1920s by Miyazawa Kenji (1896–1933). Although Miyazawa remained relatively obscure while he was alive, his poetry and children's stories gained national acclaim after his death. In his "Wolf Forest, Basket Forest, and Thief Forest" (1924), farmers, upon settling in an uncultivated land, encounter mischievous creatures—natural and supernatural—that live in nearby forests and eventually build friendly relationships with them. The story is evidently set within Japan, as indicated by a few proper place names, and there are no obvious colonial figures or symbols (exotic islands, people of different races, etc.). Yet this fairytale-like story about a group of farmers succinctly lays out the basic logic of settler colonialism. While most children's stories at the time overtly or uncritically embraced—and in so doing reinforced—an imperialist worldview as the cultural norm, Miyazawa's story, through its polyphonic text and its convoluted narrative structure, simultaneously bolsters and destabilizes that norm. The text's sophisticated strategies for critically engaging with colonialism in a deceptively simple story eloquently tell us that colonial practices overseas had a substantial impact on the culture of Japan's metropole in the 1920s.

As mentioned earlier, colonialism, which generally refers to exploitative practices in the colony, also involves the substantial participation of significant sectors of the metropole, from state apparatuses in support of the colonial enterprise to a set of enabling cultural practices and discourses. In the case of Japan, *naichi* (the homeland) was closely tied to the operation of *gaichi* (the colonial periphery) in innumerable ways: from legislative decisions related to colonial administration to the exoticisms promoted by the increasingly powerful mass media. If the practice of domination in the colony is called colonialism, the political and cultural attitudes toward the colony, as well as the general view of international relations, found in the metropole that underlie and enable such colonial practices may be called imperialism. As with colonialism, "imperialism" has been used over the years to signify a range of forms of dominance with differing nuances, but I will employ the term in this essay as a concept that refers to a condition in the homeland that facilitates, justifies, and maintains colonialism—a set of political, economic, social, and cultural institutions, domestic and foreign policies, and public discourses integral to the projection of dominating power in the international arena. I also use the term "metropole" loosely in this essay to refer to the *naichi* in general. While acknowledging differences between the metropolis and other, less urbanized areas, this essay is more concerned with the cultural consciousness of colonialism, which, aided by advanced technologies of communication and consolidated state apparatuses, was widely shared beyond the geographical metropolitan centers.[3]

There is a related critical issue that needs to be addressed before undertaking a close reading of Miyazawa's story. The 1920s are a period often associated with the phrase "Taisho democracy," and indeed the concept of democracy and liberal values were behind an education reform movement that triggered the growth of children's literature. Therefore, in studying 1920s Japan, one is often tasked with resolving the seeming contradiction of the coexistence of democratic ideals and imperialist practices.[4] In order to understand Miyazawa's story in the larger context of Japan's imperialism, I first discuss the unique triadic character of Japanese imperialism that helps us reevaluate the nature of Taisho cosmopolitanism. The reassessment will, in turn, allow us to see that the emergence of children's literature involved much more than the cosmopolitan liberalism of the metropole.

Children's Literature in the Triadic Imperialism of Cosmopolitan Taisho

Just as Orientalism shaped the Western domination of the Orient, Japan's imperialist discourses of civilization since Meiji played an essential role in "dominating, restructuring, and having authority over" the Asian Other.[5] Yet, as succinctly articulated by the well-known national slogan of the Meiji era, "Leaving Asia, Entering Europe" (*datsu-A, nyū-ō*) suggests, Japan formed its imperialist identity not solely in a dyadic relation vis-à-vis the Orient, as in Said's Orientalist model, but instead in a triadic one that involved the powerful Western Other, as well as the Asian Other. As a result, Japan's imperialism was notably complex. In his study of the discourse of savagery in Japanese colonial literature, Robert Tierney dissects this triadic structure. Tierney argues that, locked in the triad as a "colored imperialist," Japan simultaneously admired and feared the West while explicitly mimicking the Western logic of racial superiority for its own operation of the colonies in Asia and elsewhere.[6]

Japan's mimicry went beyond the theory of racial hierarchy. As a semi-colonized nation, a status imposed by the unequal treaties of the Western powers, Meiji Japan was driven to mimic, with both slippage and excess, all aspects of Western civilization in order to become a "reformed, recognizable Other" as determined by the colonial discourse.[7] While Japan's pursuit of Western standards in wide-ranging, everyday matters—from fashion, food, and entertainment to housing, education, and medicine—may not appear to constitute an imperialist project in a strict sense, within the West-Japan-Asia triad, closer identification with Western civilization served as a validation of Japan's superiority over Asia. In this sense, to complicate Homi Bhabha's formulation, the colonial mimicry of Japan was simultaneously a driving force for Japan's own imperialism.

As Japan implemented its modernization program of "Rich Nation, Strong Army" (*fukoku kyōhei*) through rapid industrialization and military build-up after Western models, and as it successfully waged two imperialist wars, against China (1894–1995) and Russia (1904–1905), Japan's colonial mimicry increasingly took on an imperialist tone. By 1911 the unequal treaties had been revised and after World War I, when Japan found itself on the victor's side due to the Anglo-Japanese alliance, Japan's colonial territories expanded to the Micronesian Islands to the south. As the Taisho period (1912–1926) came to a close, Japan's colonial mimicry was increasingly infused with the sentiment that Japan had become an able competitor to Western imperialists.[8] The inclusion of Japan in the Washington Naval Conference (1921–1922), which sought to establish an acceptable balance of armament among the Great Powers themselves, was a clear sign to Japanese that Japan was now an internationally acknowledged member of the imperialist club. Likewise, the indignant sentiment expressed in Japan over the outcome of the conference, which confined Japan to a secondary position behind Britain and the United States, unmistakably indicated Japan's perception of itself as a full-fledged competitor with the other imperialist powers.

This competitive sentiment is noteworthy. In the narrowest sense, imperialism is a policy of domination and exploitation through force, but such a supremacist project toward the Other needs an accommodating view on international relations in general in which the world is only a stage for imperialist rivalry over colonial possessions. Robert Young, for instance, observes, "Imperialism was always a product of, and always addressed to, global power politics: the increased rivalry and militarization of the main European colonial powers [was triggered by] the belated entry of the US, Germany and Japan as imperial powers."[9] In 1916, in his influential book *Imperialism: The Highest Stage of Capitalism*, Lenin identified the increasing competition among the imperialist powers over existing colonies as one of the major features of imperialism, while arguing, as is well known, that imperialism was the latest stage of capitalism dominated by finance capital.[10] Given the triadic international power relations Japan found itself in, Japanese imperialism always involved a degree of colonial mimicry, and for that reason rivalry with the West played a particularly weighty role in Japanese imperialism.

During the Taisho period, the image of Japan as a competent rival that had successfully absorbed Western norms and standards constituted one of the most prominent expressions of Japanese imperialism. The old Meiji slogan was in effect replaced with a sense of satisfaction (perhaps expressed as "Left Asia, Entered Europe"), in which Japan could be seen as being on an equal footing with the West, one among a select few. The emergence of this imperialist consciousness is perceptible in the cultural milieu of Taisho Japan. Japanese culture in the early interwar years is generally known for its urbane and cosmopolitan sensibilities and outlook, often characterized as "liberal" and "democratic." High-profile liberal social movements promoting various issues, such as universal suffrage, women's rights, trade unionism, and Japanese outcast (*burakumin*) liberation, were launched during this period, and Margaret Sanger was invited in 1922 to address the issue of birth control. Imported movies, fashion, food, art, and even schools of thought, as well as everyday goods reflecting the idea of modern life were very popular among the masses. However, consideration of the triadic imperialist context of the time compels us to take a critical second look at the benign celebratory image of metropolitan culture.

This cosmopolitanism was undoubtedly an outcome of changing political and material conditions—from the wider acceptance of Western parliamentary democracy in state governance to the increasing number of imported consumer goods—but its specific Western orientation also revealed Japan's penchant for imperial rivalry. If Japan's imperialist consciousness manifested itself in its insistence on equal footing with other well-armed nations at an international demilitarization conference, its contemporary cosmopolitanism was more about congratulating itself on the attainment of status equal to that of the West (i.e., successful mimicry) than about celebrating different cultures in a liberal egalitarian spirit. While Taisho cosmopolitanism did represent increased engagement with foreign cultures in general, it was also inseparable from the triadic structure of Japanese imperialism.[11]

A body of children's literature emerged from the liberal and cosmopolitan movements that flourished in Taisho Japan. The early modern education system established during Meiji was overtly ideological, particularly in its emphasis on duty to the state—as explicitly laid out in the Imperial Rescript on Education (1890). Remarking on the first generation of children's literature that emerged in the 1880s, as the new modern school system was being put in place in the context of rising Meiji nationalism, Maeda Ai observes that the genre "appeared on the scene as a collaborator fully affirming the state's nationalistic education policies" and attempting to instill in children a sense of duty to sacrifice themselves for the state and the emperor.[12] By the 1920s, new forms of children's culture emerged that were national in scale and consumerist in orientation under new social and economic conditions: the growing interest in education among the budding middle class, for instance, as well as the emergence of vibrant mass media, particularly a magazine industry that marketed its products to specific reader groups— housewives, the working class, children of school age, and so on—all of which were largely literate thanks to compulsory education.[13]

Under these favorable conditions, children's literature became an established field, with a number of writers who exclusively wrote for a young audience, such as Suzuki Miekichi (1882–1936), Ogawa Mimei (1882–1961), Tsubota Jōji (1890–1982), and Niimi Nankichi (1913–1943). Owing much to the advocacy of writer-publisher Suzuki, who edited the influential literary magazine *Red Bird* (*Akai tori*) from 1918 to 1936, children's literature also came to serve as the nucleus of the Liberal Education Movement. This reformist movement aimed to counter a legacy of the heavy-handed state ideology in education and advocated a more nurturing environment for children, through, for instance, art education and songs. In contrast with tales about inspirational and heroic figures common in the Meiji period, the stories that appeared in *Red Bird* were notably less didactic in tone and relied more on fairytale-like diction and imaginary settings. It would be quite appropriate, then, to recognize a liberal and cosmopolitan character in Taisho children's literature, especially in contrast with its Meiji counterpart.

Liberalism and cosmopolitanism, however, do not necessarily preclude imperialist logic. One only needs to remember how liberal intellectuals in the United States have historically supported various oppressive practices overseas and at home. In a systematic and comprehensive study of the stories that appeared in *Red Bird* in its first three years, Andō Kyōko argues that the "cosmopolitan" worldview that emerges from the stories is in fact an imperialist one, which affirms and naturalizes the hierarchy of nations and races according to the logic of Spencerian Social Darwinism.[14] The cultures and peoples from Japan's colonial peripheries are routinely presented as barbaric and inferior, while Japan itself is virtually identified with Western nations as an advanced country that shares little with Asia—conforming to the triadic orientation of Japan's imperialism. What Andō finds in the stories in the liberal *Red Bird* magazine during the mid-Taisho era hardly differs from the Orientalist discourse of "savage" and "civilization" that Kawamura observes in a wide range of materials from popular culture, mostly from the 1930s.[15] To the extent that it offered a discourse of progress and national advancement that largely presumed and affirmed a Western-oriented imperialist international order, children's literature and its "cosmopolitanism" in the 1920s played an important role in shaping the imperialist consciousness of the *naichi*.[16]

Equally significant, while children's literature was certainly a cultural site in which an imperialist worldview was often reinforced, the genre, as with many other cultural forms, also intersected with imperialism in a more critical way. Seen through the lens of modernization theory, which regards the militarist period of the 1930s and 1940s as the aberrant "dark valley" of Japan's presumably ever modernizing (equated with "democratizing") historical trajectory, Taisho would appear to be a period of stability and peace when democratic rule was in place. But, built on a triadic imperialism, Taisho Japan's identity vis-à-vis the world was far from stable. Despite its constant mimetic self-representation as a capable imperial competitor, Japan routinely faced the lamentable reminder, "Almost, but not white." The exclusion of the Japanese-proposed Racial Equality clause from the League of Nations Covenant was one such occasion. Japan's position toward the Asian Other was not necessarily steady, either. Popular, Orientalized cultural representations of non-Japanese Asian Others defined a presumably fundamental gap between Japanese civilization and other Asian countries, yet colonial administration increasingly demanded that its subjects be assimilated into the empire.[17] Japan's imperialist identity was indeed precarious, and was continuously defined and redefined by unstable discourses on the West and the Asian Others.

The instability built into Japan's imperialist consciousness made it possible for critical views of the status quo to emerge. Indeed, many of the social movements in the 1920s demonstrated that the established social arrangement could be reformed, or even built anew, and socialists, communists, and anarchists were especially active in the 1920s, pursuing a society that would not be based on imperialism, capitalism, or hierarchies. While children's literature, too, often tended to reinforce the prevailing imperialist mode of thinking, it also provided a venue in which imperialist logic could be questioned. Akutagawa Ryūnosuke, for instance, who experimented with children's literature in the late 1910s and early 1920s, wrote a satirical version of the famous folktale *The Peach Boy* (*Momotarō*) in 1924 in which the hero Momotarō (clearly marked as a Japanese male) is depicted as an arrogant, bellicose individual who goes on a rampage on Ogres' Island with his disciples, killing peaceful, innocent goblins in order to plunder their treasure. It is difficult not to read this story as an allegorical criticism of Japanese expansionism.[18] While the story's intended readers were probably not schoolchildren, we can see that the genre of the children's story allows space in the *naichi* for a different orientation toward imperialism than the one prevalent in the *Red Bird* stories. Children's literature, particularly through the allegorical mode of storytelling, could register critical assessment of, and resistance to, an imperialist order of things.

Unsettling Settlement

Miyazawa's short story "Wolf Forest, Basket Forest, and Thief Forest" is one of those stories that give form to the critical awareness in the metropole of the geopolitical reality in the colonial periphery. The story was originally published in 1924 in a book billed as a collection of Miyazawa's children's tales, and it certainly has the simple structure and rhythmic repetition expected in that genre. But, while nothing in the text refers to any particular colony or colonial subjects, the folktale-like narrative effectively sketches the basic logic of settler colonialism. Conventional studies of Miyazawa's work tend to rely heavily on hagiographic readings of his biographical data. But in recent years, critics such as Andō, Komori Yōichi, and Nishi Masahiko have challenged such dominant humanist approaches to Miyazawa's work and have called attention to the penetrating observations perceptible in many of his writings on the relations of domination that punctuate human existence.[19] Building on the works of Andō, Komori, and Nishi, I will take a close look at "Wolf Forest, Basket Forest, and Thief Forest" here in order for us to begin asking how the logic of colonialism may figure in the culture of the metropole. The story of an agricultural reclamation is told by a self-identified narrator, yet the text is polyphonic, and one of the multiple voices clearly narrativizes the farmers' encounters with their nonhuman neighbors as a story of colonial settlement. The polyphonic narration destabilizes the sense of harmony expected in children's literature and creates a subtle but unmistakably disquieting tone that unsettles the representation of the farming settlement. In addition, the text's multivoiced depiction of the settlement as a colonial process is greatly assisted by the convoluted hearsay narrative structure, and this distinctive structure also contributes to the anticolonial orientation that emerges from the story.

The story concerns a group of farmers and their families who move to an uncultivated clearing with the intention of settling there and who develop a friendly relationship with the four neighboring forests. They first ask the forests if they can move in, and the forests consent. The farmers then begin to build their community, but at the end of each fall during the first three years of the settlement, the forests create problems by taking items of value from them: Wolf Forest hides the farmers' small children in the first fall; Basket Forest hides the farmers' tools in the second; and Thief Forest hides the millet harvest in the third. Each time, the farmers confront the three forests—which are represented by their supernatural residents: wolves that speak, a basket-weaving "mountain man" with golden eyes, and a giant with black skin and long arms, respectively—and successfully retrieve the missing items. Out of these interactions, a ritual develops in which the farmers offer millet cakes to the forests every year as tokens of goodwill. This plot-line suggests a developing friendship between the farmers and the forests, and indeed, when the last incident is resolved, the narrator declares that "the four forests were all good friends with the farmers."[20]

What lies in the background of the main plot—the developing friendship between the farmers and the forests—is the arduous process of building agricultural plots. As soon as the farmers choose their site for reclamation, both men and women are seen "working frantically" to make the wilderness habitable, presumably in anticipation of the arrival of winter. During the first winter, we read that the small children, confined in what must be a makeshift shelter, cry for warmth, "pressing their frostbitten little hands on their throats."[21] Their cries remind us that, with little protection from the elements, and with no guarantee of a good harvest in the future, agricultural reclamation can be a serious business of human survival. But these harsh conditions, which must have continued after the first year, are not mentioned again. The text even seems to actively efface the difficulties of building a sustainable agricultural settlement, underscoring instead the continuing progress of the reclamation, as evidenced in the crops that "grew tall and green"[22] and the lands that "were now all vegetable fields."[23] The disappearance of the children, farm tools, and millet harvest would have posed serious challenges to the farmers. Yet, in each instance, the disappearance turns out to have been a harmless prank, or even a well-intentioned act on the part of the forests. For the most part, the forests are depicted as friendly, if childish and mischievous, neighbors who generously let the farmers move in, plow fields, and even cut down trees. The farmers, too, appear generally good-natured, laughing heartily at the resolution of each crisis.

With the voice that eschews the realistic depiction of the farmers' actual living conditions, the lively portrayals of friendly forests and farmers, and the overall sense of harmony and resolution eventually achieved, the text seems to comfortably meet the demands of children's literature. But it is difficult to ignore the unsettling feeling that underlies the story. For example, unlike other standard children's tales—perhaps like those that appeared in *Red Bird*—the story ends with a persistent sense that not all is quite well. The text announces, "After [the last disappearance was solved], the four forests were all good friends with the farmers. And they got millet cakes from the farmers at the beginning of winter every year without fail,"[24] but instead of concluding on that happy note, the story ends with the giant rock's resigned remark about the shrinking size of the millet cake offerings in recent years. There are other moments, as well, as when the rather prosaic language suggests subtle discord in spite of the ostensibly happy plot.

Certainly, the small children's cries of "I'm so cold!"[25] which bluntly speak to the inhospitable conditions of reclamation—while attenuated to a degree by the other voice that describes the steady progress of the reclamation—are a source of the somber undercurrent of the story. In addition, the sympathetic words that describe animals and nature may prompt one to identify another source in Miyazawa's well-known Buddhist-influenced view of life: that humans and nature always coexist in a tense relationship between eating and being eaten.[26] However, the subtly unsettling undertone of the story is also brought on by another voice in the text, the language of colonialism, although the colonized take the form of an anthropomorphized nature. The farmers are marked by settler-colonialist terms from the very beginning. Describing the farm tools they carry, the text employs a striking phrase, "all kinds of *weapons* (*buki*) of the mountain and field,"[27] and it even mentions that they were also carrying large *swords* (*katana*).[28] The description of the farmers as armed settlers makes sense if we see the open fields, hills, and forests north of Koiwai Farm as an *inhabited* place, instead of an empty one. "Unclaimed land" is indeed familiar rhetoric of settler colonialism that has justified violent subjugation and occupation of indigenous peoples and lands all over the world, from the North American continent to the Middle East. Discussing so-called reclamation literature (*kaitaku bungaku*), a genre closely aligned with the colonialist state agenda in wartime Japan, and which regularly chronicled with a decidedly heroic touch the struggles of Japanese settler-farmers in the colonies, Kawamura notes a similar unwillingness on the part of farmers to recognize the traces of previous farming activities in their new "unclaimed" land.[29] In Miyazawa's story, the anthropomorphization of nature—a common device in children's literature—serves to help us realize the falsehood of the "empty land" claim in the colonial settlement process. Even if there is no prior human settlement, from the viewpoint of the indigenous plants and animals, the settlers are unwelcome colonial invaders who exploit them for gain and even violently take many lives with their weapons.[30]

Thus, in telling a story about the farmers and their environment, the text speaks in multiple voices. The children cry out about the bleak reality of life in the wilderness; the language of conventional children's literature pushes for a happy story about farmers and their ultimately harmless and amicable forest friends; and yet another voice openly depicts the reclamation as a colonial process. In addition, the uneasy undertone of the story caused by those voices that are incongruent with the norms of children's literature is exacerbated by the coexistence of those voices—what Mikhail Bakhtin might call "a plurality of unmerged consciousness," which allows contradictory ideologies to exist simultaneously.[31] Understood in the context of Japan's triadic imperialism and the ongoing colonial expansion of the 1920s, the text's polyphonic depiction of the settlement process signals a conflicting narrative about colonialism, inviting us to reexamine the story from the perspective of the colonized, that is, the forests. The "thefts," for example, lose their playful aspect and begin to look like hostage-taking and serious acts of sabotage in resistance to the colonial occupation. It becomes clear that the forests' seemingly mischievous and random acts indeed carefully target three vital aspects of colonial life: future labor power (the children); the technology of repression (the farm tools); and agricultural output (the millet).

Likewise, the ritual of offering millet cakes ceases to symbolize the goodwill of the farmers and reveals itself to be their pacification ploy by which the colonial subjects are given arbitrary charity but are kept from acquiring the critical skills and technology needed for self-determination and independence. After the Wolf Forest and Basket Forest began receiving annual millet cake offerings following the peaceful resolution of the first two disappearances, the Thief Forest apparently wanted cakes, too. When it is revealed that the culprit behind the third disappearance (of the harvested millet) is the Thief Forest, Mount Iwate, who intervenes as a sort of deus ex machina, reveals to the farmers, "After all, the Thief Forest just wanted so much to make millet cakes himself. That's why he stole the millet."[32] In spite of this unambiguous revelation about the Thief Forest's desire to learn to make millet cakes himself, the settlers would only give him cakes (peppered with sand at that!) but not the crucial technical know-how, leaving the forest still dependent on them.

The forests are aware of their compromised position and are not without resentment. When the farmers come to the Wolf Forest for the third time, this time in search of the missing millet, we encounter this scene:

> With their weapons of choice in their hands, everyone went to the nearby Wolf Forest first.

The nine wolves were already waiting at the edge of the forest. Upon see-ing the families, *they gave a little chuckle* and said,
"*The millet cakes again.* There's no millet here, we swear. Come back here if nothing turns up elsewhere."[33]

The faintly mocking attitude of the wolves becomes clear when this scene is compared to the farmers' visit one year earlier. Then, the wolves simply said, "No, no. We don't have [the farm tools], we swear. Come back if nothing turns up elsewhere."[34] And they did so with "serious expressions," i.e., with-out a chuckle. The Basket Forest exhibits a similarly impertinent response to the farmers' visit through the mountain man's grinning remark, "Here come the millet cakes. The millet cakes . . ."[35]

Voicing Resistance

The inclusion of a voice that is critical of colonialism in this polyphonic text contributes to what appears to be the story's major inconsistency. In a seeming structural flaw in the story, the "unmerged consciousness" of settler colonialism becomes most perceptible. The story is first presented unam-biguously as a tale about the origins of place names. At the beginning, we encounter the following passage.

When and how the forests came to be, and why they got those odd names—the only one who knows all about it is me, bragged the giant rock in the middle of the Black Hill Forest one day; and he told me this story.[36]

Yet, in the remainder of the story, the text never tells us how indeed those forests were named. Instead, whenever the story seems to come close to re-vealing the origin of a name, it betrays the reader's expectation. When the farmers find their missing children in the first forest, they hear the wolves sing, "In the middle of the Wolf Forest / The fire roars, click-clack / The fire roars click-clack,"[37] suggesting that the forest had been named already. As the farmers search for their farming tools the following year, one of them re-marks, upon finding a large basket in the second forest, "You might think it's just natural to find a basket in the Basket Forest, but we don't know what's inside,"[38] again indicating that the forest already had a name at this point. And when the farmers search for the missing millet harvest in the third year, they walk into the Thief Forest, saying, "The name already smells,"[39] clearly signaling that the dubious name had already been established. It is, of course, possible to read those references as the story's stylized, if oblique, way of telling how those forests were named. After all, a major element of each incident of disappearance does match the name of the respective forest (with the difficult exception of the Black Hill Forest). But even if this were the case, the indirect and roundabout explanations would not sit well with the explicit statement in the opening about what the story is going to be about. In other words, the text never fulfills the promise it makes at the opening.[40]

A tale concerning the origin of a place name is ultimately a record of human intervention in nature, or of colonial settlement activities from the viewpoint of plants and animals.[41] Place names are given only by human beings, whether they are the initial settlers or are those who later assert their legitimacy by renaming the place after displacing the previous residents. The establishment of such legitimacy, or of domination over nature, is what underlies the tales of place-name origins. Those tales, told from the colonizer's position, inevitably present colonial history in a light partial to the logic of the settler. In tales that ultimately commemorate human beings' power over nature, the human violence inherent in the settling process, symbolized in the act of naming, is made invisible, and the voices of nature's inhabitants are silenced.

The seeming structural inconsistency of "Wolf Forest, Basket Forest, and Thief Forest"—a wide gap between what the narrative form (place-name origin tale) promises and what is actually delivered—indeed reveals conflicting ideologies about settler colonialism that coexist in the same text. The place-name origin narrative is a common genre in folktales, and given the frequent overlap between the folktale and children's literature, the opening remark about the origins of the forests' names represents a mode of conventional storytelling. Further, just as popular children's literature of the 1920s generally accepted imperialist norms and standards as the case of *Red Bird* demonstrates, the opening remark also reveals the text's complicity with the normalization of imperialistic sensibility in its deployment of the place-name-origin narrative. In this sense, the remark "The only one who knows all about it is me" is spoken by a voice that articulates the language of the conventional mode of thought that unquestioningly absorbed the logic of settler colonialism. To be sure, the remark is presumably first made by the giant rock, who should be recognized as a colonized subject. But subjectivity is always a site of conflicting discourses, and different, even contradictory, voices can speak through the same agent.

The structural gap of the story emerges because the voice that promises a place-name-origin narrative is countered by another that is motivated to resist and disrupt the naturalized discourse of settler colonialism. The voice of conventional storytelling, uttering remarks such as, "everyone, even the adults, pranced around joyfully"[42] and "the harvest was plentiful,"[43] presents a story of a successful farming settlement, aiming at two objectives: to produce a safe, happy tale presumably appropriate for children; and to move the text's focus away from the power relations in the story that are colonial in nature. However, the counter voice, which articulates an anticolonial consciousness, depicts the encounters between the farmers and the forests in such a way that the moment of naming never arrives. Instead, it slips in the forest names without revealing the precise naming moments, undermining the whole colonialist framework of the story. It is this subversive voice that reveals that "there was a little bit of sand in [the millet cakes]" for the Thief Forest and that "[t]hose millet cakes have become much smaller" in recent years.[44] It is also this voice that hints at the forests' impertinence, as we saw earlier in the Wolf Forest's and the Basket Forest's responses to the farmers' inquiry about the missing millet harvest.[45]

Because of the story's hearsay structure, in which the narrator tells the reader a tale originally told by the giant rock, it seems reasonable to associate the anticolonial voice with the rock's indigenous status. In this regard, it is noteworthy that the Black Hill Forest is the only forest whose name origin remains unexplained in any way. Perhaps such a "credential" gives the giant black rock the authenticity to speak an anticolonial language.[46] However, given the hearsay structure of the tale, we should not forget the role of the narrator. Ultimately, it is this human narrator who obtains the story from the giant black rock and relays it to the reader. Without the narrator's role, the story's voice of resistance would not have the same impact.

After telling the reader about the source of the story at the opening, the narrator largely disappears, resurfacing only twice to directly express sympathy for the giant rock. At the very end of the story, we read that the farmers recover their missing millet harvest from the Thief Forest through Mount Iwate's intervention, and that they make millet cakes for all four forests. This is when the narrator reappears.

> [The farmers] gave the Thief Forest the most [millet cakes]. I heard that there was a little bit of sand in them, but it probably couldn't be helped.
>   After that, the four forests were all good friends with the farmers. And they got millet cakes from the farmers at the beginning of winter every year without fail.
>   Those millet cakes have become much smaller these days. But this, too,

can't be helped, said the giant black rock in the middle of the Black Hill Forest at the end of his story.[47]

At first, the giant rock's resigned remarks on the millet cakes seem to indicate its understanding and even grudging acceptance of the deteriorating quality and decreasing quantity of the edible offering. And the narrator conveys a sense of cheerful resolution and harmony in the second paragraph ("After that, the four forests were all good friends with the farmers"). But, after the pleasant-sounding remark, with which a standard children's story would have ended, the narrator's further revelation about the shrinking size of the millet cakes serves to undermine that very harmony and resolution. The narrator's intervention here is a sympathetic one that reveals a troubling reality for the giant rock and nature in general.

The other time the narrator directly talks to the reader is when the farmers go to the Black Hill Forest in search of the missing millet. The narrator first describes how the forest answered the farmers' inquiry.

> "At dawn today I saw big black feet flying in the sky to the north. Go further north," [replied the Black Hill Forest.] I was told that the forest said nothing about millet cakes. And I wholeheartedly think that was indeed the case. Because, after hearing this story from the forest, I gathered all my copper coins—7 sen in all—and gave them to him as my thank you gift; but he would not accept them. That's how upright this forest was.[48]

Here the narrator actively vouches for the integrity of the giant rock, giving its story credence along the way.[49]

These sympathetic and respectful representations of the giant rock resonate with the narrator's speech act toward the rock, which can be aptly described as supportive. For instance, statements such as, "And it appeared that buckwheat and barnyard grass were planted," which suggest a direct observation of the farmers' activities, remind the reader that the narrator is merely retelling the story originally given by the giant rock.[50] This subtle interruption gives the rock narrative authority while placing the narrator in a position supportive of the indigenous storyteller's speech. Perhaps most revealing is the opening and ending, where the giant rock's remarks are presented. All the statements made by the characters in the story are clearly indicated by quotation marks, and there is no ambiguity as to who is speaking. However, the giant rock's remarks at the beginning and the end, "When and how the forests came to be" and "Those millet cakes have become much smaller," are indirect quotations. Because of the lack of visual markers, and because of the Japanese syntax of the quotation, which identifies the speaker after the statement (the translation in this chapter retains the word order in the original), the giant rock's remarks first appear to be attributed to the narrator, before the reader finally realizes mid-sentence who is actually speaking. Through the momentarily misidentified voice, which opens and concludes the story, the narrator lends speaking authority to the giant rock. At the end of the story, indeed, the narrator's concern about the shrinking millet cakes becomes palpable, creating the unsettling undertone previously discussed. When these textual details are examined, what the relationship between the narrator and the giant rock suggests is a form of equitable anti-colonial alliance between the colonized and the metropolitan subjects.

The hearsay narrative structure of the story gives the colonized a voice, but whether that voice effectively reaches the reader depends on the narrator-mediator, who, after all, belongs to the human family. In Miyazawa's story, the narrator exhibits remarkable fidelity to the giant rock, even talking directly to the reader about the uprightness of the rock, in addition to intervening at the end to undercut the conventional genteel conclusion. Due largely to the sympathetic narrator's intervention, the hearsay structure of the story delivers the voice of the colonized more fruitfully than would a direct address. And because of the blurred boundary between the giant rock's and the narrator's voices, the text enables the colonized subject to speak without a sanctimonious metropolitan subject speaking for him. The existence of the human narrator who serves as a supportive spokesperson for, and assures the integrity of, the colonized not only destabilizes the colonial order of things but also suggests the possibility of, if not the necessity of, anticolonial solidarity within the metropole for the liberation of the colonized.

Conclusion

Restructuring an existing story from a different perspective can be powerfully destabilizing, and even subversive. The opening of our synopsis of this tale framed the story from the viewpoint of the farmers: "The story concerns a group of farmers and their families who move to an uncultivated clearing with the intention of settling there and who develop a friendly relationship with the four neighboring forests." From the position of the forests, however, it should have been: "The story concerns four forests who engage in a difficult, and ultimately unsuccessful, anticolonial struggle against a group of armed settlers who moved in nearby." Given the textual hints throughout, the text indeed seems to invite us to adopt a destabilizing perspective. The unsettling feeling of "Wolf Forest, Basket Forest, and Thief Forest" comes not only from the bits of information that obliquely point to the somber reality of colonial dominance over nature, but also from the voice of resistance, most prominently embodied in the narrative format, that challenges the established colonial order and imperial consciousness in the metropole.

"Wolf Forest, Basket Forest, and Thief Forest" suggests that Japanese colonialism's impact on the 1920s *naichi* was not limited to the increased visibility of the exotic Other in cultural expressions. In the story, colonialism was understood on a more conceptual level as a powerful force that organized the basic structure of everyday life and, in this case, was also presented by a critical voice. The established genre of children's literature, whose narrative conventions include anthropomorphization of nature, is instrumental in the story's effective portrayal of colonialism, as well as in the insertion of a critical counter-voice. As Maeda's earlier comment about the ideological thrust in Meiji children's literature reminds us, the genre developed alongside the emergence of the Japanese nation-state. By the 1920s, the construction of the modern nation-state had led to an established national education system, a literate public, and a vibrant publishing industry—all essential ingredients of a metropolitan culture that fostered the growth of children's literature. As long as children's literature is rooted in urban middle-class life, a nationalist educational agenda, and the system of capitalist mass production and consumption, "Wolf Forest, Basket Forest, and Thief Forest," an appropriation of the children's literature genre, remains as a little story of settler colonialism that reveals substantial critical engagement with imperialism by the culture of the metropole.

Notes

I would like to thank Dustin Leavitt, Ted Pearson, Sheila Lloyd, and Priya Jha for their close reading and editing help, not to mention their camaraderie I acutely needed. Michele Mason and Helen Lee helped me, first, reconfigure my original project, then, improve my argument. Adrienne Hurley, then at the University of Iowa, provided an opportunity to present an early version of this essay. I thank her students for their insightful and earnest comments. My students at the University of Redlands have helped me carefully craft my argument. My gratitude also goes to Komori Yōichi, who let me sit in on his lectures on Miyazawa, planting a seed while I was unaware.

An earlier English translation of the story appears as "Wolf Forest, Basket Forest, Thief Forest," in Karen Colligan-Taylor, *The Emergence of Environmental Literature in Japan* (New York: Garland, 1990), 242–49. The present translation attempts to retain the story's aspects that are in dialog with Japan's imperial consciousness.

1. Recent examples include John Marriott, *The Other Empire: Metropolis, India and Progress in the Colonial Imagination* (Manchester, UK: Manchester University Press, 2003), and Catherine Hall and Sonya O. Rose, eds., *At Home with the Empire: Metropolitan Culture and the Imperial World* (Cambridge, UK: Cambridge University Press, 2006).

2. See the Introduction of this volume.

3. While Miyazawa was primarily active in the northeastern prefecture of Iwate, I treat his work as part of the larger *naichi* culture. For a discussion of the significance of Miyazawa's spatially marginal position, see Hoyt Long, *On Uneven Ground: Miyazawa Kenji and the Making of Place in Modern Japan* (Stanford: Stanford University Press, 2011).

4. Andrew Gordon has proposed the concept of "imperial democracy," instead of "Taisho democracy," in his *Labor and Imperial Democracy in Prewar Japan* (Berkeley: University of California Press, 1991). Miriam Silverberg's term "consumer-subject," as opposed to "imperial subject," also captures the problematic coexistence of democratic façade and imperialistic practices. Miriam Silverberg, *Erotic Grotesque Nonsense: The Mass Culture of Japanese Modern Times* (Berkeley: University of California Press, 2006).

5. Edward Said, *Orientalism* (New York: Vintage, 1979), 3.

6. Robert Tierney, *Tropics of Savagery: The Culture of Japanese Empire in Comparative Frame* (Berkeley: University of California Press, 2010), 14–28.

7. Homi Bhabha, *The Location of Culture* (New York: Routledge, 1994), 122.

8. The naturalization of imperialist rivalry in Japanese consciousness was already discernible in the term "first-rate nation" (*ittōkoku*), which became popular after the Russo-Japanese War (1904–1905). In the opening of Natsume Sōseki's *Sanshirō* (1908), for instance, upon seeing a few Westerners, the eccentric teacher Hirota notes, "We can beat the Russians, we can become a 'first-class power' (*ittōkoku*), but it doesn't make any difference. We still have the same faces, the same feeble little bodies." Hirota's remark shocks the protagonist Sanshirō precisely because it directly contradicts the accepted belief in Japan's competence in the ruthless imperialist world order assumed in the term "first-rate nation." Natsume Sōseki, *Sanshirō: A Novel*, trans. Jay Rubin (New York: Penguin, 2009), 15.

9. Robert Young, *Postcolonialism: An Historical Introduction* (Malden, MA: Blackwell, 2001), 28. See also Jürgen Osterhammel, *Colonialism: A Theoretical Overview*, trans. Shelley Frisch (Princeton, NJ: Markus Weiner Publishers, 1997), 21–22.

10. V. I. Lenin, *Imperialism: The Highest Stage of Capitalism* (New York: International Publishers, 1939). See also W. G. Beasley, *Japanese Imperialism, 1894–1945* (Oxford: Clarendon, 1987), 2–3. Discussing the relationship between modernism and

imperialism, Fredric Jameson notes that until the interwar years, "the word 'imperialism' designate[d], not the relationship of metropolis to colony, but rather the rivalry of the various imperial and metropolitan nation-states among themselves." Fredric Jameson, "Modernism and Imperialism," in Terry Eagleton et al., *Nationalism, Colonialism, and Literature* (Minneapolis: University of Minnesota Press, 1990), 47.

11. The decidedly benign perception of Taisho cosmopolitanism today is perhaps not a coincidence. Commenting on the lack of critical examination of the accepted image of cosmopolitan Taisho, Bruce Cumings observes that "the benign image corresponds to a very benign Japan, undercutting no one's exports and markets and acquiescing in the 1920s international system that defined America, England, and Japan in a perfect trilateral formula: 5:5:3 (the ratio of naval ships in the Pacific, but it can stand for everything else)." Bruce Cumings, "Archeology, Descent, Emergence: Japan in British/American Hegemony, 1900–1950," in *Japan in the World*, eds. Masao Miyoshi and H. D. Harootunian (Durham, NC: Duke University Press, 1993), 100.

12. Maeda Ai, *Text and the City: Essays on Japanese Modernity*, ed. James Fujii (Durham, NC: Duke University Press, 2004), 112.

13. The compulsory education system began in the early 1870s, and by the 1920s the vast majority of Japanese children were receiving six years of grade school education.

14. Andō Kyōko, *Miyazawa Kenji: "Chikara" no kōzō* (Miyazawa Kenji: the Structure of "Power") (Tokyo: Chōbunsha, 1996).

15. For a brief analysis of *Red Bird*, see also Tierney, *Tropics of Savagery*, 56–57.

16. For a discussion of childhood as a modern discursive construct, see Karatani Kōjin, *Origins of Modern Japanese Literature*, trans. Brett de Bary (Durham, NC: Duke University Press, 1993), 114–35.

17. Leo T. S. Ching, *Becoming "Japanese": Colonial Taiwan and the Politics of Identity Formation* (Berkeley: University of California Press, 2001).

18. For a discussion of Akutagawa's story as a satire, see Tierney, *Tropics of Savagery*, 136–43.

19. Andō, *Miyazawa Kenji*, Komori Yōichi, *Saishin Miyazawa Kenji kōgi* (The Latest Lectures on Miyazawa Kenji) (Tokyo: Asahi shinbun, 1996), and Nishi Masahiko, *Mori no gerira Miyazawa Kenji* (Miyazawa Kenji, The Guerrilla in the Woods) (Tokyo: Iwanami shoten, 1997).

20. Miyazawa Kenji, "Oinomori to zarumori, nusutomori" (Wolf Forest, Basket Forest, and Thief Forest), in *Kōhon Miyazawa Kenji zenshū* (Complete works of Miyazawa Kenji with various versions of texts) (Tokyo: Chikuma shobō, 1974), vol. 11: 27.

21. Ibid., 21.

22. Ibid., 23.

23. Ibid., 25.

24. Ibid., 27.

25. Ibid., 21.

26. John Bestor, for instance, describes one of Miyazawa's recurring themes as follows: "The poet stands . . . aware of himself as a single creature among countless

living creatures of countless different species, whose tragedy it is to live by preying on each other." Miyazawa Kenji, *Once and Forever: The Tales of Kenji Miyazawa*, trans. John Bestor (Tokyo: Kodansha International, 1993), x.

27. Miyazawa, "Wolf Forest," 19 (emphasis added).

28. See Komori, *Saishin*, 41.

29. Kawamura, *Ikyō no Shōwa bungaku* (Showa Literature of the Strange Homeland) (Tokyo: Iwanami shoten, 1990), 32–33.

30. See Komori, *Saishin*, 41–43.

31. Mikhail Bakhtin, *Problems of Dostoevsky's Poetics*, ed. and trans. Caryl Emerson (Minneapolis: University of Minnesota Press, 1984), 26.

32. Miyazawa, "Wolf Forest," 27.

33. Ibid., 25 (emphasis added).

34. Ibid., 24.

35. Ibid., 25.

36. Ibid., 19.

37. Ibid., 22.

38. Ibid., 24.

39. Ibid., 26.

40. It should be noted here that Miyazawa is well known for his meticulous, multiple revisions of his manuscripts, often executed in pens of different colors. Given such scrupulous attention to the text, it would be difficult to argue that the discrepancy is simply Miyazawa's oversight.

41. See Komori, *Saishin*, 37–38.

42. Miyazawa, "Wolf Forest," 21.

43. Ibid., 23.

44. Ibid., 27

45. While examining "Wolf Forest, Basket Forest, and Thief Forest" through a framework different from the present essay's—as a story of ecology rooted in the necessary negotiation between the wild and the civilized—Gregory Golley calls the work "a geographical biography," a tale "*told by the land itself*" (italics in the original). *When Our Eyes No Longer See: Realism, Science, and Ecology in Japanese Literary Modernism* (Cambridge, MA: Harvard University Asia Center, 2008), 228. The implications of Golley's study, which sees the farmers' settlement as the beginning of civilization, for our inquiry are rather heavy: Is human settlement, or civilization, itself a form of colonialism?

46. Komori suggests that the tale told by the giant rock, which remains nameless, delivers the voice of nature resisting human control. *Saishin*, 38.

47. Miyazawa, "Wolf Forest," 27.

48. Ibid., 26.

49. It should be noted that the narrator makes its point by stressing the fact that the rock/forest refused the offer of money for telling the story. What is upheld by the refusal is the act of speaking, or telling of a history, as something not to be commodified.

50. Miyazawa, "Wolf Forest," 21.

CHAPTER SEVEN

TEXT

Manchu Girl

KOIZUMI KIKUE

CONTEXT

Manchuria

CRITIQUE

Imperializing Motherhood: The Education of a "Manchu Girl" in Colonial Manchuria

KIMBERLY T. KONO

A CCOMPANYING her army officer husband to Manchuria in early June 1935, Koizumi Kikue lived in Mukden (now Shenyang) and later Shinkyō (now Changchun) until 1938. Little is known of her personal life, but the works Koizumi published during the war reveal a woman of varied interests. After *Manchu Girl* (*Manshūjin no shōjo*, 1938), featured in this chapter, Koizumi wrote *Revealing Women's History* (*Joseishi kaiken*, 1941)— an examination of the roles women played in Japanese history. She also engaged contemporary political debates in *The East Asia League and People of the Showa Era* (*Tōa renmei to Shōwa no tami*, 1940), which advocated economic and military cooperation among Japan, China, and Manchuria. Deeply influenced by Nichiren Buddhism, Koizumi also penned *What Are the Doctrines of Nichiren Priests?* (*Nichiren shōnin no kyōgi to wa donna monoka*, 1941) and *Tales of the Lotus Sutra* (*Hokekyō monogatari*, 1944).

Koizumi's *Manchu Girl* is based on letters she sent to a friend in Tokyo during her stay in colonial Manchuria, which coincided with a period of heightened anti-Japanese sentiment and resistance, particularly following the Marco Polo Bridge Incident in July 1937. In this narrative, "Manchu" maid Guiyu learns the Japanese language and customs under Koizumi's tutelage and not only changes her critical attitude toward Japanese but eventually wants to "become Japanese." Early sections of the work, translated here, describe the linguistic, cultural, and ideological barriers that complicate their developing relationship. At the end of the text, Koizumi relates that their relationship has deepened to the point that both she and Guiyu refer to her as Guiyu's "Japanese mother" (*naichi no okāsan*).

Manchu Girl

KOIZUMI KIKUE

TRANSLATION BY KIMBERLY T. KONO

"I have decided to buy a young Chinese girl."

When my husband spoke those words, I was shocked. He then explained that a co-worker who was going to be transferred to Harbin wanted to pass on to us the fourteen-year-old girl that he had bought from rural Andong three months ago.

"Did you just say that he 'bought' her?" I exclaimed in surprise.

We discussed the details such as how much to pay each year within a three-year contract. Although it is rare nowadays, there are people in Manchuria who sell their children. Of course, you may think that as a Japanese subject who silently allows the practice of daughters being sold off as mistresses, I am hardly one to talk. And yet, this point is brought home by the fact that, here in Manchuria until recently, people walked along the streets with infants in baskets hanging at each end of a pole and tried to sell them. The year before last, along Kasuga Street, the main thoroughfare in Mukden, a cute boy around six years of age sat wearing a "Kid for Sale" sign that explained in detail why he had to be sold for 100 yuan. When purchased, the boy would have worked as a servant for the rest of his life. With those images in mind, I interpreted my husband's utterance—*kattekita*—as meaning "bought." However, upon closer consideration, I realized that the word *karitekita* (rented) is rendered *kattekita* in certain dialects, and perhaps such phrasing was meant to imply hiring the girl. Nevertheless, I was shocked to hear such words.

Some time before our conversation, I had hired a twenty-one-year-old Manchu woman. Three years earlier, she had married her nineteen-year-old husband, who had left her in the countryside and gone to Mukden to work as an errand boy in a government office. The young woman had never encountered a Japanese before and did not understand a word of the Japanese language. She said she had never gone to school. Even so, because I was exhausted from stoking the fireplace and taking care of the housework by myself every day, I hired her. I thought that since she didn't understand Japanese, I would try to learn Manchu. Because I had to rely on books and physical gestures in my attempts to communicate, this was a period when I sometimes felt like bursting into laughter. Yet, I started to feel as if I would be better off without any household help. It would have been easier if she had been literate in Chinese, but we could not even communicate by writing Chinese characters. Also, since my husband and I were the first Japanese she had ever met, she had no way of understanding our lifestyle. I could tolerate her stepping into the entryway with her indoor slippers, but she would do things like spit and blow her nose into the kitchen sink, the bathtub, wherever she happened to be. She would pull out the rice chest to sit on it. And because she could not even distinguish between a sponge and a mop, I was about to have a nervous breakdown and she—Suishi was her name—she grew increasingly silent at each reprimand. In cases where she would do things like cut corners while mopping the floor or take off the lid while cooking rice, I carefully and patiently taught her the correct methods. As for her unsanitary behavior, however, I could not tolerate any of it. For Suishi, working here must have been like a silent religious practice, an intensely painful time because she could not express her feelings or thoughts.

During our time together, she gradually came to understand my strange attempts to speak Manchu, and in the evenings with a Japanese-Manchu dictionary between us, we even began to have comical conversations. Yet, she increasingly took on a strange attitude close to hysteria and inexplicably would pick quarrels with me. As a result, by the eighth day, I sent her home. I realized that I too had felt anxious, because afterward I thought to myself "At last!" I felt utterly exhausted.

Not one month had passed since this experience with Suishi. So, when my husband mentioned a new girl, I told him, "I have had enough of hiring Manchus when I don't even understand the Manchu language." Upon hearing these words, he gave me a surprised look and said, "This one has attended high school. While working for Mr. O, who is quite skilled at Manchu, she has become familiar with the Japanese lifestyle. He said that she's got a good head on her shoulders and most important, unlike the other maid, she is still a child. I think that our efforts will have a great effect upon her. By taking care of this child and helping her to understand the proper viewpoints of Japanese through our way of living, isn't this working for goodwill between Japanese and Manchu and the practice of what you call 'faith'?"

After hearing him out, I was speechless and bowed my head. I was truly ashamed of myself.

In this way, Li Guiyu came to our home on November 27, 1936. Due to these initial conditions, my feelings toward this young girl were resolute, something much more than the usual feelings toward a Japanese maid. I understood quite well that the work was too much for someone like me, a mere housewife awkward with even the fundamentals of everyday life. Yet, I vowed to present myself as I am and convey to this child the faith of an average Japanese housewife. I would try to offer my immature faith without forcibly demanding success, or rigidly glossing over the differences in customs and language.

Guiyu was a cute young girl. Since July she had spent five months at the O household, and had taken care of their two- and three-year-old daughters. When O brought her to our home for an introduction and said it was her "debut," Guiyu wore Japanese clothing and looked exactly like a Japanese. O said, "She learned the basics of Japanese in high school, and can write all her *katakana*. Her mother is a Christian employed by the church and is a solid, reliable person, so this girl is also bright and remembers what she has been taught." Sitting properly next to O, she bowed politely and said in Japanese, "Thank you very much," when I offered her teacakes. Her excellent manners made it difficult to believe that she had spent all of her time taking care of the children. Mr. O only complained that she tried to do everything on her own because she was quite stubborn.

On the evening that Guiyu finally came down the snow-covered path to our home, she wore a small thin Manchu dress. When our former maid Suishi lived with us, she prepared and ate her food on her own. In contrast, I was relieved to hear that Guiyu ate Japanese food. But on the first night that she arrived, she cried and refused to touch the meal that I cooked for her. After fretting over what to do, I tried to make a fried dumpling with wheat flour by drawing upon my memory of watching others prepare this traditional Chinese dish. I served it to her saying, "I'm not very good at cooking and probably can't make something as delicious as your mother's food, but please try a little."

She sobbed, saying in broken Japanese "My mother no prepare such food for me. We not even have one grain of wheat flour. My mother just eat sorghum. We not even eat a grain of rice. My mother's hands, thin. Aiya! Father small too. He's always ill. Japanese all eat rice. Japanese all fat. Big. Japanese forty or fifty years of age, not old. My father fifty, very very old. My mother ate little sorghum. Church gave mother four yen a month. Father went to mountain, boss give him two yen per month. We no eat rice with meals."

Soon thereafter, she said, "Madam. Japanese people, many don't know, rice delicious. Aiya. Rice IS delicious. Rice smells good. In the beginning, when I ate rice and sweets, and then everything, I thought of my father, mother, older sister, and younger brother."

She cried when she first arrived at our home because she was saddened by thoughts of her parents. In the same way that Koreans add the phrase "Aigo" in speech, Manchus readily say "Aiya." They say it at times when Japanese say "Ara ma" or when one says "Ahhh" in admiration. I can see the influence of her mother in each instance of Guiyu's honesty, her filial behavior, and her determination to improve herself. I can see the influence of her mother's mother, who was the first family member to convert to Christianity. When Guiyu did not have any tasks at hand, she would read the Bible in her room. I have never seen her pray, however.

Her home was in a rural town called Huanren. Trains do not yet pass through this town, which is in the heart of the mountains on the eastern side of the Andong-Mukden line. It is said that the area around Huanren, Donghua, and Kuandian is a region with many rebels, but I can't imagine what sort of place it must be. In that small town, there has been a church for over thirty years, and an instructor (a priest, perhaps?) travels between churches in Donghua and Kuandian and educates the citizens. Guiyu wrote on a piece of paper that the priest was a person from Tankoku and showed it to me. Certain Chinese characters are used to signify Germany, but where is this country that Guiyu calls "Tankoku"? When I showed her the globe, she pointed to Belgium and said "I think it is here." She also explained that the instructor had a frightening expression with which he gazed at everyone. "If you tell lies, smoke opium, or steal, you will become a devil after you die." Hearing this, Guiyu was afraid.

These Christian beliefs and the anti-Japanese sentiment she had learned in school had both become fixed in her mind. Sometimes it was clear how these beliefs overlapped. As a result, I felt that I must always directly confront the strong ethnic consciousness that had been cultivated in her.

Gradually, she came to understand the workings of the household, and by the end of the year, when she grew accustomed to her chores, I began to teach her how to knit socks. In the afternoons, winding balls of yarn, we racked our brains and awkwardly tried to speak to each other. As the days passed, Guiyu, who had already taken her first steps in learning the Japanese language, became quite skillful in conversing in Japanese. My husband frequently traveled to the countryside on military expeditions, and I also went out on occasion to do things like visit wounded soldiers, welcome the returning troops, and mourn the deaths of those killed in action. Consequently, such activities naturally became topics of conversation. Also, because she came from the Huanren region, where there were many rebels, and I wanted to know her feelings and the attitude of the local community toward the Japanese army, there were times where I consciously shifted the conversation toward these topics.

The term "traveling bandits" refers to, well, spies who informed the rebels about the movements of the suppressing Japanese forces. In these parts, one often hears the phrase "separation of the rebels and people" but to the extent that such efforts must be made, there seems to have been no distinction between rebels and good people. If a person is starving, he will join the rebel army. And if he doesn't profit as expected, he will return to being a farmer. Others are coerced into joining the bandits or drawn by greed, and there are probably those who take on the role of a spy without any difficulty. But even if a person does something bad, all his misdoings are erased once he is punished. Since neither the person himself nor his acquaintances have problems with this practice due to their cultural background, someone who had been a bandit one day could go work in the fields the following day, and everyone would pretend not to know. The work of subduing the bandits is an extraordinary challenge, or so I have heard.

Some time ago, I read a newspaper article about a noble-looking young man about twenty years old who walked through the town of Andong holding a cat in his arms. When a sensitive official caught and interrogated him, it turned out the young man was the deputy leader of the rebels and had come to survey the condition of the Japanese subduing forces. This winter, while we were staying at a dormitory in Mukden, we were surprised by the sound of five or six gunshots in the middle of the night. The next day I heard that rebels had appeared at a nearby Manchu home and set the house on fire. Since Mukden is just like a bustling, miniature version of Osaka, it seemed strange and I was skeptical, but I had no idea about how to find out the true identity of the rebels. For the first six months we were in Manchuria, I was troubled at my inability to figure out who the rebels were. But recently, I have come to understand that there are many types of rebels. The rebels who suddenly interrupted my dreams with gunshots in Mukden are like thieves in Japan. A few of those who are generally called former rebels and have been caught by the Japanese military or left for other reasons, disappeared into the cities. Some became cooks at dormitories and for half a year or so hid from the public eye. Others became rickshaw drivers or chauffeurs, but in reality they were the violent leaders of the rebel groups.

One rebel leader, who posed as a lady, was arrested in the middle of the city, surprising everyone. However, compared with the infiltration of thieves and other extremists through every part of Japan, the presence of rebels throughout the cities is not surprising in the least.

I'm sure you've heard of Fujiwara Yoshie's record, "Subdue the Rebels." One lyric notes, "The mud that seems to be everywhere." The words were written by the poet Yaginuma Takeo, who grew up in Manchuria and actually hid in the muddy swamps near the Xing'anling Mountains with Japanese troops. For those of us who live in Manchuria and are affected by the hardships of the imperial army, hearing that record causes tears to roll down our cheeks. At the point in the song that says, "No food for three days, two nights, perhaps it is the cold of a night of hunger," anyone in the Ginza district in Tokyo must perceive these to be the events of a faraway dream. For myself and others born in Tokyo, pleasant images of our homeland sometimes appear to us, and we can see the bright eyes of cheerful and carefree young men and women amidst the various crowds of the Ginza. To me, they all are as innocent as babies.

And yet, when I think that there are natural limits to that carefree attitude, I am somehow saddened. "The soldiers have returned from the battlefront!" shouted children gripping the *hinomaru* flags of Japan as they rushed to the front of the nearby military office. On that day, I too rushed behind them, my heart filled with emotion. The soldiers, their skins tanned to deep brown, were wearing their soiled uniforms with pride. When I saw them marching in time to a bugler, I felt I could hear the formless sound of the footsteps of the many young people who were not of this world anymore. Moved by the thought of the war dead, I screamed with all my heart, "Thank you. Thank you for your efforts!" The young lieutenants and other officers grew beards like the samurai Katō Kiyomasa and laughed that they were souvenirs from their military service. After their laughter, an air of refinement seemed to linger. When I think that around that same time of year, other young people were in college or caught up in dancing, those carefree attitudes weighed heavy on my heart. Even so, Japan will grow larger and take on a new shape. Those of us in Manchuria believe that we should not force these hardships onto them. And knowing that those in Japan have such luxuries would be a comfort to those living on the deadlocked frontlines.

. . .

Since the China Incident, the world has been quickly transformed. Today while it is appropriate for someone to sing "Subdue the Rebels" in the middle of the Ginza district in Tokyo, other things weigh down the hearts of those going off to war. One can hear on the radio the intense support of the Tokyo residents on the home front! Someone said that these days, the people coming to observe Manchuria would be surprised at how quiet it seems compared to Japan. As I reflect back on the past years, I have many different thoughts and emotions.

Manchuria is a foreign country. Moreover, it is a young, newborn nation. It must develop into the bond that links Japan and China together. The more challenges Japan faces in Manchuria, the more it uses all of its passion and strength to work for the complete construction of Manchuria. Aren't they showing respect for the Emperor as well as love for the motherland? Even during the period before the China Incident when Tokyo was radiant, here in Manchuria the tension of the frontline became the basis for building "the imperial way, the peaceful land." Until the day that Japan, Manchuria, and China become unified, until true peace is established in East Asia, even if Manchuria seems tranquil, the importance of Manchuria as the frontline in this effort and the duty of Japanese who work in Manchuria will not change. Even for an unimportant person like myself, when the North China Incident expanded into the Sino-Japanese Incident, and then transformed into the China Incident, I felt Japanese should join our spirits with the people of Manchuria, and we all should open up our hearts to each other.[1] It is my strong belief that we must begin to support each other in a much deeper and more solid manner.

However, forging such bonds is difficult. I could bring up young Guiyu! Considering even that impulse, I briefly became exhausted. I thought I couldn't do it. There were two or three nights when I was unable to sleep because I was immersed in thought. There were days when I prayed in front of the Buddhist altar and could do nothing but cry. There were times when I lost all confidence; I was told that my way of doing things was bad, and nodded my head in agreement. I was tormented by these thoughts for many days. Told that my ideals were too high, I could not respond. Those who know it is in my nature to go to the limits of all my strength can certainly imagine how I was at that time. But, please do not worry. Nowadays, I am filled with the exaltation that comes after such pain. I have traversed a high peak. My heart that moves on the waves of emotion has arrived at a place where I have the leisure to look back thankfully and see that I was merely an ordinary person among other ordinary people. Being ordinary actually enabled me to do the difficult work of assimilating a Manchu; I could convey the true feelings of the heartfelt friendship of Japanese who tried to embody the ideals of nation-building. But our destination is still far ahead, and there are many peaks we must climb. Although the end is still far, it has become clear that my desire to assimilate Manchu people to Japanese ideals would be challenging but not impossible. I won't become disappointed or exhausted like the last time.

. . .

Let's return to my story and continue on.

I knew that Guiyu had lived in and around Huanren, Donghua, and Kuandian in Andong province where many rebel groups with especially strong leaders were reputed to be hiding out. One day, when I spoke of the ideological rebels (Communists), she said "They are not rebels." I was surprised by her solemn interjection. When I inquired what they were and she responded, "They are patriotic troops," I was startled. I'm embarrassed to say this but my hand began to tremble in fear. I then asked her to explain how to differentiate them from the rebels, and why they were patriotic troops. Guiyu replied, taking a firm, and what I would even call proud, attitude.

"The rebels steal things from good people. They wear dirty clothing and don't have good guns. The patriotic troops don't steal from good people. They even give money to the poor. They have splendid uniforms like the Japanese army. They also have guns. They are not rebels."

This conversation occurred about a month after she had come to live with us. I became so frightened that I considered dismissing her. However, to do so would be a mere stopgap, like putting a lid on something giving off a foul odor. On the one hand, I was overflowing with the passionate feeling that, without making an imperial subject of this one girl, how could I as a Japanese subject reciprocate the precious trust of the Emperor? It is said that when one leaf falls, we anticipate the approach of autumn. Yet, on the other hand, my mind cries out, doesn't this young girl's proud attitude signify the existence of solid roots? If she were a spy, I wondered, could she change from poison into medicine? I could not deter my single-minded wish to affect this child and respond to the influences that caused her to feel this way. While I gazed at my trembling hands, I reminded myself that I must not be hasty. Every day after that, we spoke of such things as the bandits, the significance of building Manchuria, and the existence of countries trying to prevent the growth of Manchuria. We also discussed the source of the advanced weapons that the ideological troops possessed and what their source is demanding in return for that supply. During one of our talks, Guiyu, smiling meaningfully, said, "But Manchuria, just three years old. China, very old." When we spoke of such things, this cute young girl's eyes filled with doubt, and she became silent. She transformed into a cool, hard being who, like a human made out of steel, would rebuff one's advances. Her behavior puzzled me, and later on that night I secretly told my husband that this kind of child could become a member of the anti-Japanese female military.

Another time, she stood in front of a map of East Asia hanging on the wall, and laughing, said, "Aiya, Japan so small!" Her words made me want to say, "You little brat!" This matter was different from others. When I thought my country was being laughed at, my competitive spirit appeared on my flushed cheeks. I tried to hold back and wait until the appropriate moment instead of giving in to the temptation of a temporary victory. With feelings of regret sinking into my flesh and bones, I felt even more determined to carry out my intentions until the very end.

Gradually, she became used to her daily chores of cleaning the house, doing the laundry, and cooking. Yet, in terms of spiritual beliefs, as she grew increasingly familiar with me, she exposed her true character, the seeds of which lay in her anti-Japanese education. Because she was smart, she bombarded me with questions. However, since she asked without hesitation, no matter how frank the question, I was happy that I had succeeded in taking the first steps to becoming closer. Nevertheless, because Guiyu was the kind of person who would grow up and fight for a cause and I am a person who is a devout believer in the "Faith" sect of Nichiren Buddhism, we were able to have conversations that were like serious competitions where sparks flew from our hearts. If we had limited our discussions to things like cleaning and cooking, I would have only come to see her as an adorable young Manchu girl. If she were the type of girl who did not ask direct questions, I too would not have made an effort to speak about anything. I find that thought to be quite frightening. The coolies filling up city streets, the children clad in tatters—I was unable to overlook these things even for a moment. In addition to the surprising words that came out of her innocent mouth, the thoughts behind those words, and her manner which absorbed, like blotting paper, all the things that Japanese say and do, her observations of the contradictions between Japanese words and deeds and her unsparing critiques made me believe completely that each and every Japanese who comes to Manchuria must live according to the purely divine spirit that long ago accomplished the great feat of founding our nation. I told my friends as many of these ideas as I could. We must watch our speech and our actions, as if each Japanese lived in a crystal palace, because even a young girl—no matter how ignorant she may seem—pays attention to every action of the Japanese. What burdens do those who work for the building of Manchuria immediately face? Many Japanese who came simply to make a profit will hinder the "good work" of others. All this became clear to me.

Because Guiyu was to a certain extent faithful to her anti-Japanese education, she was a difficult child in terms of ideology. But, due to the goodness that she gained from her Christian mother, Guiyu felt ashamed of the belief that thievery was common among Manchu. Also, because she was just a child, her own budding faith had not been damaged through contact with the faith of others. I have heard that the faith of humanity does not get through to the Manchu and Chinese peoples who suffered corrupt politics for hundreds of years. But this child has a pure heart. I believe that her mother's religion prevented the corruption of Guiyu.

I thought about cultivating her innocence and helping her to experience the sincere faith of Japanese. At first, before and after attending memorial ceremonies, I began discussing the loyal and patriotic actions of those who died in battle. It wasn't as though I planned such topics beforehand and then discussed them with her. Rather, I was so moved after paying my respects to the soldiers who had died at the battlefront that these feelings somehow transformed into words. Because I had to inform her of these activities, the words came out in quite a natural way. Once able to talk to her about these matters, I was surprised to learn of the difference between Japanese and Manchu-Chinese attitudes toward soldiers.

I said to her, "In this way, I too will try my best to bring up my son Yoshio. When the mothers of those who died on the battlefront think of their sons' lives of twenty odd years, it will all seem like a dream. Oh, what good Japanese mothers. Even today telegrams were sent that say 'Rejoice that your child could be helpful in the war effort. Respectfully wait for his ashes to be sent home.'" Guiyu responded by asking, "Your son won't be sent off to war, will he?"

I replied, "Well, we need to raise him to have a healthy body, so he can become a soldier."

"Why do the sons of rich families become soldiers?" she asked in a puzzled voice.

I remembered hearing that only desperate and hopeless individuals join the military in China, and thought, "I see!"

If she could not comprehend the honor and splendid nature of the soldiers, how could she understand the gratitude I felt toward those holy young men who died on the battlefront? I thought she could not understand the hearts of Japanese who get dressed up and go to honor the wartime deaths of soldiers. From that time on, I began telling her stories about the most exceptional people joining the military and the dignity of the imperial troops.

"The soldiers who are chosen for the imperial forces have all attended elementary school. There are many who graduate from high school and university."

Guiyu exclaimed, "Aiya!" and made a facial expression typical of Manchu and Chinese showing surprise. "University graduates joining the army—In Manchuria, there aren't any soldiers like that," she sighed.

Then, a while later, she pointed at a soldier who was bringing horses to a neighboring house and escorting officials in an automobile and said, "Is that soldier the son of an important man? Did he go to university?"

Due to the passion and interest with which she stared at the figures of the soldiers covered in dirt and sweat, I began to wonder whether such cases of elite or educated Japanese soldiers were unusual and reconsidered the true character of the imperial troops.

Afterward, when I went out to a memorial service, she furrowed her brows and said things like, "The rebels are bad. Did the Japanese soldiers die?" Another time, she waited for me to return home and asked, "Did the father and mother come to the service? The bride, did she cry?" I told her that nobody cried at a memorial service when we visited the parents and the young wife of a deceased soldier from Mukden. In surprise she said, "Aiya, why no one cry!"

I've heard that in Korea there is a custom of hiring men and women to cry and yell out "Aigo!" at funerals. I've also seen a female crier once before. Here in Manchuria they don't seem to have this custom, but it is viewed as beautiful when the parents and the couple cry loudly on top of the coffin. Even if I explained the deep sensibility of Japanese who internalize their emotions, she probably would not have understood. I thought "If we continued to follow our Japanese lifestyle, won't she naturally understand the feelings that come out of this way of living? Even if she cannot have the same feelings as a Japanese, she will probably understand how and why Japanese express such feelings." Therefore, I treated her as if she were an uneducated Japanese and decided that I wouldn't simply assume "She can't understand because she is Manchu." No matter what I say, with the difference between our long histories, and because we are of different ethnic groups affected by our varying geographical environments, and because even hereafter we cannot eliminate these historical and geographical differences, I understood it would be unnatural to treat her the same as a Japanese person and would in fact be unnecessary. In order to teach the Japanese spirit to this young girl, who has deeply internalized an anti-Japanese education under a certain plan, I had to make her learn through experience with a pure Japanese lifestyle so that she could become Japanese by sharing those Japanese feelings of daily life. And without such a process, no matter how much I talked or corrected what she had already learned in school, I thought it would be impossible to teach her the Japanese spirit. I didn't know how long we would be in Manchuria, but in the short time she was in our household, I would try as much as possible to have her become Japanese. I didn't know how this child would view her current experiences as she grew up. That is, of course, her own free choice, but I worried that this was the only means I had for teaching her about Japan. Also, as for basic beliefs, everyone has a heart and a Buddha nature like the Buddha. This stemmed from my belief in the Buddha's teaching that the faith deep in people's hearts is equal. There was also the Nichiren belief that Buddha nature and that faith are not at all abstract entities, but take shape and exist in our daily lives.

.   .   .

[Translator's Note] *Several months pass with Koizumi and Guiyu growing closer. Koizumi arranges for Guiyu to take Japanese lessons and continues to "educate" the young woman in the Japanese lifestyle. Guiyu begins to criticize individual Manchus and specific Manchu cultural practices (e.g., arranged marriages, attitudes toward money). The death of her father prompts her to ponder her place in the world and in Manchuria, and to further question her education.*

.   .   .

This smart girl began to sigh at how her previous education differed from her actual experience with Japanese. She listened to me talk about my own experiences in Japan—learning how to sew a kimono in elementary school, how schools in the countryside gave vocational guidance, and how junior high and high schools taught cooking and childcare.

As the days passed Guiyu came to have a strong trust in me. While sometimes feeling a burden that was difficult to endure from this child who was upfront about everything, I also began to have a soft spot for this naughty child as if she were my own.

In March, because we were moving to Xinjing, I offered to have some simple Manchu travel garments made for Guiyu. She responded that she didn't like Manchu clothing.

"Japanese kimono are pretty. Warm, too. Manchu clothing is inexpensive, but it's not pretty at all."

Upon her saying this, I gave a pained smile, and because we had made her a kimono for New Year's Day, I decided to give her a kimono overcoat and undergarment, thronged sandals, tabi socks, a shawl, and gloves in order to complete the outfit. She was thrilled, of course, and kept asking me how much each item cost.

I taught her the proper way to fold a kimono. When I would return home from errands, she would sit by my side while I changed clothes and took pleasure in folding everything. Then she would say, "Aiya, so pretty it makes my eyes hurt. It's expensive, right? How much is it?"

When I would tell her how much the garments cost, she would shake her head and exclaim, "Aiya, madam! Japanese are scary. Do you really wear such expensive things? There aren't Manchus who would do that!"

"That's not true. Some rural Manchu are frugal, but the wives of elites wear beautiful new clothing every spring and every autumn. Unlike Japanese, they make quite expensive earrings and rings and bracelets. This kimono was made ten years ago and this kimono coat has been re-dyed twice already. My *obi* is from when I was a young girl."

Once I explained this to her, she was wholly impressed and the soft touch of the silk and the beautiful unique hues of the Japanese fabric all must have given her a girlish pleasure. She would carefully smooth down the fabric and fold it for me.

The pleasure that she seemed to derive from possessing the red muslin kimono, *haori*, and the felt slippers—it was something I could not understand. She would stare at the items lined up in the corner of the room and sleep with them beside her pillow.

Around that time, she grew irritated at being seen as a Manchu when taking orders. She declared that her current hairstyle didn't look good with Japanese clothing and began to grow her hair out. She pinned up her bangs with a comb even though she was ashamed of her wide forehead. Since that was how she felt, I thought it was fine. I let her do what she wanted, but then one day, she said to me, "Madam, I will be Japanese in three years!"

I laughingly replied, "Oh, really?" It seemed as if she had her own plans.

Because she was an adorable child with a continental nature and a boldness borne from a clear ethnic consciousness shaped by poverty, and her trust in me was such that nothing could come between us, people often mistook us for mother and child. This was probably a delight for Guiyu. Sometimes I would go out with her and Yoshio and sometimes with my husband too, and we played the Corinth Game for relaxation in the evening. At those times, she would say, "Well, now it's mother's turn. Hurry!" or "Father, the red ball went in again. Too bad, ha ha ha." Together with Yoshio, she would call us father and mother.

Because she was this kind of child, she was cool and collected even when we were riding on the "Asia" observation car or going to the dining car, and when we fed her Western food at the Yamato Hotel, she would quietly watch what I would do and then calmly use a fork. There was no comparison to the restless subservience of Japanese girls who had just come from the countryside. I admired her attitude, which came from taking her education seriously into her soul, whether the education was correct or incorrect. Indeed, the way she marveled at her new experiences was more intense than the average person. She would stop cleaning and tell me that she planned to write a letter to her younger brother and tell her friends about the dining car in the express train or the dazzling hotel chandeliers. Moreover, she would wait until we returned home to express these feelings.

Shortly after arriving in Xinjing, when my husband was out of town, I took Yoshio on a field trip from Dalian to Harbin. Because we had a secure, corner apartment on the second floor, I had Guiyu stay by herself to house-sit for three days. I didn't have any concerns except that she might be lonely. Guiyu must have felt that we left her with the entire household. When we returned home, she asked me to read a letter she wrote to her mother. Since it was a custom from her previous house, I read it aloud to her with curiosity. It turned out that Guiyu wrote that the entire family was absent and she was left to protect the entire house. Within that letter, I discovered the Chinese characters, "Japan and Manchuria trust each other." Although Guiyu was a little shy, I felt intensely shocked. Truly, there is no greater virtue for a child than trusting others. During the three days of solitude, this girl shared in the delight of this expansive trust. She even cleaned up the entire house.

Imperializing Motherhood:
The Education of a "Manchu Girl"
in Colonial Manchuria

KIMBERLY T. KONO

In comments to the All Manchukuo Women's Federation in 1933, General Koiso Kuniaki, head of the Kwantung army, recognized the importance of "women's kindness" in bringing together Japanese and Manchu (*Nichi-Man yūwa*) and praised the "encompassing love of the mother toward humanity transcending national boundaries."[2] Koiso urged Japanese women's organizations to "become the nurturing mother of the greater nationality (*daikokumin*) of Manchukuo."[3] His remarks are notable for their portrayal of motherhood as a way for Japanese women to contribute to Japan's colonial project in Manchuria. The evocation of motherhood would have been familiar to Koiso's audience of Japanese women, who throughout the modern period were subject to the Japanese government's use of maternity to recruit women for the purposes of the nation. At the same time, however, Koiso's speech diverged from a nation-centered form of motherhood to emphasize women's responsibilities for serving both the nation *and the empire* as loyal, imperial(ist) mothers while in Manchuria. In other words, Koiso's reconfiguration of gender points to a broadening of expectations for Japanese women and represents one example of the central focus of this essay, imperialist motherhood.

During the first half of the twentieth century, motherhood represented one of the main avenues for Japanese women to perform loyalty to the nation and achieve recognition as national subjects.[4] Beginning in the Meiji period (1868–1912), the Ministry of Education advocated the notion of good wife, wise mother (*ryōsai kembo*), which formulated women's work in the private sphere (e.g., childbirth, domestic labor, caretaking of children and the elderly) as service to the nation.[5] As mothers, Japanese women were expected to perform roles as both biological reproducers, creating potential subjects of the nation, and as cultural reproducers, maintaining and protecting the family.

Official nationalist discourse throughout the Taisho (1912–1926) and early Showa (1926–1989) periods continued to situate women as mothers within the private sphere, but also began to reformulate motherhood for the public sphere.[6] As Japan established its status as a modern nation-state in large part through colonial expansion, expectations for women as national subjects transformed, creating venues for Japanese women to support and contribute to Japan's imperialist projects. For example, militarized forms of motherhood began to appear during this period with wartime propaganda exhorting Japanese women to care for both their biological male offspring and other "sons of the nation" through their support of the military.[7] Mass media coverage of Manchuria during the early 1930s regularly featured "military mothers" supporting all "sons of Japan" in the war effort.[8] Organizations such as the Patriotic Women's Association (Aikoku fujinkai) and the National Defense Women's Association (Dai Nippon kokubō fujinkai) mobilized women for such activities as sending off troops to the warfront, raising funds for the war effort, and visiting injured soldiers in the hospital.[9] These examples highlight the expansion of both women's roles in society and the boundaries of their spheres of influence.

Kathleen Uno describes the recruitment of women for these nationalist purposes as "imperial motherhood."[10] According to Uno, imperial motherhood "calls attention to the nationalist motivations for its genesis and the infusion of nationalist aims in normative values and behavior for the female gender."[11] In other words, the practice of motherhood—giving birth to and bringing up children—was reformulated as an integral part of Japanese women's responsibility to their nation. This essay builds on Uno's notion of imperial motherhood by proposing the related concept of "imperialist motherhood," which will be elaborated on in the discussion to follow.

Throughout the years of colonialism (1869–1945), Japanese women in the colonies received messages similar to those given to their counterparts in the metropole about the importance of both educating their own children to become "good imperial subjects" and supporting the military, the "sons of the Japanese empire." Yet, maternal practices changed in the translation of ideas about motherhood into the colonial context. While Uno's notion of imperial motherhood emphasizes maternity in the service of the nation, imperialist motherhood identifies a different construction of mothering that was performed *within the colonies for the purpose of propagating empire.* This difference, then, acknowledges the disparate conditions between the metropole and the colonies, including the different audiences within those locales as well as their oftentimes divergent perceptions of empire itself. In other words, the notion of imperialist motherhood takes into account the ways that nationalist and imperialist ideologies were manifest differently in the colonial context than in the metropole as a result of the varied concerns and experiences of colonizing and colonized subjects living in the colonies. In order to facilitate colonial rule, the colonial government identified colonized peoples as potential imperial subjects and imposed assimilationist policies upon them. Thus, imperialist motherhood integrated several enterprises: mobilizing women for the purposes of the nation/empire, asserting colonial hierarchy, and managing colonized subjects through assimilation.

Reflecting these heightened expectations for women in the colonies, Koizumi Kikue's *Manchu Girl* represents one example of the deployment of "imperialist motherhood" in the colonial context. This work is based on letters Koizumi sent to Japan describing her experiences living in Manchuria with her husband and young son. The narrative focuses on a young Chinese girl—Li Guiyu—who worked as Koizumi's maid for a year and half when the family lived in Mukden and Xinjing (*Shinkyō*).[12] Through her relationship with Guiyu, Koizumi attempts to bridge cultural differences between Japanese and Chinese or enact "ethnic harmony" (*minzoku kyōwa*) by "educating" the young girl. Not only does Koizumi work to familiarize her maid with Japanese cultural practices but she also tries to counter the anti-Japanese education Guiyu received as a young girl and convey the "truth" about the Japanese military and the war effort. Thus, from the onset, the relationship between Koizumi and Guiyu is framed not simply as that of employer and employee but rather of teacher and student or, even more revealingly, as will become more apparent, surrogate parent and child.

Manchu Girl represents an especially provocative example of the mobilization of the trope of familial relationships, widely used not only to exhort Japanese women to play a limited yet active role in imperial expansion, but also to obfuscate the nature of the relationship between Japan and colonial Manchuria. Moreover, the multiple versions of this work suggest some telling strategic differences between depicting the Japanese empire in the metropole and the colonies. A close reading of this text within the larger field of imperial rhetoric highlights the complex power relations wherein Japanese women simultaneously were shaped by and shaped discussions of maternal practices, national citizenship, and empire.

Contextualizing Manchu Girl

Manchu Girl originally appeared in 1938 in serialized form in the Nichiren Buddhist journal *Faith* (*Makoto*). Later that same year, it was republished in the general interest magazine *Manchuria Monthly* after Koizumi's return to Japan, and subsequently compiled in a book by Manchuria Monthly Publishers in December 1938. Several years later, in 1942, an expanded and revised edition was published under the title *Manshū shōjo* by Zenkoku shobō in Osaka.[13] The book was also the basis for a radio drama broadcast in Dalian in 1940, further increasing the audience for Koizumi's narrative.[14] The multiple versions of the text speak to both its popularity and influence.[15]

During this period, reportage from the colonies frequently appeared in Japanese newspapers and other publications. In such women's magazines as *Radiant* (*Kagayaku*) and *Family Light* (*Ie no hikari*), for example, Japanese women recorded their experiences traveling or living abroad. These essays provided a domestic readership with a glimpse of life in the distant colonies and frequently reinforced the promotion of the colonial project in Manchuria. The serialization of Koizumi's work in both *Faith* and *Manchuria Monthly* were part of this wave of writing, a fact that undoubtedly shaped Koizumi's crafting of her narrative.

This essay refers to the first bound version of *Manchu Girl* published in Xinjing, Manchuria, in 1938. Like many other publications from the colonial period that were destroyed or lost in the wake of Japan's defeat in August 1945, the serialized versions of the text are no longer available. The Manchuria-published version retains few obvious traces of the segmentation of serialization, suggesting that Koizumi may have made revisions between serialization and publication in book form. Although it is difficult to accurately assess how the text may have changed between these two formats, it seems possible that the larger audience afforded by the book format could have expanded the scope of Koizumi's text. Specifically, the text may have shifted attention away from a Nichiren Buddhist focus to the broader project of promoting colonial relations. The version published in Manchuria contains a few references to Nichiren concepts such as faith (*makoto*) but ultimately centers on the importance of the interactions between Koizumi and Guiyu in the expansion of empire. Yet, without the original serialized versions, the possibility of revisions to the text remains conjecture.

Because the work is based on Koizumi's time in Manchuria, *Manchu Girl* is frequently described as a record of her experiences or impressions and labeled as a memoir or nonfiction. While the text may draw upon Koizumi's encounters on the continent, it is important to keep in mind authorial privilege (and prerogative) and the ways in which Koizumi shapes the narrative to craft a specific message, namely the support of Japan's presence in colonial Manchuria. For example, despite the detailed descriptions of Guiyu's changing attitudes toward Japan, these evaluations are based in conjecture rather than fact as the young girl's words and actions are perpetually mediated through Koizumi's own authorial (and imperialist) gaze. As a result, the labeling of this text as "nonfiction" elides the inherent biases of the author and misleadingly identifies its contents as "fact." This ambivalence points to the insufficiency of the categories of fiction and nonfiction and necessitates readers' critical awareness of the author's subjective assessments in their engagement with the text. Despite such biases, however, readers at the time most likely viewed *Manchu Girl* as nonfiction, in part because of their minimal knowledge of life in Manchuria and their amenability to Koizumi's message of imperialist motherhood.

Educating a Manchu Girl

The opening lines of the text immediately establish the narrator as a maternal figure, concerned with the welfare of children. This first passage centers on a misunderstanding between Koizumi and her husband, who are discussing the prospect of hiring a Chinese maid.

> "I have decided to buy a young Chinese girl."
> When my husband spoke those words, I was shocked. He then explained that a co-worker who was going to be transferred to Harbin wanted to pass on to us the fourteen-year-old girl that he had bought from rural Andong three months ago.
> "Did you just say that he 'bought' her?" I exclaimed in surprise.[16]

Koizumi's initial shock diminishes when she rationalizes that her husband must have been using dialect to talk about "hiring" a young girl rather than actually "buying" one. Specifically, because the words for "hiring" *kariru* and "buying" *kau* are both rendered *katte* in certain strands of colloquial Japanese, the narrator supposedly misunderstood her husband's initial declaration. Subsequently, Koizumi launches into a discussion of how, in the past, impoverished Chinese and Japanese families sold their children while also expressing her horror at the idea of such a practice. By acknowledging

Japan and China's shared past, Koizumi establishes her ability to empathize and understand the reasons behind the practice. At the same time, she positions herself as a modern subject, removed from the antiquated practice of child labor. As a result, this opening establishes the narrator as both maternal, through her concern for the welfare of children, and civilized, through her critique of the anachronistic custom of selling children.

The opening passage adds to this maternal identity by characterizing Koizumi and her husband as benevolent parental figures. Even after Koizumi recovers from the shock of the initial misunderstanding, she resists hiring this young girl due to difficulties with a previous maid, a twenty-one-year-old Chinese woman who lacked Japanese language skills and never learned how to clean the house "properly." In response to his wife's resistance, the husband evokes their responsibilities as Japanese subjects:

> "This one has attended high school. While working for Mr. O, who is quite skilled at Manchu, she has become familiar with the Japanese lifestyle. He said that she's got a good head on her shoulders and most important, unlike the other maid, she is still a child. I think that our efforts will have a great effect upon her. By taking care of this child and helping her to understand the proper viewpoints of Japanese through our way of living, isn't this working for goodwill between Japan and Manchuria and the practice of what you call 'faith'?[17]

The phrase "taking care of this child" (*kodomo o sewashite*) with its emphasis on Guiyu as a "child" makes the couple seem as if they are considering adoption rather than hiring a servant. Such wording identifies Koizumi and her husband as prospective parents and not potential employers. In addition, the husband's justification for hiring Guiyu further elucidates the nationalist and imperialist aims of such parenthood. He emphasizes the appeal of getting a child who is young and thus pliable enough to educate, as opposed to their previous maid, who was too old to train. By bringing Guiyu into their home, they will have the chance to mold her and ostensibly facilitate imperial relations in Manchuria. Thus, this passage portrays Guiyu as a young subject in need of guidance and care, and affirms Koizumi and her husband's status as representatives of the Japanese empire.

This characterization of the relationship between Guiyu and Koizumi as resembling that of parent and child functions as national allegory. Guiyu represents the young nation of Manchuria in need of supervision by the mature, modernized Japan, as embodied by Koizumi. Similar familial tropes appear in reference to Manchuria in popular publications, particularly journalistic works, of the metropole. For example, propaganda on emigration to Manchuria depicted Japan as a parental figure to the developing nation of Manchuria in order to extend Japan's authority into the colonies.[18] Tropes of family and marriage also appeared in literary explorations of colonial relations by both Japanese and colonized subjects.[19] By establishing Koizumi's maternal role in the narrative, the opening passage of *Manchu Girl* augments this body of journalistic and literary work and situates imperial relations in a familial framework.

Koizumi further asserts her qualifications as an imperialist mother by enacting her loyalty to the Japanese military and the emperor. In passing, she notes that she regularly "visit[s] wounded soldiers, welcome[s] the returning troops, and mourn[s] the deaths of those killed in action."[20] Later in the text, she elaborates her own passionate feelings of indebtedness toward the returning Japanese troops.[21] Furthermore, by engaging in discussions about these activities with Guiyu, she shares her patriotism. For example, after attending the memorial services for soldiers killed in battle, Koizumi talks to Guiyu about the "loyal and patriotic actions of those who died in battle," and how mothers of the deceased will be honored for sacrificing their children for the war effort.[22] Guiyu inquires about Koizumi's willingness to allow her own young son, Yoshio, to enlist in the future. Koizumi responds that she would be honored if her son were to serve in the imperial army. Since she was the daughter of a military official, and wife of a soldier, her passionate support of the Japanese troops and the nation hardly comes as a surprise. Even so, her stance was not unique as Japanese women throughout the metropole were enacting military motherhood. Koizumi's declarations of patriotism and sacrifice affirm her identity as a staunch supporter of the military and loyal subject of the emperor.

Manchu Girl's narrative also suggests Koizumi is keenly aware of the differences between Japanese in the metropole and their counterparts in the colonies in terms of the latter's awareness of the conflicts in Manchuria. In one passage, she discusses a popular song, "Subdue the Rebels," which is based on a poet's experiences accompanying Japanese troops in Manchuria.

> For those of us who live in Manchuria and are affected by the hardships of the imperial army, hearing that record causes tears to roll down our cheeks. At the point in the song that says, "No food for three days, two nights, perhaps it is the cold of a night of hunger," anyone in the Ginza district in Tokyo must perceive these to be the events of a faraway dream. For myself and others born in Tokyo, pleasant images of our homeland sometimes ap-

pear to us, and we can see the bright eyes of cheerful and carefree young men and women amidst the various crowds of the Ginza. To me, they all are as innocent as babies.[23]

The immediacy of the experience and urgency of the imperial project on the continent contrast with the perception of such events as "faraway dream[s]" by those in Japan. By describing her counterparts in the metropole as "innocent as babies," Koizumi highlights their ignorance of the events on the continent and identifies a disjuncture between the romanticized visions of Manchuria and the harsh realities. In addition, her firsthand information about the challenges of colonial life, such as relations with colonized subjects and the dangers of living near the warfront, demarcates the significant difference between lived experience and popular imagination.

As previously noted, Koizumi views her maternal responsibilities as extending from her biological son and the other "sons of the nation" in the military to Guiyu, her surrogate daughter. Throughout the text, Koizumi describes her attempts to "bring up" Guiyu (*shōjo keigyoku o sodateru*) and help her to assimilate (*dōka saseteyuku*). Her endeavors at cultivating Guiyu included attempts to familiarize Guiyu with a Japanese lifestyle in order to facilitate understanding between Japanese and Chinese. Koizumi teaches Guiyu about such things as Japanese food and clothing and even takes her to an exhibit on the "modern" practice of proper hygiene.

However, Koizumi's attempts at cultural reproduction do not simply entail the teaching of specific cultural practices. They also require conveying the *emotions* that accompany such activities. Koizumi devotes much attention to the importance of Guiyu's "understanding the feelings of Japanese." The ability to comprehend "Japanese feelings," according to Koizumi, will ostensibly allow Guiyu and other Chinese to then understand Japanese actions, specifically the efforts to develop the Japanese presence in Manchuria. The focus on intangible, subjectively defined feelings allows for the goal of cultural assimilation to remain perpetually out of reach for colonized subjects. Moreover, mobilizing the power of sentiment also renders Koizumi's "sentimental education" as an emotional, filial, and intimate gesture rather than a politically motivated strategy and thus conceals the threat of "imperialization."

While the content of their discussions reflects the ideas that Koizumi perceives as important, the presentation of these conversations, specifically Guiyu's language use, shows the progress of this "reeducation" project. In the beginning of the text, the maid's comments in broken Japanese reveal a limited vocabulary and contain missing particles and numerous other grammatical mistakes. Because her only form of expression in the text is in Japanese and her minimal knowledge of Japanese limits her abilities of expression, she is consistently confined within an infantilized state of mind. Her ungrammatical Japanese reinforces her image as a child as well as accentuates her lack of knowledge about Japanese language and culture. As the narrative continues, and Guiyu grows increasingly enamored with Japanese culture, her language abilities greatly improve. While this advancement of her powers of expression might be read as "natural" in the context of living with this Japanese family, her increased abilities are also significant in terms of the relationship between language and identity. Her improved language skills demonstrate her successful assimilation into Japanese cultural practices, with linguistic fluency serving as a marker of cultural knowledge. At the same time, Guiyu's developing Japanese language abilities serve as a barometer by which Koizumi measures her own "accomplishment."

The positive transformation of Guiyu's attitudes toward Japanese culture is accompanied by a negative shift in her attitudes toward her own Chinese identity. When Koizumi offers to have some travel garments made for Guiyu, the girl rejects Chinese clothing in favor of Japanese kimono. Koizumi describes how Guiyu "would stare at the items lined up in the corner of the room and sleep with them beside her pillow."[24] Guiyu's pleasure at viewing these garments, a feeling that Koizumi "could not understand," represents a shift in the girl's attitude toward Japanese and Chinese culture.

> Around that time, she grew irritated at being seen as a Manchu when taking orders. She declared that her current hairstyle didn't look good with Japanese clothing and began to grow her hair out. She pinned up her bangs with a comb even though she was ashamed of her wide forehead. Since that was how she felt, I thought it was fine. I let her do what she wanted, but then one day, she said to me, "Madam, I will be Japanese in three years!"[25]

The excerpt above reflects Guiyu's desire, according to Koizumi, to become Japanese. By this point in the narrative, Guiyu has criticized other Chinese, rejected her identity as Chinese, changed her appearance, and expressed a preference for Japanese kimono; in Koizumi's eyes, she is well along in the assimilation process.

While Guiyu's embrace of Japanese cultural practices indicates her successful assimilation, her attitude toward Koizumi and her family provides further confirmation. On occasion, Guiyu and Koizumi are mistaken for mother and child, a fact that Koizumi states "was probably a delight for Guiyu."[26] The passage continues with Koizumi noting that while playing with the family, Guiyu would call Koizumi and her husband, "mother" and "father." Koizumi portrays this as evidence of Guiyu's desire to be included within their family, but it takes on added resonance as a reflection of a colonized subject's alleged desire to be included as a member of the Japanese empire.

It is important to note here that Guiyu's definition of a Japanese identity may differ from that of Koizumi's. Guiyu bases her image of Japanese upon her experience with Koizumi and her cohort, a community of elite subjects with privileges and resources that were unavailable to most Chinese. For Guiyu, the appeal of kimono and other "Japanese" cultural practices may lie, not in their association with the Japanese empire per se, but rather with a particular class status associated with a modern lifestyle. In other words, Guiyu's declared goal of becoming Japanese may reflect a desire to elevate her class position within colonial society and gain access to the privileges and material accoutrements of such status. By contrast, Koizumi's definition of a Japanese identity is inextricably intertwined with the imperial project and in particular, loyalty to the nation and its military efforts. As a result of these vastly different notions of "Japanese" identity, Koizumi misreads Guiyu's attraction to things Japanese as an embrace of empire rather than an attempt to improve her class status.

Manchu Girl portrays the "successful" education of Guiyu as an assertion of Japanese civility, but Koizumi's preoccupation with this educational enterprise suggests her own unstable position in the colonial context and within the empire. That is, her recognition as a national subject is contingent upon her successful performance of the officially sanctioned role of motherhood. Her status as a subject of Japan is not preexisting or inherent, but rather is produced *through* her interactions with Guiyu. Koizumi realizes her own identity as a Japanese citizen-subject by means of the very process of educating this girl. Postcolonial theorist Albert Memmi discusses the interdependence of colonizing and colonized subjects and emphasizes the colonizer's reliance upon the colonized for her production of identity. Memmi notes that the "colonialist's existence is so closely aligned to the colonized" that she cannot reject the colonized without also erasing herself.[27] Viewed in this light, Guiyu is integral to Koizumi's self-assertion as a maternal figure, a gendered national/imperial subject. Without the young girl, Koizumi cannot fulfill the role of "imperialist mother."

Even though Koizumi benefits from the alleged success of her reeducation of Guiyu by affirming her own imperial(ist) subjectivity, it is difficult, if not impossible, to gauge the effects of these interactions upon Guiyu herself, the object of Koizumi's attentions. Citing the lack of resistance evident in the text, Kawasaki Kenko suggests that Guiyu's assimilation is not forced.[28] Whether or not this may be the case, readers cannot adequately assess Guiyu's own perceptions of the relationship as a result of the mediated nature of the narrative. The girl's voice is always contextualized or modified by the author through the act of writing the text. Koizumi appropriates Guiyu's voice and experience in the service of the colonial project by portraying the young woman as a naïve, misinformed child who blossoms in the author's care. Guiyu's eventual conversion into a willing subject of empire serves as an allegory for the transformation of Manchuria itself into a part of the Japanese empire. Thus, the "successful cultivation" of Guiyu allows Koizumi to both claim her own status as a loyal Japanese imperial subject and allegorically render the relationship between Japan and Manchuria as beneficial to both parties.

Late in the narrative, Koizumi herself reciprocates Guiyu's familial feelings when she considers adopting Guiyu after the girl's mother falls ill taking care of Guiyu's older sister. By this point, Guiyu's father has already passed away and once Guiyu's sister dies of scarlet fever, the girl is left with only her ailing mother and young brother.

> The girl's mother could die. And her seven-year-old brother, who would be left behind, might also die without anyone to take care of him. . . . Ay, because nobody is watching him, even now he may have already been killed playing in the street. . . . I thought about what would happen if this child's mother died. I decided that in that event, I would consult with my husband about adopting this girl and her brother. Feeling the inextricable bonds of fate, I had made up my mind to do just that.[29]

The parental benevolence delineated in this scene overlaps with colonialist rhetoric at large. The colonial partnership between China and Japan was often articulated in terms of an ailing, ancient China in dire need of the guidance or protection of Japan. A well-intentioned Japanese surrogate parent waits in the wings to help the young China survive. Even though Guiyu's mother eventually recovers and the adoption does not occur, Koizumi's consideration of adoption suggests the pervasive power of familial tropes.

Rewriting Motherhood for the Empire

The multiple versions of *Manchu Girl* attest to the value of this text that reinforces both popular and official conceptualizations of Japan as the leading imperial power in Asia. As mentioned earlier, this work was serialized twice, first in the journal *Faith* in 1938, and then several months later in another journal, *Manchuria Monthly*. At the end of that year, in December 1938, the text appeared in book form under the title *Manshūjin no shōjo* (Manchu Girl) published by Manchuria Monthly Publishing in Xinjing. In 1942, the volume was published in an expanded version in Japan as *Manshū shōjo* (Girl of Manchuria) with additional sections detailing Koizumi's experiences in Manchuria and Guiyu's life after leaving Koizumi's employ.[30]

While these versions of the text differ in context and format, they also reveal multiple purposes and intended readerships of Koizumi's narratives. The book published in Manchuria in 1938 is described in the preface by poet Ishihara Gantetsu as a "textbook for Japanese on the continental development of Chinese and Manchu."[31] This version focuses solely on the author's relationship with Guiyu while in Manchuria and, appropriately for something recommended as a textbook, has pronunciation guides (*furigana*) on all of the *kanji*, or Chinese characters. The use of *furigana* suggests that the target audience involved subjects who were not completely literate. This intended readership may have included colonized subjects who were learning the Japanese readings of Chinese characters. Koizumi could convey the good intentions of some Japanese in Manchuria not just to Guiyu but also to a colonized audience. Koizumi's efforts to "educate" thus extended well beyond Guiyu, reaching other colonized subjects throughout Manchuria and Japan. In addition, Japanese settlers may also have been a potential target. For these readers, *Manchu Girl* served as an inspiring example of possibilities and implicitly provided guidelines in developing relations with Chinese. As previously noted, Koizumi embedded critiques throughout the text regarding the exploitation of colonized subjects such as her condemnation of child labor in the opening of the text. She also comments on how Japanese should model the appropriate behavior of an imperial subject. The labeling of the Manchuria-published version as a "textbook" seems especially apt because of its potential use as a primer for many colonial subjects. The didactic function enables Koizumi to extend her role as imperialist mother by educating not only her Chinese maid, but also a colonial readership composed of Japanese settlers and colonized subjects.

The second book version of the text, published in Japan proper, fulfills the function of a travel narrative, giving the ostensibly Japanese readership voyeuristic access to the experience of life in the colonies. In addition to the Manchuria-published version's description of Koizumi's life with Guiyu, the version published in Japan contains an introductory chapter with meticulous descriptions of life in Manchuria. Such detail suggests that the audience for this expanded version of the text would include individuals unfamiliar with Manchuria. In addition to these particulars, the Japan-published version also continues the story after Koizumi returns to Japan, leaving Guiyu behind in Manchuria, and greatly revises the possibilities presented at the conclusion of the first version of the text.

By the end of the Manchuria-published version, Guiyu now identifies by the Japanese name Keiko, consisting of a Japanese reading of the first character of her name (*Gui* in Chinese and *Kei* in Japanese) plus a second character (*ko*), making the name typically Japanese. When Koizumi returns to Japan with her family, Guiyu/Keiko vows never to forget what she has learned and to pass this knowledge of Japan on to Chinese children. In other words, in Koizumi's absence, Guiyu volunteers to take her place as an imperialist mother and continue the "work" of Koizumi. The possibility of a Chinese "girl" taking on imperialist motherhood and thus imperial subjecthood certainly represents a surprising turn. And yet, in the revised and expanded version of the book published in Japan, Guiyu is prevented from assuming this role. In a chapter added to this second version, Koizumi describes the death of 19-year-old Guiyu in childbirth several years later while in Keijō (present-day Seoul).[32] While Guiyu becomes a mother through the birth of her child, the possibility of becoming an imperialist mother is eliminated. This ending adds to the melodrama of the Japan-published version of Koizumi's text but also resonates as a commentary on the fate of colonized subjects, and colonized women in particular. Despite promises of imperial subjecthood, colonized women remained in the position of objects, not subjects, of imperialization—a complicated destiny that prevented future censure as collaborators but also limited attempts at asserting agency. While cultural assimilation was possible, as evidenced by the example of Guiyu, achieving a Japanese identity was not.

Imperializing Motherhood

The portrayal of imperialist motherhood in *Manchu Girl* highlights the importance of both the domestic sphere and the roles of Japanese women in the colonial project. By showing how colonialism played out in gendered spaces, the text illustrates how some Japanese women, despite their political disenfranchisement, were active participants in empire-building. Through their relations in the home, these women acted as agents in the process of imperialization and advocates of the colonial project to both colonizing and colonized subjects alike. Their contact with colonized subjects in the domestic sphere afforded them opportunities for (re)producing empire in ways that differed from the imposition of empire in the public sphere.

The use of motherhood as a means of enacting imperialism maintained conventional expectations for Japanese women and provided a rationale for their colonialist behavior. In the context of a mother-child relationship, Koizumi's "educating" Guiyu is seemingly motivated by maternal sentiment rather than the imperialist desire to expand the Japanese influence in Manchuria. Rendering Koizumi's behavior in familial terms thus naturalized the relationship and justified these attempts at cultural assimilation as the responsible behavior of a concerned "parent." Conveniently, the expectation of mothers teaching their children meshed well with the colonialist framework of colonizers "educating" colonized subjects and provided further support for efforts at imperialization. Within this colonial construction of women's roles, the object of mothering widened from biological children and Japanese soldiers to include the "children of empire," colonized subjects.

The familial tropes, centered on the imperialist mother, conceal the realities of the relationship between Koizumi and Guiyu. That is to say, the violence in the colonial relationship is masked by the symbolic union of mother and daughter. In so doing, *Manchu Girl* evokes the qualities traditionally associated with families and transforms the colonial project into a harmless, sentimental endeavor. Not merely a representation of colonial relations, the text creates a social space that authorizes the enactment of imperialist motherhood. Whether as a text or radio drama, the narrative serves the greater mission of the empire by "educating" its audience about the importance of cultural assimilation and the responsibilities of all subjects of empire. By providing guidelines on the path toward imperial subjecthood,

Manchu Girl continues the process that Koizumi begins with Guiyu and further promotes the colonial project by extending its maternal attentions to all corners of the empire.

Notes

There exist a number of versions of the story *Manchu Girl*. The excerpts translated herein are based on the 1938 book version, published as *Manshūjin no shōjo* by Gekkan Manshūsha. Koizumi Suzuko and Shirato Koshiko have graciously granted permission for this English-language translation.

1. It is unclear to what exact incident Koizumi is referring in each of these three cases. At the time she wrote *Manchu Girl*, designations for these incidents, some of which would later be known as wars, were not consistent. Today, it is widely accepted that the Marco Polo Bridge Incident on July 7, 1937, instigated the second Sino-Japanese War (1937–1945), and it is this general history that Koizumi is touching on.

2. Koiso Kuniaki, "Zenman fujin dantai rengōkai kai'in shoshi ni tsugeru no sho" (Letter to All Our Sisters of the All Manchukuo Women's Federation), in *Zenman fujin dantai rengōkai hōkokusho* (Report of the All Manchukuo Women's Federation), ed. Ishikawa Shinobu (Dalian: Zenman fujin dantai rengōkai, 1933), 6. As cited in Prasenjit Duara, *Sovereignty and Authenticity: Manchukuo and the East Asian Modern* (Lanham, MD: Rowman and Littlefield, 2003), 150–51.

3. Duara, *Sovereignty and Authenticity*, 151.

4. National subjecthood refers to inclusion in the national community and acknowledgment of that status through access to certain privileges. For more on the construction of gender and national identity, see Nira Yuval-Davis, *Gender and Nation* (London: Sage, 1997); Anne McClintock, *Imperial Leather: Race, Gender and Sexuality in the Colonial Contest* (New York: Routledge, 1995); Partha Chatterjee, "The Nation and Its Women," in *The Nation and Its Fragments: Colonial and Postcolonial Histories* (Princeton, NJ: Princeton University Press, 1993), 116–34.

5. Sharon H. Nolte and Sally Ann Hastings, "The Meiji State's Policy toward Women, 1890–1910," in *Recreating Japanese Women, 1600–1945*, ed. Gail Lee Bernstein (Berkeley: University of California Press, 1991), 152. On motherhood and nation/empire, see Anna Davin, "Imperialism and Motherhood," in *Tensions of Empire: Colonial Cultures in a Bourgeois World*, eds. Frederick Cooper and Ann Laura Stoler (Berkeley: University of California Press, 1997), 87–151.

6. In the metropole during the 1930s and 1940s, Japanese women enacted "motherhood-in-the-interest-of-the-state" (*kokkateki bosei*) and contributed to the nation through biological reproduction. Yoshiko Miyake, "Doubling Expectations: Motherhood and Women's Factory Work under State Management in Japan in the 1930s and 1940s," in *Recreating Japanese Women, 1600–1945*, ed. Gail Lee Bernstein (Berkeley: University of California Press, 1991), 267–95.

7. Cynthia Enloe refers to this transformation of motherhood as part of the "militarization of women's lives." Cynthia Enloe, *Does Khaki Become You?* (London: Pluto, 1983).

8. Louise Young, *Japan's Total Empire: Manchuria and the Culture of Wartime Imperialism* (Berkeley: University of California Press, 1998), 171. See also Wakakuwa Midori's analysis of wartime images of motherhood in *Shufu no tomo* (The Housewife's Companion), in Wakakuwa Midori, *Sensō ga tsukuru joseizō: Dainiji sekai taisenka no Nihon josei dōin no shikakuteki puropaganda* (Images of Women Constructed by War: Visual Propaganda of the Mobilization of Japanese Women during World War II) (Tokyo: Chikuma shobō, 1995).

9. Hikari Hori, presentation at Five College Women's Studies Research Center, "Mobilizing Women: Wartime Visual Culture and Gender in Japan, 1931–1945," Hadley, MA, November 2006.

10. Kathleen Uno, *Passages to Modernity: Motherhood, Childhood, and Social Reform in Early Twentieth-Century Japan* (Honolulu: University of Hawai'i Press, 1999), 148.

11. Ibid.

12. The titles of both works refer to Li Guiyu as a "Manchu" girl, despite the fact that she is Chinese. Mariko Tamanoi has discussed the use of the term "Manshūjin" in Mariko Tamanoi, "Between Colonial Racism and Global Capitalism: Japanese Repatriates from Northeast China since 1946," *American Ethnologist* 30, 4 (Nov. 2003): 537.

13. Saitō Hideaki notes that in addition to these versions, a version with a different binding and cover was published in 1939 and a paperback version appeared in June 1945. Saitō Hideaki, "Manshū no shōjo" (Manchu Girl), in *"Manshūkoku" bunka saimoku* (The Details of Manchurian Culture), ed. Nishida Masaru (Tokyo: Fuji shuppan, 2005), 240.

14. Radio in colonial Manchuria, which began in Dalian in 1925, initially served a Japanese audience and only later came to provide programming for Chinese listeners. *Rajio nenkan, Showa 13-han* (Radio Annual, Showa 13), Nihon hōsōkai, ed. (Tokyo: Seibundo, 1938).

15. This essay refers to the first book version published by Gekkan Manshūsha in 1938. Koizumi Kikue, *Manshūjin no shōjo* (Xinjing: Gekkan Manshūsha, 1938).

16. Koizumi, *Manshūjin no shōjo*, 3.

17. Ibid., 5.

18. Young, *Japan's Total Empire*, 367.

19. Japanese writers Sakaguchi Reiko and Yuasa Katsue, among others, used tropes of family and marriage to comment on the status of colonial relations in Taiwan and Korea, respectively. See Kimberly Kono, "Writing Colonial Lineage in Sakaguchi Reiko's 'Tokeisō,'" *Journal of Japanese Studies* 32, 1 (Winter 2006): 83–117.

20. Koizumi, *Manshūjin no shōjo*, 9–10.

21. Ibid., 13.

22. Ibid., 20–21.

23. Ibid., 13.

24. Ibid., 53.

25. Ibid.

26. Ibid.

27. Albert Memmi, *The Colonizer and the Colonized* (Boston: Beacon, 1965), 54.

28. "Gyōsei ni yoru mono dewanai." Kawasaki Kenko, "Manshūkoku ni watatta joseitachi: Bungei undō o tegakari ni" (Women Travelers to Manchuria: Clues in Their Literary Activity), in *Onna to otoko ni jikū: Nihon joseishi saikō 5 Semegiau onna to otoko, kindai* (TimeSpace of Gender: Redefining Japanese Women's History, Volume 5: Women and Men in Conflict, Modern Period) (Tokyo: Fujiwara shoten, 1998), 82.

29. Koizumi, *Manshūjin no shōjo*, 80–81.

30. While the first title, *Manshūjin no shōjo*, identifies the girl as Chinese or Manchu, the second title, *Manshū no shōjo*, is slightly more ambiguous, implying that the girl is Chinese or Manchu, or is simply in Manchuria.

31. "Nippon minzoku manshi tairiku hatten no kyōkasho." Koizumi, *Manshūjin no shōjo*, 2.

32. Ibid., 288–89.

CHAPTER EIGHT

TEXT
The Adventures of Dankichi
SHIMADA KEIZŌ

CONTEXT
The South Seas/Micronesia, Taiwan, China, Korea

CRITIQUE
Popular Orientalism and Japanese Views of Asia
KAWAMURA MINATO

MANGA ARTIST Shimada Keizō (1900–1973) began his career as a political satirist, but turned to children's manga in the early 1930s, continuing to work in that field after World War II. Together with Tagawa Suihō's *The Soldier Dog* (*Norakuro*, 1931–1941), *The Adventures of Dankichi*, Shimada's best-known work, is generally recognized as the most popular manga before the appearance of those by Tezuka Osamu (1928–1989) in the postwar era.

Reflecting the diversity of manga art at the time, *The Adventures of Dankichi*, serialized in the *Boys' Club* (*Shōnen Kurabu*) magazine from 1933 to 1939, is written in the picture-story format in which each page is split into narrative and illustration sections. The story depicts the adventures of Dankichi and his mouse friend, Mister Kari, on a tropical island. Dankichi and Mister Kari fall asleep while fishing, drift to the island of dark-skinned "barbarians," and find themselves on the run. However, with his own quick wit and Mister Kari's resourcefulness, Dankichi beats back the natives and becomes their king.

Regularly calling himself a cultural critic (*bungei hyōronka*) rather than a scholar, Kawamura Minato writes on various genres of texts, including manga, and on a wide variety of subjects, often those that complicate conventional notions of Japanese culture. He is well-known for his pioneering works that examine the relationship between colonialism and modern Japanese literature, but this important contribution should be understood as only one expression of his consistent interest in defamiliarizing the familiar. His numerous publications include *Showa Literature as Literature of the Other* (*Ikyō no Shōwa bungaku*, 1990), *Japanese Literature of the South Seas and Sakhalin* (*Nan'yō/Karafuto no Nihon bungaku*, 1994), and *The Collapse of Manchukuo* (*Manshū hōkai*, 1997).

Kawamura's essay "Popular Orientalism and Japanese Views of Asia" (*Taishū orientarizumu to Ajia ninshiki*, 1993) offers a helpful synthesis of a number of crucial issues covered in this volume and reflects his ability to deftly navigate diverse genres and contexts.

Note Regarding Discriminatory Language and Imagery

The manga that follows, *The Adventures of Dankichi*, is included in this volume as a historical document. Its discriminatory language and imagery were typical of the time it was created and do not reflect the views and opinions of the editors or Stanford University Press.

Given that an overarching aim of this anthology is to consider the pervasiveness of imperial ideology, the visuals and wording of this manga, while disturbing and offensive to a modern audience, manifestly reveal the extent to which such ideas were naturalized at every level of Japanese society.

Permission to translate and publish this text was graciously granted on the condition it appear with Kawamura Minato's essay "Popular Orientalism and Japanese Views of Asia," which properly contextualizes its moment of production. We strongly advise against any unlawful reproduction of this work.

It was a bright, clear day. Until now, Dankichi had been fishing in his boat. Not catching a single fish, Dankichi became sleepy.

"Oh my gosh! Dan-chan, have you fallen asleep?"[1] Before long, the eyes of Dankichi's good friend, the black mouse Mister Kari also glazed over.[2] So the boat began drifting along with the waves and the breeze.

1. *Chan* is a diminutive suffix, which is attached to the end of names and indicates friendliness and closeness. Thus, Dankichi and Dan-chan are the same character.

2. In Japanese the mouse is called Karikō, *kō* meaning "Sir" or "Mister."

Suddenly Mister Kari awoke, and, looking around, he saw that the boat had drifted to a strange land; the scenery was unfamiliar. What's more, the boat was teetering atop a large rock. "Oh no! We're in quite a pickle here! The boat was pulled by the tide, and now it's stuck on top of this rock. Oh man, this is bad," exclaimed Kari.

Surprised, the ever-responsible Mister Kari looked at Dankichi, but the boy was still pleasantly snoring away. "Jeez, what a sleepyhead!"

Just then a strange wind started to blow from behind them. "Yikes!" When Mister Kari turned around, there was a strange and mysterious bird swooping down at Dankichi. "Holy smokes! Dan-chan, look out!"

Dankichi opened his eyes at the sound of Mister Kari's absurd outburst, exclaiming, "What's the matter with you? You're so loud." "I'm not loud! Look!" When Dankichi looked, he saw a frightening and mysterious bird with its beak wide open, flying straight at him. "Oh my goodness! Th-this is so terrible!"

The boat was stuck on top of a narrow rock, so it shook with every move they made. "Aah! Oh gods, please help me!" Dankichi pleaded. Isn't it funny how people only ask the gods for help when they're in a pinch?

In a panic Dankichi and Mister Kari tried to hide in a corner. The boat, along with the two friends, fell from atop the high rock with a banging and rattling noise.

"Just as I thought, the gods are good for something," said Dankichi.

The boat had completely turned upside down during the fall, saving Dankichi from the sharp beak of the mysterious bird.

"In such a close call, it's amazing you remembered the gods," said Mister Kari with his heart still pounding and the overturned boat still covering Dankichi. "Dan-chan, the mysterious bird is not here. Come on out!"

Finally crawling out from under the boat, Dankichi carefully surveyed his surroundings. Dankichi said, "Hey, this is a tropical land. That's one big palm tree." While looking around restlessly at the surrounding area for strange things, Kari suddenly plunged into the forest and brought back a handy-looking branch and a piece of strong-looking vine. "Now Dankichi please make a bow with this. Nothing worries me more than being in a place like this without a weapon."

"I bet you're hungry, I'm pretty hungry myself. I wonder if there's any food around here," said Dankichi.

"The tropics are full of food! There are coconuts, bread fruit, pineapples, bananas, and various other things. Hey look, there're some coconuts. Let's eat 'em."

"But I'm not very good at climbing trees."

"Why not shoot it down with the bow we just made."

"Wow Kari, you really are smart!"

He took aim, released the arrow, and scored a splendid hit on the coconut. The coconut fell.

"Ouch! Who's there? What's the big idea hitting me with this in the middle of my nap?" came a roar from the jungle. Neither Dankichi nor Mister Kari could have known there were lions living on the island. Unaware of this, they had carelessly shot down the coconut.

"Oh no, Kari, this is bad. It's a lion!!"

Wild animals such as lions will usually run away from people, but when attacked they will fight back. The offended lion was angry. If you could understand lion-language, this is what you would have heard: "Wait 'til I get my paws on you, you rascal." The lion chased them.

"Aah. It's dangerous! Run! Run!" Dankichi turned to shout, already ten yards ahead.

Dankichi had the strong legs of a marathon runner, something that can't just be bought in a department store. Running around the mountains in confusion, they saw signs of people. "Kari, there are people! There are people! There are a lot of houses." They were ecstatic that this time they would be saved by people not gods. "Hey! Help us!" shouted Dankichi, making the biggest mistake of his life. Sure they were people, but they weren't helpful people. They were people who ate people.

"Aah, cannibals!" Even the athletic Dankichi felt his legs shake. "Kari, what should we do?"

"What should we do?? Stop talking already and run!"

"So... it's more running?"

"What choice do we have?"

Since they didn't have any weapons there wasn't much else they could do. Behind them, the lion! In front, the cannibals! They dashed to the right.

"Phew, we're finally in the clear," gasped Dankichi.

"What a shock! But we aren't out of the woods yet, Dan-chan; the natives know this area really well. They'll find us for sure. Hey! Why don't you use mud from this river to disguise yourself?" said Mister Kari.

"Disguise? But how?"

"Just dissolve some of it in the water and plaster it on your skin. Then you'll become a blackie!"

"Jeepers! Great idea Mister Kari!" Dankichi said as he set about applying his blackie camouflage.

"Oh wow, you did it!" cried Mister Kari.

"You think this'll be good enough to fool them? I bet I look like an honest to god blackie."

"For sure, you did a super job!"

"Well then, I think it's time to make an appearance over at the camp."

"You think it'll be ok?"

"Don't fret, it'll be fine."

Dankichi is a Japanese man, and on top of that, the "Dan" in his name stands for "danger," so he fears nothing.

"Duuum, a little blackie is heading this way. Hey, little black boy, where are you going?" said a guard at the gate of the natives' camp.

"Do you know who I am? I'm the Chief's aunt's father's son. You lot are clearly inferior to me, so show me to the Chief," Dankichi proclaimed.

"Huh? Oh really…that's kind of weird, but okay," the guard said and proceeded to guide Dankichi to the Chief. He was able to hoodwink the Chief as well and a massive feast was brought out. Dankichi and Mister Kari proceeded to stuff themselves. As they feasted, the sky suddenly clouded over and it started to pour.

"Yikes! It's raining," said Mister Kari as he suddenly realized that they were completely wet. Dankichi's disguise had washed off, and he had returned to his original white appearance. Unaware, Dankichi continued to happily munch on his banana.

The Chief's suspicious face quickly melted into an expression of great anger. "Dummm. That's a white boy. He really fooled me," said the Chief.

Previously, Dankichi had disguised himself as a blackie and snuck into the natives' camp to have a feast. However, his identity was revealed when his disguise washed away in the rain. The Chief, realizing he'd been fooled, was so furious he looked like steam was going to shoot out of his ears.

"You rat! How dare you deceive me, the King!"

"Jeepers Creepers!" yelped Dankichi as he had only just now realized he had turned back into a white boy. But it was too late; the Chief was charging at them with a spear in hand. The two friends dodged the spear and ran off into the dense jungle foliage. Mister Kari began to scramble around for something to use and found a strong vine.

"Kari, we're in a quite a hurry here. What're you doing, picking that thing up?" asked Dankichi, a little worried.

"With this we'll capture the Chief. Now I'm going to make a loop, so please hold this over there."

As they hid in the shadows of the trees, the Chief ran up with puffs of steam shooting from his head. At that instant, his foot was caught perfectly in the loop the two had made and, like a football, he tumbled head over heels with a great *thud!*

It is true that savages are simply lacking in wisdom. After all, the Chief was caught alive.

"Hey Mr. Barbarian, you can't match the wisdom of the white man. If you promise you won't eat us from now on, I'll forgive you."

"Yes! We most certainly will not eat the white master. We've had quite enough." Tears like great lumps of charcoal flowed from the Chief's eyes as he apologized. At this, Little

Dankichi unfastened the vine, seizing the crown and spear.

"As usual, Dan-chan never fails to amaze."

"Kari, you yourself are quite amazing as well."

The crown Dankichi captured was the symbol of the king. With this crown he could rule over the savages. "Yahoo! From now on I am the King of this island, you know!" Lost in his happiness, Dankichi sang, "Yay! Yippee!" and celebrated with a native's dance. At that moment, a roar loud enough to topple a mountain came from behind them. Startled, Kari turned around only to see... trouble! It was an elephant! A most enormous elephant!

Of course the elephants found in zoos, circuses, and the like are quiet and rather tame, but as for the elephants of the wild, they are bad-tempered beyond belief. One will trample and crush anything that is in its path. Swinging a trunk the size of a chimney, it bounded closer, and the startled Dankichi was horrified. With a "Yikes!!" he suddenly made as if to run into the field, but Kari hastily shouted out, "Dan-chan, it's dangerous to run that way, escape this way between these thick trees!"

Following Kari's command, Dankichi dove between the two trees.

"Heyyy stupid Elephant. Hey! Over here." Kari, with the wisdom of a seasoned general, stood between the two trees and ridiculed the giant elephant thousands of times bigger than himself. In a rage, the elephant flew towards him. This was Kari's plan. The elephant was sandwiched between the two trees and was unable to move.

"Long live Dankichi... even the elephant was caught alive!"

Once again saved from a jam by the quick thinking of Kari, Dankichi returned to where he'd disguised himself as a blackie since he needed to get his clothes.

"Kari, it was just around here, wasn't it?"

"Yeah it was just by the stream over there."

When Dankichi looked forward, he was surprised by what he saw. It seemed that earlier, someone up in a tree had seen Dankichi in his clothes. Wobbling around and looking very odd was a monkey, wearing Dankichi's clothes and swinging around a pair of pants.

"What the heck!? What should we do, Kari?"

Unfortunately, because the monkey was quick, it was able to escape. "Hey, it's going over there!" squeaked Kari. Then the monkey stopped, not sure where to go.

"Alright! Let's catch him, Kari!" Dankichi jumped across with great concentration. The monkey was surprised. He had never seen a white person wearing the Chief's crown. He was bewildered and climbed up a tree to hop across the river.

"That darn monkey! But I can jump over that river no problem!" exclaimed Dankichi.

"Are you sure that's a good idea?" asked Mister Kari.

"Don't worry about it. Watch this!" Dankichi got on his mark. He started running. He made a splendid jump!

Usually Dankichi wouldn't have any problems with a jump like this. However, sometimes things don't go quite as planned. The spear sank into the muddy river bottom, and Dankichi was stuck hanging over the middle of the river.

"Dang!" cursed Dankichi, but saying that wouldn't be any help to him now. Hanging from the spear like a piece of laundry on a clothes- line, Dankichi looked down and saw that this time the danger was very real.

Below him was a huge alligator with its mouth open wide, waiting for Dankichi to fall. Surely if he had known there were alligators in this river, he might have reconsidered this plan. "Kari! I'm in real trouble now!"

Kari, observing the events, thought, "Hmm, what can I do?" Soon enough, the wise Kari had something in mind. He quickly ran up a tree, stick in hand, and threw it at the alligator.

Kari's aim was true and the stick landed on target in the alligator's gaping mouth. They had escaped that deadly situation by a hairsbreadth.

Dankichi's weight pulled him down towards the alligator's mouth at the same time as the branch landed. Naturally, the alligator, unable to close its mouth with the stick there, was frantic. In that instant, Dankichi and Kari crossed the river.

"Thanks, Kari, you saved me."

As the two friends searched here and there for the mischievous monkey, it started to get dark.

"Kari, it's getting dark, what should we do?"

"We don't have any choice but to sleep here tonight; but we're in the wilderness, so wild animals will probably come out during the night. We should make a fire to frighten them off."

Kari truly is a loyal friend. He gathered some branches together and made a fire.

Gradually, the sun sank below the horizon of this untamed land. The awful shriek of a strange bird searching for prey and the howls of the wild beasts wandering through the jungle made Dankichi feel very uneasy.

"Kari, that was a horrible sound, wasn't it? I wonder if we'll be okay..."

"As long as we keep the fire going, we'll be fine. It'll scare away the beasts of this island."

These two had fought off danger all afternoon, so they were completely worn out, and they went straight to sleep.

As night fell, the crackling fire slowly burned down to embers, to the peril of Dankichi and Kari. You see, this is an island crawling with hungry wild beasts. When the fire went out all of the beasts that had been waiting gathered in close as a pack. Our heroes were awakened by a loud noise in the surrounding bush. They rubbed the sleep from their eyes only to see....

Our adventurer Dankichi, who had drifted ashore a barbaric

tropical island and had gone on to have many exciting adventures, was now celebrating the New Year. You see, this land was so hot that all the people had been burnt black, so even when the New Year came they could still walk around naked.

"Ah, is everyone here?"

In the early morning on New Year's Day, Dankichi gathered all his men in the field in front of the palace.

"Today, I'm going to tell you about an interesting plan I've made."

The plan was to make an elite trooper corps from the ten strongest men, who could perform military duties from now on. The selection method was a strange form of sumo, in which the last ten men remaining would be chosen for the corps.

A sumo wrestling ring was made. At last, the ridiculous forehead sumo began. "In this type of sumo you can't make use of your limbs, only your forehead," said Dankichi.

"Come on Number Twenty! Pull yourself together!" cheered Dankichi.

"Looks like Number Eight also lost…"

You see, this is sumo where you cannot move your arms and legs. In this strange sport you can only move your head around blindly, like a cow.

THUMP!

The men were stubborn, so they continued to hit their heads together. Both contenders had lumps

on their heads and were on the verge of tears. All throughout, the others cheered noisily and the fight continued.

"I want all ten champs to line up!" ordered Dankichi. On his command, the ten men got in a line.

"Men, from this moment forward, you will be known as the New Army Elite Troopers. You get the honor of wearing this cap," Dankichi proclaimed.

The caps that Dan-chan proceeded to proudly place on their heads were actually coconuts cut in half with a star insignia drawn on to show honor.

The natives were overjoyed. With their special caps and armbands, their loyalty to King Dankichi grew and their resolve strengthened.

"Our next mission is to raise our glorious Japanese flag at the highest point on this island. I know it seems like a difficult mission, but I'm asking you all to give 110%!" Dankichi declared.

The preparations were made.

"Alright, let's move out!"

Since becoming King of the island, Dankichi hadn't explored his territory at all. He had no idea where they were going. "Kari, is the flag safe?" he asked.

"For sure, I'm keeping it wrapped around me."

They walked for a while and ended up at a dead end where a river blocked their path. The current was strong and there was nothing to cross on.

Dan-chan is an excellent swimmer, but it wouldn't do to get the Japanese flag wet.

"Your Highness! I've thought up a neat plan. Just leave it to us," said trooper Number One. After some discussion, the troopers leaped into the river one by one and grabbed on to each other. In the blink of an eye, a human bridge had formed.

"Gee whiz! These elite troopers are the cat's pajamas! Let's go ahead and cross," said Dankichi.

With Number One's valuable stroke of genius, they were able to cross the river without any trouble. The group had been walking along a difficult path and was now close to a mountain's peak. But then they arrived at a steep cliff and had to stop again.

"I aim to hang the flag on the tree at the top of that cliff, but it doesn't seem like we can get up there," said Dankichi. Of course, the cliff wasn't really that tall, but Dankichi was just too good to get dirty while climbing.

"Have no fear, Your Highness, we can surely be of use to you. We'll build a stairway that you can use to climb up," said Number One. He had received three stars on his gold stripe from Dankichi and was still giving it his all.

Number One yelled out a strange command. "Alright you lot, let's become a stairway for His Highness!"

Dankichi and Mister Kari watched as the natives climbed on each other's back one by one, gathering together into a jumble of black bodies and spears. Before long a ladder of black men was made.

"Wow, simply amazing! But the man at the very the bottom must be quite something. Well, Mister Kari, climb on up after me then!" Dan-chan began to climb up with ease.

"The distance between the spears is a bit too far, so I'm going to borrow your heads for just a moment," said Mister Kari as he used the heads of the natives as stepping-stones, climbing up the ladder with small hops.

"Wow, just as I'd expected of the highest point on the island! What a great view!"

Having reached the peak of the mountain, Dan-chan looked all around and let out an "Oh no!" when he looked at the base of a palm tree. There, napping lazily, lay an unbelievably huge lion!

"Mi…Mister Kari, it's a lion! Wha…what are we going to do?!"

"We're in a pretty tight spot, huh?"

Even the great Dan-chan, unable to approach any closer, was at a loss. If he could just call the natives to drive it away, all would be well. But if he raised his voice, the lion would awaken. It'd be perfect if it would just wake up and wander off, but if it were to chase after him, he would surely be lunchmeat.

"Hey Dan-chan, I thought up something great." Mister Kari quietly whispered. Then, he quietly approached the lion holding a length of rope.

After attaching the rope to the lion's tail, Mister Kari tightly fastened the other end to the palm tree.

"Dan-chan, you're fast on your feet, so rouse the lion and run some laps around that tree!"

"Gotcha."

Dankichi understood Mister Kari's plan completely. He woke the lion right away and ran round and round the tree as the lion chased him.

Completely unaware that his tail was tied to a rope, the roused lion chased Dankichi around and around, only to be mortified to find himself immobile.

"Ha ha ha! Mister Lion, you've been beat after all, haven't you! Since you're there, allow me to borrow you as a foothold."

Having finally climbed to the top of the tall pine tree, Dankichi, along with Mister Kari, was able to unfurl the Rising Sun flag into the New Year's morning breeze.

Ah, the fluttering of the Rising Sun in the morning breeze, how nostalgic! The natives, who had climbed up as well, stood admiring Dankichi, whose eyes glistened with tears.

"Even after coming to this savage island, and becoming the King… in the end I'm still Japanese," thought Dankichi.

"Long live the Rising Sun!" Dankichi shouted out at the top of his lungs.

"Long live the Japanese Empire!"

Popular Orientalism and Japanese Views of Asia

KAWAMURA MINATO

TRANSLATION BY KOTA INOUE & HELEN J. S. LEE

I. Barbarity and Civilization

1. ADVENTURES OF DANKICHI'S GLOBE

Billed as a "delightful comic tale," Shimada Keizō's *Adventures of Dankichi* was serialized in the magazine *Boys' Club* for six years, from 1933 to 1939. While fishing in a boat, the young protagonist Dankichi falls asleep and drifts away to a tropical island thickly forested with palm trees—an "island of barbarians." The story develops around Dankichi's adventures as he, helped by the quick wit and wisdom of Karikō the black mouse, who serves as his judicious consultant, becomes king of the island. *The Adventures of Dankichi* was a very popular comic that mesmerized Japanese children at the time.

Adventures embodies possibly the best expression of images held by Japanese—in a general sense—of the "tropics," "blackies," "the South Seas," "the uncivilized," and "barbarians" during the 1930s (although adventure and expedition stories for boys set in the South Seas, such as Nan'yō Ichirō's *The Green Desert Island* and *The Roaring Jungle*, had been serialized in *Boys' Club* and other magazines since the late 1920s and were enthusiastically received). *Adventures'* frequent use of discriminatory terms that would be avoided in contemporary society, such as "cannibals," "blackies," "savages," "natives," and "cannibal-savages," only indicates the shallowness of social consciousness regarding racial discrimination in this period, and the use of those words should not be regarded as a sign of the text's particularly blatant prejudice. As the author himself admits, he had a preconceived idea that "the tropical region in the South Seas was a place where dangerous beasts and wild birds roamed in the jungle and where dark-skinned headhunters lived."[1] Reflecting this image, the story consists of a mishmash of animals from all over the world that would generate the image of the "tropics" and "uncivilized lands"—not only do African animals such as lions, elephants, giraffes, and crocodiles appear in the story, but so do animals such as orangutans, sea turtles, and camels from the Southeast Asian tropics, Arabian desert, South America, New Guinea, and India.

The story conveys a sense of what can be called Japanese "Orientalism" toward "the southern region," "the South Seas," and the "tropics," collectively.[2] The author creates a tale of an imaginary and fantastical "tropical region in the South Seas" that is markedly different from the reality in Africa and Southeast Asia. Such a lack of national specificity was, of course, not deemed problematic by the general public because the story was merely a type of comic, a form of children's amusement. Comics were granted the privilege of ignoring the geographical restriction of a story, be it Africa, Sumatra, Borneo, New Guinea, Samoa, or the Marshall Islands. The mode of expression called children's comics was at the bottom rung of pop culture, and one can say that its status as a marginalized genre helped justify its preposterous content.

However, *Adventures'* Orientalism toward "the tropical region in the south" has a clear origin in its political and social context. The author, Shimada Keizō, states that the idea of *Adventures* was "an extension of the dream I've always had since my boyhood." He continues: "Back then, all boys seemed to share the same dream of becoming a cabinet minister or a general, but for some unknown reason, an absurd dream sprouted in my little head." Shimada further explains his "irrepressible wishes, which were growing like mushrooming clouds": "The dream was to go somewhere in the south where the climate was mild . . . and become a king on a deserted island . . . where I'd be accompanied by animals as retainers . . . with no worries about money . . . and no homework." Shimada comments, "At that time, the South Seas Islands were under Japan's colonial mandate, and the political idea of southward national expansion was on the rise in the name of development projects. All eyes were on the southern region, so I figured that a southern island would be the best setting for my Dankichi story."[3] He suggests that his original idea to set the story in a "tropical region in the south" was because he envisioned the Micronesian Islands, which were Japan's colony at the time. Mori Koben, a Japanese pioneer of South Seas development, who was active in the Truk Islands (present-day Chuuk in the Eastern Caroline Islands of Micronesia), is often said to be the model for Dankichi, and this is perhaps because it is highly likely that Dankichi would have fetched up on one of the Micronesian Islands.[4] As an aside, it should be noted that Yamanaka Minetarō's *300 Miles across the Enemy Territory*, published by Kodansha in 1931, includes a novella called "The Boy King in the South Seas." It is a fiction set in the actual South Seas, in which a boy named Ōtaki Kenkichi becomes king of an island in the Solomon archipelago by conquering the people in the island using "tools of civilization," such as mirrors, fertilizer, and pistols. It appears that *Adventures* was directly inspired by the boy king of this "Kingdom of Daiken," which was named after the protagonist.[5]

Of course, in the South Seas, with the exception of Palau (Belau), which has crocodiles (which were likely brought in from the outside), there are no wild beasts such as lions, gorillas, or panthers, let alone primitive peoples who could be described by a discriminatory term such as "cannibals." On Dankichi's globe, the tropical region in the South Seas included the "dark continent" of Africa, remote Borneo and Sumatra, the dense forests of New Guinea, and the Amazonian jungles. All together, this was the world of "primitives," "barbarians," and "natives."

Viewing *Adventures* in this light, it is hardly meaningful to discuss what the actual setting of the barbarian island was, or who the model for the protagonist was. It is true that the South Seas Islands provided inspiration for the creation of Dankichi's island, but the tale was mostly created by the author's wild imagination. Or to put it in a critical light, the "delightful comic tale" continued to be produced by his Orientalist images of the South Seas, which were shaped by ignorance and popular misconceptions.

. . .

It is possible to view *Adventures* as a propaganda text endorsing Japan's expansionism and colonial domination, or as a text that underscores Japanese superiority grounded in racial prejudices. Given the limited level of public consciousness in the 1930s, however, it is hard to pass judgment by concluding that the content of *Adventures* was particularly expansionist, colonialist, or racist. The frequently used racist expressions mentioned earlier were part of commonly used everyday language, and they do not suggest that Shimada had stronger racist inclinations than others.

However, what *Adventures* introduced into the underlying mentality of the culture—literally, underground culture, rather than subculture—of the late 1920s and early 1930s Japan was the very theme of "barbarity" discovered by "civilization." In other words, a Japanese boy, Dankichi, who dons only a grass skirt, appearing practically identical with the naked "savages," symbolizes "civilization" in contrast to the "barbarity" of the "blackies" by the very fact that he wears a wristwatch and shoes. The watch and shoes are evidence of his civilized self. And it is the small accessory—a wristwatch— that functions as the symbolic device that decidedly separates the characters into a hierarchal culture: Dankichi as the king, on the one hand, and the "barbarian retainers" on the other (Shimada never forgot to draw Dankichi's watch on his left wrist, even in the smallest frame; this has already been pointed out in Yano Akira's *Japanese Views of the History of the South Seas*).

Dankichi is the one who rules "time" on the barbarian island, and it is his unitary control and rule over "time" that becomes the source of his power on the throne. Dankichi introduces to the uncivilized island—now his island—schools, hospitals, a military, a postal system, and money, and tries to civilize his "barbarian retainers." But what lies at the root of this "civilization" is none other than the watch, a sophisticated device that controls "time." Perhaps the watch also indicates that his superiority comes from his familiarity with numbers and letters, which allows Dankichi to become king among the "natives" (Dankichi does not want to be bothered by the names of his "blackie" retainers, such as Banana, Pineapple, and Betel Nut, so he writes numbers on their chests, calling them "Number One," "Number Two," and so forth).

Wearing a watch (or wearing shoes), as Dankichi does, however, was a relatively new phenomenon in modern Japanese history. In Meiji (1868–1912) and Taisho (1912–1926) Japan, it was almost inconceivable for children to wear watches, and even in 1933 (the first year of *Adventures*' publication) it was probably very rare to see a child with one. If a watch is a reflection of civilization, it should be noted that Japan's own civilization and enlightenment did not have such a long history for Dankichi to boast of to his "barbarian retainers." Conversely, only by discovering the "barbarian retainers," as well as other "savages" on the "barbarian island" such as the "Kūroi" tribe, "Burakku" tribe, "Kankara" tribe, and "Yami" tribe,[6] could Dankichi, as a Japanese, become a "civilized individual." By discovering the external "barbaric Other," one can find "civilization" within. In other words, it is fair to say that by acquiring the "barbarous" colony that was the South Seas Islands—or, by incorporating "uncivilized" savages and barbarian islands into its own territories—Japan, for the first time, came to have an awareness of itself as a first-class, "civilized nation."

2. DISCOVERING THE "NATIVE"

In Lesson Two of the ninth volume of the state-approved grade school Japanese language textbook (of the third edition, which ran from 1918 to 1932) is a reading entitled "A Letter from the Truk Islands." It reads as follows:

April 10

Dear Shōtarō,

. . . It's been three months since I came to the Truk Islands, and I now have a good grasp of the lay of the land here. Both winter and spring are close to summer in the Japanese mainland. I've heard that it's as warm as it is now throughout the year, and contrary to my initial worries, this seems to be a pleasant place to live. Also, the islands in this area are governed by our country, and many Japanese people have moved here, so I don't feel lonely in the least bit. The first thing you would notice upon arrival here is the plants. Especially rare among them are the coconut palm trees and breadfruit trees. Among the palm trees, the tall ones can reach as much as ninety feet. Leaves that look like the wings of birds are clustered at the top of the trunk, where bunches of fruit grow the size of an adult's head. [. . .]

The natives are not very civilized yet, but they are meek and easily take to us. Because our country has built many schools in recent years, the native children have learned to speak very good Japanese. I saw a girl about ten years old singing the Japanese anthem *Kimigayo* the other day.

I will write again soon. Please give my best regards to your father and mother.

Your Uncle

The mandate of Micronesia was handed over to Japan from Germany in 1920, and it did not take long for the islands to be used as a topic in Japanese textbooks. (Volume nine of the textbook was edited in 1920.) Takagi Ichinosuke, the author of this "letter," was a scholar of Japanese literature who worked as the editor of school textbooks for the Ministry of Education. He later recounted that he composed the piece "without any direct knowledge of the Truk Islands" and wrote it "solely relying on guidebooks of the islands."[7] Remarking, "It bothers me after all that the letter introduces a story about the 'natives' at the end in an awkward manner," he went on to offer self-criticism saying, "Especially the line, 'I saw a girl about ten years old singing the Japanese anthem *Kimigayo* the other day,' is very much an abstract expression. You can write these conceptual things with flare if you're writing from a dogmatic standpoint, but they have nothing to do with reality."

Setting aside Takagi's self-criticism, it is undeniable that these colonialist materials were used in elementary school education and that they planted in the minds of young subjects of the Japanese empire images of the "natives" and the colony: unusual vegetation—such as palm and breadfruit trees—and "yet-to-be-civilized" "natives" in a strange and unfamiliar landscape. It is not far-fetched to say that the natives that appeared in grade school textbooks prepared the way for "barbarian retainers" in *Adventures* and "violent savages" in *The Green Desert Island*. And just as Dankichi ruled the "barbarian world" in the name of "civilization," it was the Japanese language in schools and the nation-state system of the "Japanese empire," symbolized in the Japanese anthem, that governed the uncivilized.

The Micronesian "natives" under Japan's mandate were not the first group of "natives," "uncivilized people," or "barbarians" that modern Japan discovered. In fact, they were the last. Over the course of Japan's modernization (that is, on its way to the national goal of "Civilization and Enlightenment"), the barbarous and uncivilized "natives" that stood in stark contrast to the "civilized" Japanese were constructed one after another. They were the Ainu, who were perfectly preserved as "former natives" in the law entitled "The Hokkaido Former Natives Protection Law," the "natives" who lived in Otasu Forest near present-day Poronaisk in Sakhalin (that is, the northern ethnic minorities such as the present-day Uiltas, Nivkhi, Yakuts), and the "natives" who were called the "Takasago tribe" or "native savages" in Taiwan, which became Japan's colony soon after the Sino-Japanese War (1894–1895).

. . .

The natives of the Truk Islands described in the textbook were "meek" and "easily took to [Japanese]." Needless to say, these expressions conversely presume that there were natives who were "not meek" and did not "easily take to [Japanese]." For example, they point to the existence of ferocious and vicious "savages" like the "natives" in the Marshall Islands depicted by Suzuki Tsunenori in his *True Record of the South Seas Expedition*.[8] Suzuki and others headed out to the Marshall Islands to investigate a group of shipwrecked Japanese fishermen and, as suggested by information passed on by an English ship, concluded that the shipwreck was indeed caused by an attack from "natives." He describes so-called Marshallese "natives" in the following terms:

> The natives are very idle in nature, and more docile characters are hardly ever found. However, they are unable to discern right from wrong and have no sense of honor or judgment at all. They still exhibit a friendly and sociable manner with each other, as though they were relatives, and very rarely fight each other. Their deference to the king of the island is comparable to that of a god, and the way in which people look up to him is more akin to worship than paying respect. If a foreigner pays a visit and brings rare gifts or food, they share it with their neighbors and friends. However, the custom from

the barbaric era persists in the way in which men oppress women. Men treat women no differently from the way in which slaves were treated during the Roman empire—quite close to the handling of furniture or property.

On the islands of Manowa[9] and Arno in the archipelago, the atmosphere is quite brutal, and the residents have not given up the custom of cannibalism. Some of the inhabitants on other islands are also vicious and evil, having a particular taste for human flesh. When they discover starving drifters on their islands, they feed them food and make them believe that they have been rescued. However, the islanders secretly slaughter the drifters later, bury the dead bodies in the sand, wait until the middle of the night when there is no one around, and dig up the bodies and eat them. This is what I have heard. When I asked how they ate human flesh, I was told that they tear off small pieces, wrap them with pandan leaves, and grill them on a strong fire until the surface is roasted and turns the color of charcoal. Then they take the grilled flesh out of the fire, peel off the roasted leaves, and eat the human flesh inside that has turned white and become like tofu. The taste of human flesh is said to be marvelously delicious.

The "barbaric customs," characterized by cannibalism, idleness, adultery, superstition, and tattooing, are definitive images of the "natives." "South Seas natives" has conjured these images of an uncivilized world, such as "barbarians" and "savages," ever since Suzuki's time. Even when Japan later took possession of the whole Micronesian region—including the Marshall Islands—as a colony, the generalized image of the "natives" as uncivilized and barbaric was handed down largely unaltered.

Taiwan's "Takasago tribe," which staged the Wushe Incident, left even more grave and alarming marks of barbarism in the Japanese psyche than the Marshallese "natives."[10] As a result of the Sino-Japanese and Russo-Japanese wars, two wars of colonial expansion, Japan acquired colonies such as Taiwan and Korea, but it also met with large-scale resistance from the indigenous peoples in the process of colonization. By the fact that those resistance movements have been trivialized as disturbances and riots and have not been understood as a part of the larger anti-Japanese, anticolonial struggle, we can see the tendency to disregard accountability for Japan's modern colonial policies.

The Wushe Incident refers to the uprising of the "Takasago tribe" in October 1930, in the indigenous village of Wushe, located in the mid-region of Taiwan. On October 27, about two hundred Takasago people from six hamlets stormed into the playground of the Wushe local school on Sports Day, killing Japanese and attacking police and governmental offices. One hundred thirty-four Japanese were killed. It appears that the incident was understood on the Japanese mainland as a case of revolt by "the barbaric" against "the civilized," rather than an outcome of the anti-Japanese movement in the colonies. The Takasago were generally known as "savages" who practiced headhunting, adorned their bodies with tattoos, fought among their clans, and continued to live in strife and conflict. Images of the Takasago swinging their machetes at the Japanese overlap with the scenes frequently seen in comics or films in which "cannibalistic natives" attack explorers and travelers. Collectively delineated in these scenes are the reactionary attacks of the "savages" on "civilization" through which Japanese soberly recognized the presence of "barbarians" within the borders of their own nation.

In his book, *The Governor-General Office of Taiwan*, Huang Zhaotang explains that "the cause [of the Wushe Incident] was an eruption of resentment that had built up over the years against the military expeditions and punishments meted out by the Governor-General's Office, in addition to forced labor, insults against Takasago women, and dissatisfaction with the arrogant local police."[11] However, the majority of Japanese at the time, including intellectuals, saw the incident as a manifestation of "barbarity" caused by the innate bestiality, infantile emotions, and truncated thought processes of the "barbarians." In her travelogue entitled *Korea, Taiwan, and South Seas Harbors*, for instance, Nogami Yaeko, who had visited the site of the uprising in Wushe, wrote the following about the cause of the incident as told by a Japanese who was a policeman at the time.

Hōbo is one of the native hamlets located near Meishi at the foot of the mountains. A man named Piposappo was an adoptee.[12] His wife was an exceptionally licentious woman and even ventured out to Puli in search of young Japanese men from the mainland. Piposappo could not blame or punish his wife. Instead, he was captivated by a strange heroism uniquely inherent in the Taiwanese savages. He thought he could regain her love if he demonstrated his manliness by hunting the heads of despicable mainland Japanese men.

In the meantime, Chief Mona Rudao of the Mahebo clan had a new problem, besides the one with his younger sister, who had just been divorced by a Japanese police officer. A group of people led by his two sons insulted two Japanese policemen as they happened upon them while deer hunting. It was an explosion of frustrations that young people in general harbored. The Japanese authorities had planned to quietly quash this incident, but not knowing this, Mona Rudao worried about the possible punishment that might befall his sons. Piposappo seized on his fear. His idea was to convince the chief, who was respected by all native villages, to back his plan to rise up against the Japanese authorities before Mona Rudao's sons were humiliatingly punished, and, utilizing the opportunity, to engage in headhunting and earn his wife's praise.[13]

Needless to say, this was an account completely in line with the official documentation of the incident. What is illuminated most forcefully in this passage, however, is Nogami's preconceived notion that the real cause of the incident was the "barbarism" of the Takasago, characterized by their brutality and infantilism, by heroism that only strikes the civilized as "odd," by cowardice and suspicion, sexual promiscuity, inferiority, and a hasty, self-centered thought process. She writes, "Even though the Japanese authorities had planned to quietly quash this incident," the Taiwanese savages rose up, propelled by their own mysterious, infantile, and foolish heroism and cowardice. The responsibility of Japanese police authorities is not addressed. It is assumed that the entire incident was a product of the imagination of the "barbarian natives," and was, in essence, rooted in their barbaric brutality and lewdness.

One of the fictional depictions of the Wushe Incident is Nakamura Chihei's "Foggy Native Village," included in his *Collected Taiwan Fictions*.[14] This story offers a more detailed depiction of the process leading up to the "barbarian" uprising than Nogami Yaeko's text, and it offers as the remote cause of the incident the broken marriage between a native woman and a Japanese police officer, who suffers torment over his interracial marriage. Nakamura takes a rather sympathetic view of the Takasago by emphasizing the obstacles that emerge from the lack of understanding between two ethnic groups. In essence, however, he sees the Wushe Incident as desperate resistance against "civilization" by the cornered "barbarians."

> Japan's policies toward the Taiwanese natives are gradually achieving success, and the natives' unadorned wild nature is now being tamed in the face of what we call culture. And their ethnic brutality and primitive lifestyle are already beginning to deteriorate, just like the vitality of a menopausal woman who is finally losing her biological female functions. [. . .] It was the case that the Taiwanese savages galvanized what little wild or violent nature they had left in them in order to recklessly attempt to fight, for the very last time, the lifestyle incompatible with their character; that is, civilization.

Nogami and Nakamura observe the "barbarians" (*yabanjin*) from the position of the "civilized." Their over-determined assumption—that they are on the side of "civilization" and the Taiwanese natives are on the side of "barbarity" (*yaban*)—naturally never wavers.[15] Even for Nakamura, who dramatized the Wushe Incident as a tragedy between two ethnic groups, the solution was for the civilized nation of Japan, which now included such "barbarians," to "civilize" and "enlighten" them faster, if only by a little, and to demonstrate to an even greater extent the depths of Japan's good intentions. In other words, there was no other way to educate the "barbarians" than to treat them with paternalistic sympathy, compassion, and protection in the same fashion as the policy of segregation and protection suggested by the legal framework in the Hokkaido Former Natives Protection Law for the Ainu.

3. THE MODE OF THOUGHT THAT FRAMES "BARBARISM"

In terms of the Wushe Incident's impact on the cultural psyche of the Japanese "mainlanders," however, one must point out the awakening of the Japanese—who had undergone civilization and enlightenment themselves—to their "inner barbarity." One fine example is Ōshika Taku's anthology entitled *The Savage*, which includes short stories centering on the themes of the native settings and peoples of Taiwan.[16] The stories include "Tattaka Zoo," "Savage Women," "Zhang's Desire," "In the Forest," "The People of the Inlands," and "The Savage," among others. "Tattaka Zoo" was published in 1931, "Savage Women" in 1933, and "Zhang's Desire" and "The Savage" in 1935. Ōshika began writing his "Takasago Tribe" stories one year after the Wushe Incident, and this stream of "savage literature" was produced around the same time that the heroic stories of Dankichi and his barbarian retainers were published in *Adventures*.

In the collection, the title piece, "The Savage," best exemplifies Ōshika's predilection for the concept of "barbarity." The young Japanese protagonist Tazawa joins a labor dispute in a Chikuho coal mine in Japan that his father owns and engages in a fierce protest, even instigating the miners to flood a portion of the mine. Practically disowned by his family, he is forced to relocate himself to the "native land" of Taiwan. Tazawa, who is betrayed by his trusted friend during the labor struggle, "feels as though he has lost the foundation of his spirit," and "almost as an act of self-abandonment," comes to work at the police station that guards the Taiwanese savages. He then meets the native girl Taimorikaru, who possesses wild and unadorned charm. She is looking for a Japanese husband from the mainland, and he ends up reciprocating her simple, passionate advances.

A riot among the Taiwanese natives erupts in a nearby community. Tazawa joins in the "punitive expedition forces," and in the heat of the moment, with a machete, ends up beheading a native who attacks him. This marks the surfacing of the barbarity that was latent in Tazawa, the petit bourgeois intellectual and highly educated idler. Now, Tazawa has to recognize the wild, primitive nature and the barbaric essence inside him. However, he is forced to admit that these traits are nevertheless restrained when compared to the real "barbarity" displayed by Taimonamo, the younger sister of Taimorikaru, who puts a curse on the severed head of the enemy that Tazawa had brought back by saying, "Bring here the heads of your parents and siblings. I'll let them live with you here." This passage follows:

> Witnessing this attitude of Taimonamo, who was only 15, Tazawa was unequivocally made aware of his weakness. He couldn't simply believe that this was all because the rough customs of this place affected her mind. He felt as though he had caught the choking smell of barbarism handed down through the blood. "No, it's not just barbarism. That barbarism is like the solemn pulse that throbs into the indomitable spirit of a giant tree—a colossal tree that spreads its chest while suffering from merciless Mother Nature, yet sustained by its acerbic compassion. The sap continues to run throughout the tree, and it gushes out from the tip of even a small branch. Compared to this, I am only a feeble sapling, just transplanted.

It can be said that this passage depicts the catalyst for the transformation from "civilization" to "barbarity." While Tazawa is a young man who "dropped out of school in Tokyo," there is no question that he is a fellow traveler, would-be intellectual who shows sympathy for labor organizing. But the same Tazawa, the "civilized man" who possesses a higher intellectual ability than most people, engages in an instinctive fight and carries out an act of "headhunting" just like the Taiwanese natives. It proves that the regression into barbarism from civilization can happen among Japanese, or those from the mainland. However, such barbarity is still tinged with a delicate shade compared to even Taimonamo, the native girl. If her wild, barbaric nature is something that has put down its roots deep into the ground, Tazawa's awakening to a "wild nature" is merely that of a transplanted sapling. And of course, all this means nothing but the rediscovery of modern Japan's "civilization and enlightenment" as a "transplanted civilization," as well as an awakening to the true, wild barbarity that existed before Japan's modernity.

. . .

In the early Showa period (1926–1989), the Japanese could confirm their own "civilized self" by finding "barbarity" and "untamed nature" in the "natives" and "savages" of the colony. But, within themselves, who were supposed to be thoroughly civilized, they also were to discover a "barbarity" as their hidden and secret passion. Tazawa chops off a man's head with a Taiwanese native's sword and triumphantly comes home with it, and Dankichi subdues powerful enemy natives, pirates, and rascals with his military power. In other words, this is a calling from an "untamed instinct" within and an awakening of "barbarism."

That such an awakening of "wild nature" and "barbarity" was the other side of contempt and fear toward the native and savage is apparent without being examined in the context of modern Japanese history. The awareness of the tenuousness of transplanted Western civilization in Japan, on the one hand, and the discovery of the "barbaric nature" of Japanese themselves, which they had ostensibly expunged by introducing modern, systematic ideas, on the other, were one and the same thing. The problem inherent to modern Japan was that its own appropriation of a foreign culture and civilization and its project to modernize and civilize native cultures—that is, the "Orientalization" of the surrounding Asian and Pacific cultures and the de-Orientalization of Japan's own traditional/Asia-Pacific culture, which was rooted in the Asia-Pacific region—had to occur simultaneously.

This is to say that the discovery of "barbarity," as in the case of Ōshika, did not open a path to critique and overcome the "civilization" of the West by uncovering Japan's own uncivilized nature. Instead, it only valorized barbarism as defined within the existing framework of civilization itself (Ōshika himself regretted that his work was regarded as explorations of "mere barbarism"). The ultimate goal of modern Japan, "Leaving Asia, Entering Europe," could not be achieved only by modernizing, civilizing, and Westernizing Japan. It was also deeply implicated in treating other Asian and Pacific ethnic groups and countries as uncivilized and in regarding them as primitive and barbaric. In other words, Japan's enlightenment and civilization meant the transformation of other Asian-Pacific ethnicities and countries, which historically had much in common with Japanese culture, into a primitive and barbarous existence.

It is widely accepted in the study of world history that the divide between the imperial master and the colony never occurred where there was no gap in stages of civilization. Countries and ethnic groups that were on a similar level in their cultures could never develop imperial-power-and-colony relationships with each other. Japan's colonial acquisitions followed the Western model—examples include England and India, France and North Africa, Holland and Indonesia, etc.—and were always accompanied by cultural invasion and deprivation in which other ethnicities and countries were thoroughly despised, looked down upon, and regarded as "barbarous," while their customs, cultures, and conventions were degraded as uncivilized. In some ways, the fanatic inculcation of Japanese spirit and emperor ideology in the colony was an expression of the inferiority complex felt by the Japanese themselves toward the transplanted Western civilization. Such inculcation, functioning as a hot house for arrogant cultural chauvinism and narrow-minded cultural nationalism, prepared for the absurd, yet calamitous, situations in the regions under Japan's colonial rule.

II. "Natives" in Asia

I. COOLIES, BEGGARS, AND OPIUM ADDICTS

The steamer came alongside a stone wharf that reminded me of the one at Iida.[17] It did so with such precision that I should never have believed I was at sea. On the pier, there were crowds of people; most of the people there, however, were Chinese coolies. Looking at any one of them, I had the immediate impression of dirt. Any two together were an even more unpleasant sight. That so many of them had gathered together struck me as most unwelcome indeed. Standing on the deck, I contemplated this mob from my distant observation point and thought to myself: "Goodness! What a strange place I've come to!" [. . .]

I looked along the pier and noticed the horse carriages drawn up on the landing place. There were also a large number of rickshaws. However, they were pulled by the same crowd of bellowing men, so business did not appear, compared with Japan at least, to be particularly good; most of the horse carriages also seemed to be operated by the same people. Consequently, all that was there was a load of dirty vehicles clanking away. Of the horse carriages in particular, it had been rumored, at the time when the Russkies had evacuated Dalian during the Russo-Japanese War, that the Russkies had very carefully dug holes and buried the vehicles in order to prevent their falling into Japanese hands. Afterward, the Chinks walked about everywhere sniffing the ground; when they found the right smell, they nosily disinterred one carriage, then another, in the same manner. Very soon, Dalian was teeming with growling, muttering diggers of holes. These, of course, were just rumours, and I do not know what really happened. In any event, of all the rumours circulating from that time, this seems one of the cleverest, and anybody could see with his own eyes that these carriages were indeed covered in mud.[18]

Invited by Nakamura Korekimi (often known as Zekō), his friend and then-president of the South Manchurian Railway Company, Natsume Sōseki visited Korea and Manchuria for a month and a half, from September to October 1909, and serialized his travel essay *Travels in Manchuria and Korea* in a newspaper. The quotation above is the scene in which O.S.K.'s *Tetsureimaru*, with Sōseki on board, sails into the port of Dalian, the entry point to Manchuria. There are some who argue, based on this scene, that Sōseki harbored disdain toward Asia and a discriminating sentiment toward the Chinese, but here I simply want to point out that the colony "Manchuria" was first recognized as a very dirty place in the eyes of a representative intellectual and writer from Japan. In this context, coolies are equated with crowds of bellowing men, which are equated with "Chinks"; therefore the whole of "Chinks" is represented by the "filthy," "unsightly" coolies. Sōseki's first impression during his Manchuria-Korea trip was griminess and strangeness, and from here, it would not have taken much to reach the generalization of "dirty Chinese" and "filthy China."

If the text simply stated that there were many grubby coolies in China, it could be an objective statement, although tinged with a sense of disdain for poor hygiene and filthiness. But one cannot help feeling in Sōseki's rhetoric a dehumanization of coolies, or, frankly, a gaze that treats them as animals rather than as humans. One has to assume an unconscious intention to represent the coolies as subhuman animal-like creatures in sentences like, "The steamer passed alongside the shore in a calm and dignified manner, skimming close by that curious throng of coolies, and finally coming to a halt. As soon as we had docked, the crowd of coolies started buzzing and swarming like angry wasps,"[19] the frequent use of the phrase "crowd of bellowing men," or the expression "the Chinks walked about everywhere sniffing the ground; when they found the right smell . . ." in the above passage.

In the interest of comparison, let us turn to *Unbeaten Tracks in Japan*, written by the British woman Isabella Bird, who visited Japan in 1878. The following is a scene in which her ship enters the port of Yokohama.

The first thing that impressed me on landing was that there were no loafers, and that all the small, ugly, kindly-looking, shriveled, bandy-legged, round-shouldered, concave-chested, poor-looking beings in the streets had some affairs of their own to mind. At the top of the landing-steps there was a portable restaurant, a neat and most compact thing, with charcoal stove, cooking and eating utensils complete; but it looked as if it were made by and for dolls, and the mannikin who kept it was not five feet high.[20]

It is not easy to say whether the Japan of 1878, when Isabella Bird arrived at Yokohama, was more "civilized" than the Manchuria (China) of 1909, when Natsume Sōseki entered Dalian. But one has to conclude that in the area of racial and ethnic prejudices, Sōseki scores higher. Of course, this is not to say that Bird was completely free from racial prejudices. Upon meeting Ainu in Hokkaido, she wrote, "They are uncivilisable and altogether irreclaimable savages." The words "uncivilised" and "savages" appear frequently in her travel writing to describe the Ainu people. But she expresses disapproval of her interpreter Ito's extremely discriminatory words, "Treat Ainos [i.e., Ainus] politely! . . . They're just dogs, not men."[21] She also writes the following immediately after the earlier quote about the "irreclaimable savages":

> . . . yet they are attractive, and in some ways fascinating, and I hope I shall never forget the music of their low, sweet voices, the soft light of their mild, brown eyes, and the wonderful sweetness of their smile.[22]

Although the Japanese regard the Ainu as subhuman (dogs, indeed!), this British woman with a great deal of curiosity writes about the attraction of the Ainu as humans, all the while suffering from "filthiness," such as swarms of fleas and an unbearable stench. It is possible, of course, to identify here the mental tendency toward the worship of the wild state and the natural—as exemplified by the notion of the "noble savage"—in post-Rousseau Europe. But even considering that, it is perhaps justified to say that Bird's gaze fairly captures the Ainu as "humans." This British woman attempted to overcome the gap between the civilized and the primitive by the concept of universal humanity, but the Japanese (who were supposed to be only marginally civilized themselves) tried to paint the "uncivilized" peoples with the images of "dogs" and animals that were sniffing around the ground.

. . .

Let us consider another example. Imaeda Setsuo's *Strange Stories from Manchuria* was an astonishing best seller as a Manchurian guide book, reprinted twenty-four times in five years after first being published in 1935 by Gekkan Manshūsha. Unlike official guides to Manchurian immigration or textbook-like introductions to Manchuria, it reports on the hidden side of each Man-

churian city—prostitutes, opium addicts, thieves' markets, and so on—
while underscoring the bizarreness of it all. It is an interesting book that
depicts the underbelly and unknown side of Manchuria, which was strongly
associated with official slogans such as "Cooperation of Five Peoples" and
"Asian Paradise by Moral Rule." The book is written in the form of a conversation between a host and a guest. The following is an exchange in the
book's section on Dalian, the entry port to Manchuria.

> "Look at the main square. All kinds of cripples are clinging there like scabs.
> Now, a Western lady might come out of the hotel and be pleased by the
> flowers and the smell of the acacia along the boulevard. But she wouldn't
> find it easy to go out often if a cripple keeps pestering her the whole block,
> would she?"
> "In the olden days, they used to do a 'beggar sweep'—shipping all those
> picked up to Shandong peninsula in a boat and dumping them there."
> "All sent back to where they came from, you mean?"
> "They were all kept on deck, of course, but one year, the boat was hit by
> a storm. It tipped 45 degrees. Crashing waves were washing the deck. . . . Do
> I need to say the rest? These guests on the boat were missing hands or legs,
> you see. By the time the storm passed and calm clouds finally floated in the
> sky, the deck was sparkling clean, just like when VIPs come aboard, I hear."
> "Geez! It must have been a screeching hell, literally!"

This is the tone of the conversation throughout. What is depicted is the
hidden side of the Japanese colony Manchukuo and its dark, social aspects,
valued entirely for its sensationalism. The content of the book was originally
serialized in the magazine *Manchuria Monthly* under the title *Guide to the
Manchurian Special Scenic Zones*, and it is nothing more than popular reading material that largely relies on exposé realism. However, compared to
the empty formalistic reports and travelogues written by mainland writers
and journalists who visited Manchukuo on junkets sponsored by the South
Manchurian Railway Company or newspaper companies, perhaps the
book's value should be recognized, if only paradoxically, just for its mockery
of the official state slogans, such as "Cooperation of Five Peoples," "Asian
Paradise by Moral Rule," and "The Whole World under the Emperor."

Of course, this is not to say that the book offers any fundamental criticism or negative perspective of the puppet state Manchukuo. The only
thing that can be found in the book is a gaze of the curious and the bizarre
that seeks things exotic, ugly, vulgar, peculiar, and rare; and it is nothing
but a gaze that fully intends to de-familiarize Manchuria, Manchukuo, and

Manchurians. Thieves' markets, brothels, opium dens, underground scenes, etc. fill the pages. Along with the "Manchurian sunset" and warlords, these were the images of Manchuria shared among the Japanese masses, and they often came from popular travelogues and travel essays of this kind.

. . .

Let us examine other material, a book called *Dissection of Taikan'en*. No colophon, author's name, or publisher's name can be found in the book. The front cover bears the two characters for "Top Secret," and the title page states, "Social Field Work on the Han People, Volume One." This is a report on the building and facilities called Taikan'en in Fujiaden, the so-called "Manchurian residential zone" in Harbin. The book declares that here can be found every kind of vice and misery imaginable.

> From under the carved letters "Taikan'en" a cave-like pathway opens up heading north. Once you pass this gate, you will find yourself led into a dark world filled with foul smells, profanity, and terror. Two-story buildings that house flophouses, fortune-tellers, morphine dealers, and miscellaneous stores occupy both sides of the pathway. The conspicuous staircase in the middle of the path leads to the flophouse upstairs. Naked corpses are often found behind the staircase, but we see none today. The women, who are standing, as if dazed, in small groups in front of the flophouse and near the staircase, are the prostitutes who live in the hotel. Due to syphilis, their eyes are clouded white, and their faces are blue-black and emaciated because of excessive sex and drugs. The noisy crowds that surround them are those who are haggling down the already miserable price of 40 *sen* apiece.[23]

The author depicts the world of the "foul smells, profanity, and terror" of Taikan'en with the calmness of a surgeon and thoroughly objective investigation and analysis: morphine addicts, sex workers, gambling, vagabonds, opium dens, morphine dealers, beggars, thieves, and corpses. Fujiaden, the representative of the largest criminal underground of Manchukuo, and Taikan'en, the symbol of its vice, immorality, filth, and degeneracy, were nothing but the exact opposite of the ideal of "Asian Paradise by Moral Rule."

But what we need to be aware of is that the author connects the existence of Taikan'en and Fujiaden with the ethnic character of the Han. Any country or ethnic group, to a varying degree, has a criminal underground, as well as a dark side, such as brothels and slums. Its degree corresponds to the level of political and economic development of the country, and it is now common sense that it has nothing to do with ethnic or national character.

But this author discusses the issue as a problem of ethnic culture. Thus we find a passage like this one: "Contrary to the state and culture of the Japanese race, which always attempts to keep individual character pure, the Han race's society and culture are thoroughly instinct-based. They always seek to live in wild abandon, as they are led by their instinct. Therefore, there is a bad tendency in the social structure of Han society from the beginning that tends to ignore national policies. The only decisive element in Han society is the deep-seated instinct that ignores human will and sneers at normal efforts by human beings."[24]

In other words, the discriminatory gaze toward the Han race, that is the Chinese, is dressed up in the attire of cultural comparison and is offered as an observation of cultural difference between Japan, which seeks "pure character," and China, which is "thoroughly instinct-based." Needless to say, the discriminatory gaze toward China, disguised in this type of seemingly objective cultural argument, intentionally conceals the grossly inhumane and perversely immoral criminal acts committed on a national scale by Japanese who conspired to obtain large sums of money by taking advantage of the vice, corruption, fear, and immorality in China: as exposed by Eguchi Keiichi's 1988 book *Sino-Japan Opium War*, the Japanese military and merchants were actually behind those Koreans and Chinese who participated in the morphine and opium dealings. The opinion of *Dissection of Taikan'en*'s author, that the result of "seek[ing] to live in wild abandon as they are led by their instinct" is embodied in the opium addicts and sex workers, and that such is the instinct of the Han people, can amply prove how much narrow-minded chauvinism and racism may be hidden in the objectivity of cultural theory and cultural comparison.

These three writings on the Manchurians—a travel essay by a literary author, a popular travel guide, and social research—are unlike each other in their genres and periods. But what they have in common is the unconscious/conscious sense of discrimination that seeks to place the Manchurian or Chinese people in a position inferior to the Japanese by emphasizing their "dirtiness," "misery," "filth," "foul smell," "immorality," and "instinct." It is nothing other than a gaze that regards all peoples other than its own as subhuman and as animalistic, instinct-driven "natives."

Of course, Japan has a long history of fondly regarding China as a developed, civilized country, and of respecting it as if it were an older brother. During the modern period, the reversal of the relationship of the "civilized" to the "uncivilized" made it possible for Japan to colonize China. China was the source of the powerful Chinese culture. Japan was influenced by the overwhelming Chinese culture in all aspects of life, such as Chinese characters, Confucianism, Buddhism, codes of etiquette, cultural artifacts, arts, clothing, city planning, and social institutions. And that is precisely why Japan had to treat modern Chinese, the Han race, as "native." Historical, cultural inferiority could not be overcome without proving Japan's cultural superiority. Therefore, finding "Chinese" culture in coolies, beggars, and opium addicts was necessary for the sake of maintaining the fiction and vanity of the civilized nation of Japan.

2. CULTURE AND DISCRIMINATION

The tendency to dismiss non-Japanese Asians as "native," especially to treat indigenous peoples in colonies or occupied lands discriminatorily, gradually intensified as Japan accelerated imperial indoctrination based on an emperor-centered historical view. Shibusawa Keizō lists the Ainu, Pacific islanders, and Taiwanese natives as the "three major primitive peoples" within official Japanese boundaries.[25] Needless to say, the term "native" was originally used in referring to these groups generally—they were also called "former natives of Hokkaido," "South Seas natives," and "Taiwanese natives," respectively—with contempt.

An 1878 notice by the Hokkaido Development Commissioner officially renamed the Ainu "former natives"—they were earlier also called "Ezo natives," "Sakhalin natives," and "Kurile natives." The notice reads as follows: "While the former Ezo people should be treated in the same way the general population is treated for family registry and other matters, when a distinction needs to be made in certain situations, 'old subject,' 'native,' or 'former native' have been used for them, which was confusing. Therefore, from now on, they should be called 'former natives.'"[26] The Ainu were, in effect, "elevated" from "native" to "former native" at this point, but it actually meant the transformation of the Ainu, who were "native," into "common people." As Murai Osamu has pointed out, the concept of "former natives" emerged in modern Japanese history in tandem with that of "new common people," the term the Meiji government gave exclusively to former outcastes, in effect giving a new name to the old discrimination.[27]

The notice from the commissioner reveals that "native" was not a neutral term, but much later, in 1922, a literary work was published in which the Koreans under Japanese colonial rule were called "native." The novel, Nakanishi Inosuke's *New Buds in the Red Soil*, receives ambiguous reception today.[28] Written by an author who was well known as an early proletarian writer, it is a serious, socially conscious novel that depicts a Japanese news reporter's anguish and Korean farmers' suffering in a multilayered fashion. One could highly praise it as a rare work by a Japanese writer who realistically depicts Koreans as large as life, but at the same time one could identify the author's unconscious ethnocentrism and methodological error in his use of the term "native." Here is an example.

> It was winter in Colony C. It was [censored] of the powerful country N in the east. About 100 houses of the natives stood in the small settlement. A stormy wind with yellowish sand blew from the west of the continent and without restraint threatened the lives of the inhabitants, who had lived a life of inertia and lethargy on this peninsula since ancient times. The natives lived in small houses made of coarse mud—they were like sturdy caves—in order to protect themselves from the storms. The houses seemed like shelter that had progressed very little since the prehistoric age. Their roofs were thatched with an abundant amount of straw and sorghum stalks. On those roofs, or near the entrance of each house, blotchy snow covered the lids of the large clay pots for pickles. Under the eaves hung chili peppers that were redder than nandina berries, as well as dried gourds the size of human heads. The chili peppers were the only spice the natives possessed to fend off the unbearable cold, and the gourds were used to scoop water to wash the white robes that the natives regularly wore.

It would be difficult to defend the use of the term "native" here by saying that it only refers to indigenous people or aborigines. The sentence, "The houses seemed like shelter that had progressed very little since the prehistoric age," clearly equates "native" with "primitive" by association, and in this case the term "native," it can be said, is full of negative value judgment. The attempt to turn the setting of the story into an abstract one through such expressions as "Colony C" and "the powerful country N" can be attributed to the author's intention to lessen the scrutiny of the censor, but such consideration cannot be detected in references such as the one that introduces the protagonist, "the native Kim Ki-ho."

Furthermore, in these descriptions in which the term "native" and, specifically, Korean culture are linked, there is naturally the danger that a cultural gap and cultural comparison lead to a culturalist hierarchy. Words such as "large pots for pickles," "chili pepper," "gourds," and "white robes" are all expressions referring to Korean culture in the realm of clothing, food, and shelter, but they end up leaving a strange and bizarre impression of the "natives' customs."

We may point out the sense of contempt for and ethnic superiority over the local people and indigenous Koreans among the Japanese immigrants in colonial Korea after the annexation of Korea in 1910. Discrimination against the indigenous people of Korea (they were called "peninsula people" or "those from the peninsula," but not Koreans) existed officially and unofficially, with differing degrees of bluntness, in contrast to such slogans as "Same Love for All" and "Japan-Korea, United Body." At the root of this treatment festered a perverted ethnic sentiment of the Japanese that sought a sense of superiority over those of the same nationality but of different ethnicity, even though they had been "annexed" to Japan. The Japanese who tried to shut out the bad friends of Asia and the modern Japan that attempted to achieve "Leaving Asia, Entering Europe" created a mental structure that allowed them to regard non-Japanese Asians as "native" in an attempt to negate their own origins and to adopt Western modernity.

Hey, even the police are all Korean constables, I'm telling you. They're all in cahoots with each other and mocking us Japanese. When we came here from Japan for the first time, it wasn't like this at all. Koreans were so afraid just to pass in front of us. That all changed since the war. "Koreans are Japanese, too," I keep hearing. We are too nice to them, so they are getting cheeky these days and think it's OK to jump a bill at a Japanese restaurant. They won't learn a lesson unless we beat them up real good. Heck, it's OK if we kill 'em.[29]

This is a passage from Tanaka Hidemitsu's *Drunken Ship* (1949), in which a Japanese restaurant owner is hitting a Korean boy who tried to eat and run at his *oden* stew restaurant. This is probably one expression of honesty among ordinary Japanese immigrants in Korea about official slogans such as "Same Love for All" and "Japan-Korea, United Body." "Koreans *should* feel afraid just to pass in front of a Japanese," and "It's OK to kill those bastards who disobey or mock Japanese." These are merciless utterances of ethnic discrimination. However, we should see them as quite candid expressions of some of the Japanese immigrants in Korea, rather than regard them as exceptions. It is true, of course, that there were some Japanese in Korea, such as Asakawa Takumi and Abe Yoshishige, who consistently treated Korea, Koreans, and Korean culture with love and respect. But it cannot be denied that many Japanese harbored ethnic prejudice against Koreans in one way or another.

We must recognize that the function of journalism then was to discuss cultural differences between Japan and Korea (or China)—not to end the prejudice and discrimination but rather to promote it—and moreover, to provide arguments for a hierarchical cultural comparison or a cultural gap between the civilized and the uncivilized. Just to mention one instance, the book entitled *Complete Collection of Strange Customs in the World* has a section on "Bizarre Marriage Customs," where there is an entry on "Strange Taiwanese Ways" after sections on India and China.[30] It states, "There are natives and aborigines in Taiwan, but the barbaric way of the aborigines is truly awful. Readers will probably have heard of some examples, but I'll begin with the natives' customs." It proceeds to describe unusual marriage proposals and engagement presents, as well as marriages for sale. The "Taiwanese natives" in this case are actually the Han people, known as mainland Chinese. It then introduces as "barbaric customs of the aborigines" the coming of age ceremony, the adoption system, and then the "extremely barbaric" custom in which headhunting is assigned to the prospective son-in-law as a condition for a marriage. After this section comes another, on "Strange Korean Ways." It first remarks, "Since Korea is Japan's territory today, perhaps all things small and large may become Japanese style in ten years, but the old ways cannot be dispensed with today or tomorrow. Therefore, there are still some exceptionally strange practices intact, and marriage customs are especially peculiar." It goes on to describe the unusual custom of "son-in-law hazing" and the practice of marrying older wives.

These unusual, strange, peculiar, and immoral customs are introduced based solely on sensationalism. They are none other than "world customs" that are viewed through curiosity, prejudice, a discriminatory consciousness, and titillation-seeking sensibilities. Here, cultural differences are turned into an order of superiority, and we can detect cultural chauvinism that unquestioningly presupposes the superiority of the author's own culture. Obviously, the differences in marriage customs should be discussed as cultural divergence without value attached. But the book clearly depicts Taiwanese natives' headhunting customs and the Korean custom of "son-in-law hazing" as "primitive" practices, and inevitably discusses cultural differences in folkways, customs, and traditional rituals in a discriminatory manner. (In addition, these types of marriage customs can be observed in rural Japan; and as for headhunting, the book intentionally overlooks the fact that samurai regularly competed for the head of the enemy for rewards.) The introduction of the customs of various Asian ethnic groups and regions, such as India, China, Taiwan, and Korea, was not done in order to bridge the cultural gaps among ethnicities. We should understand that such moves were intended to exaggerate and underscore savagery, bizarreness, strangeness, and peculiarity in order to somehow prove the cultural superiority of the Japanese.

It should be acknowledged that academic disciplines such as anthropology, ethnography, and folklore have contributed to interpreting these cultural differences within a comparative hierarchy, assuming the existence of superior and inferior cultures or differing achievements of progress. We have already seen how *Dissection of Taikan'en*, which claims to be a field survey of Han society, actually argues for a fixed, fatalistic cultural gap from an ethnocentric viewpoint, and that it "enlightened" the Japanese about the Han ethnic group. In this sense, it cannot be denied that modern Japan's views of Asia, in various fields including literature, was distorted by the persistent impetus to "leave Asia."

.   .   .

The Japanese discovered the "native" in the South Pacific, Taiwan, and Sakhalin. And at the same time, they also discovered the "native" in China, Korea, Manchuria, and Southeast Asian regions. Needless to say, however, there was no acknowledgment that the Japanese themselves were "Japanese natives" living in the Japanese archipelago (although Kita Ikki and others cynically called Japan a "country of natives"). Bunching together those who are culturally inferior, backward, strange, or bizarre, as primitive, barbaric, and "native-like" people certainly helps foster a sense of pride that "we" are civilized.

In that moment, the commonsensical notion that there were various cultures, and that one cannot easily establish the superiority or inferiority of any ethnic culture, custom, or language, is thrown away. And the historical perspective that Indian and Chinese civilizations, as well as Korean culture, have greatly influenced Japan is also abandoned. Though the advantage they enjoyed in military and economic matters was only temporary, the great error of wartime Japanese lay in their belief that this advantage was the sign of their cultural or ethnic superiority. And the belief was not limited to military officers, merchants, or immigrants. Those who were called writers, too, were not completely immune to the groundless idea of ethnic and cultural superiority.

(What an attitude! He's sitting with his legs wide open while I'm squeezing myself into this narrow space. Why can't he be more considerate?)

That would have been the sentiment if I verbalized it. Then it gradually changed into this.

(What an attitude, you native! Sitting with your legs wide open, you lowly native! Know your place as a native and be considerate of Japanese!)[31]

The protagonist in a story thus silently curses a Javanese, who is insolently occupying extra space in a bus with his outstretched legs. This is a scene from Takami Jun's novel *Ethnic Peoples*. After experiencing ideological conversion from the proletarian movement, Takami traveled to Indonesia (occupied by the Dutch at the time), and began his career as a professional writer with *On a Fine Day*, *Ethnic Peoples*, and other works that were based on that trip. In other words, one might say that Takami attempted to recover his encounters with people living at the forgotten bottom of society, the experience he had during his proletarian activist days, in the form of another encounter with a foreign culture and the foreign people living in the area called the South Seas and the Southern Region. Perhaps one can say that he began a new life as a writer by writing about those regions and people. It would be reasonable to assume that this trajectory had some influence on his later work as a novelist, but we cannot ignore the fact that his experiences in encountering foreign ethnic groups, and of interacting with foreign cultures, were for him something that could be expressed in the inner voice that curses, "What an attitude, you native! Know your place!"

Of course, I do not quote a passage from Takami's work in order to denounce him for ethnic discrimination. I do so because I think the curse "native," which remains unvoiced by the protagonist, probably existed as a word that resonated inside Takami, an ideologically converted writer. This abusive language illustrates how common it was for those Japanese who went to Asia during the war to mistreat Asians as "natives"—whether as an actual practice or as a sentiment. At the same time, it precisely describes the unfortunate encounter between the Japanese and other Asians. Hopefully it is now obvious that the invective is more than an emotional word of explosive anger against a few impertinent Asians: it actually has a deep, cultural and historical background. Takeda Taijun was mobilized to the Chinese front as a soldier of the Japanese Army. He wrote a short essay called "The Faces of the Dirt Peasants," describing the faces of the Chinese he met there, and printed it in 1938 in the literary journal *Chinese Literature* that he and his friends were publishing.

No matter how gently the Japanese army approaches, the Chinese people on the warfront won't open their hearts so easily to us. Even when they come close to us armed soldiers, we must assume that they have mentally prepared themselves. We saw many farmers who did not seem perturbed at all in spite of their extreme facial expressions. Even when they were crying or joyful, their eyes would be fixed at something unspecific in the air. The faces of the dirt peasants are deeply tanned and appear uncomplicated, but their hearts seem lost in a deep, blue-black chasm. Even the children hide their quick minds! The Chinese we soldiers interact with are all these poverty-stricken dirt peasants who have minds like these.[32]

Chinese history and culture form a layered "deep chasm" in the tanned, simple faces of the "dirt peasants" whom Takeda met as a soldier of an "invading army." He saw in those faces the culture of "dirt peasants," that is, "people who live with the earth." The "poverty-stricken dirt peasants" may appear similar to those "natives" without culture that the Japanese encountered as invaders and colonialists, but, needless to say, they are not. Between "natives" and "dirt peasants" it becomes necessary to recognize a gap and divergence between two different views of Asia by the Japanese upon their encounter with other Asians.

The Japanese called Europeans and Americans "demon-beasts" and described Asians in the colonies and occupied territories as "natives." These names were derived from the overbearing pride of the Japanese, who defined themselves as "humans" and "civilized people." However, it is obvious that their pride was tied to narrow-minded chauvinism. Furthermore, it is clear that those appellations were the result of their intentional attempt to forget the fact that Japanese had made extracting themselves from the "native kingdom" in the backwaters of Asia and achieving the goal of "Leaving Asia, Entering Europe" their ardent goal. The "Japanese" versus "native." Now, half a century after the 1930s, when the perspective exemplified by Dankichi's globe dominated, the Japanese are being questioned seriously by wider Asia about the responsibility for their own barbaric and primitive "native"-like behavior.

Notes

[Translator's Note] *The Adventures of Dankichi* was a reading I, Helen J. S. Lee, taught in an advanced reading class at the University of Florida during spring 2006, and I would like to give credit where it is due—many thanks to David Elam, Eyal Maidan, Kathleen Owens, and Simon Yu.

Two versions of Kawamura's essay exist. It first appeared as "Popular Oriental-ism and Japanese Views of Asia" (*Taishū orientarizumu to Ajia ninshiki*) in Ōe Shinobu et al., eds., *Iwanami Seminar, Modern Japan and the Colonies* (*Iwanami kōza kindai Nihon to shokuminchi*), 8 vols. (Tokyo: Iwanami shoten, 1993), vol. 7: 107–36. A slightly modified version with a new title, "Colonialism and Oriental-ism: *Adventurer Dankichi's Globe*" (*Koroniarizumu to orientarizumu: "Bōken" Dan-kichi no chikyūgi*), was included in Kawamura Minato, *Japanese Literature of the South Seas and Sakhalin* (*Nan'yō, Karafuto no Nihon bungaku*) (Tokyo: Chikuma shobō, 1994), 21–58. Our translation is based on the original version, but we have incorporated most of the changes made in the second. All ellipses in the essay are in Kawamura's original text and have not been added by translators or editors. We would like to thank Leslie Winston and Dustin Leavitt for carefully reading the drafts in different stages, sometimes in spite of rather ungodly time constraints due to the time difference between the translators. The translation has greatly benefited from their discerning eyes.

1. Shimada Keizō, *The Complete Collection of the Adventurer Dankichi Comic* (*Bōken Dankichi manga zenshū*) (Tokyo: Kodansha, 1967). See preface.

2. Instead of narrowly signifying aesthetic Oriental taste or a study of the Orient (*tōyōgaku*), the term "Orientalism" refers to the concept Edward W. Said developed in his *Orientalism* (New York: Vintage Books, 1979). For instance, "The Orient is an integral part of European *material* civilization and culture. Orientalism expresses and represents that part culturally and even ideologically as a mode of discourse with supporting institutions, vocabulary, scholarship, imagery, doctrines, even co-lonial bureaucracies and colonial styles" (2). Reconceptualizing this Orient into the larger non-Western world, including the South Seas, I define modern Japan's col-lective expressions and representations about Asia and the South Seas regions as Japanese "Orientalism."

3. Shimada, *The Complete Collection*. See preface.

4. Kobayashi Izumi, *The Small Nations of Micronesia* (*Mikuroneshia no chīsana kuniguni*) (Tokyo: Chūō kōron sha, 1982), 5. Yano Akira has described the con-nection between Dankichi and the image of the "South Seas natives" as "the Ad-venturer Dankichi Syndrome." See Yano Akira, *Japanese Views of the History of the South Seas* (*Nihon no nan'yōshikan*) (Tokyo: Chūō kōron sha, 1979), 154.

5. [Translators' Note] Abbreviated, the boy's name would be pronounced "Daiken," following Japanese phonetic rules.

6. [Translators' Note] These tribal names Kawamura cites from *Adventures* ap-pear to be Shimada's creation. "Kūroi" (black), "Burakku" (black), and "Yami" (darkness) all refer to dark shades of color.

7. Takagi Ichinosuke, *Japanese Language Reader for Normal Grade School* (*Jinjō shōgakkō kokugo tokuhon*) (Tokyo: Chūō kōron sha, 1976), 87–90.

8. Suzuki Tsunenori, *The True Record of the South Seas Expedition* (*Nan'yō tan-ken jikki*) (Tokyo: Heibonsha, 1980), 78, 88. The original publication was by Hakubunkan in 1892.

9. [Translators' Note] *Manowa* is the transliteration of the word as it appears in the text, but we can find no evidence of the existence of an island with this name.

10. [Translators' Note] The Wushe Incident is also known as the Musha Incident. *Wushe* is the Mandarin pronunciation and the latter the Japanese rendering of the name of the area in which the rebellion took place.

11. Huang Zhaotang, *The Governor-General Office of Taiwan* (*Taiwan sōtokufu*) (Tokyo: Kyōikusha, 1981), 128.

12. [Translators' Note] Hōbo and Piposappo are transliterations of the Japanese words as they appear in the text. Given that they are rendered in katakana, we are unable to confirm the accurate spelling in the original language.

13. Nogami Toyoichirō and Nogami Yaeko, *Korea, Taiwan, and the South Seas Harbors* (Chōsen, Taiwan, kainan shokō) (Tokyo: Takunansha, 1942), 222.

14. Nakamura Chihei, *Collected Taiwan Fictions* (Tokyo: Bokusui shobō, 1941), 39.

15. [This note was originally embedded in the main text.] The character for *ban* in *banjin* is different from the *ban* in *yaban*, and, consequently, the first *ban* signifies something different from the second. The first *ban* means a place covered with thick grass, and should not be confused with the second *ban*, which denotes barbarity.

16. Ōshika Taku, *The Savage* (*Yabanjin*) (Tokyo: Sōrin shobo, 1936). A separate volume with the same title was published by Hakuōshoin in 1949, but its content differs from the earlier collection. The original book includes "The Savage" (*Yabanjin*), "Savage Women" (*Banfu*), "Tattaka Zoo" (*Tattaka dōbutsuen*), and "Zhang's Desire" (*Sō no yokubō*). The later edition does not have "Zhang's Desire," but includes "In the Forest" (*Shinrin no naka*) and "People of the Inlands" (*Okuchi no hitobito*) instead. The quotation in this section is from pp. 32–33 of the Hakuhō shoin edition.

17. [Translators' Note] An embankment on the Kanda River in Tokyo.

18. [Translators' Note] The translation of this passage comes from Natsume Sōseki, *Rediscovering Natsume Sōseki*, intro. and trans. Inger Sigrun Brodey and Sammy I. Tsunematsu (Folkstone, Kent, UK: Global Oriental, 2000), 38–40.

19. [Translators' Note] Ibid., 39.

20. [Translators' Note] Isabella Lucy Bird, *Unbeaten Tracks in Japan* (London: John Murray, 1881), vol. 1: 17.

21. [Translators' Note] Ibid., vol. 2: 47.

22. [Translators' Note] Ibid., 74.

23. As mentioned in the text, no colophon is provided in the book, and author's name, publisher's name, and the publishing date are unknown. It is widely believed that the book was edited by the Security Bureau of the Police Agency in Manchukuo in the 1930s.

24. *Dissection of Taikan'en*, 3, and preface, 1.

25. Shibusawa Keizō, *Collected Works of Shibusawa Keizō* (*Shibusawa Keizō chosakushū*) (Tokyo: Heibonsha, 1992), vol. 1: 63.

26. Yamakawa Chikara, *Politics and the Ainu* (*Seiji to Ainu minzoku*) (Tokyo: Miraisha, 1989), 77.

27. Yamaguchi Masao, Karatani Kōjin, Murai Osamu, and Kawamura Minato, "Collective Discussion: Colonialism and Modern Japan" (*Kyōdō tōgi: shokuminchi shugi to kindai Nihon*), *Critical Space* (*Hihyō kūkan*) 7 (Oct. 1992): 37.

28. Nakanishi Inosuke, *New Buds in the Red Soil* (*Shakudo ni megumu mono*) (Tokyo: Kaizōsha, 1922), 2.

29. Tanaka Hidemitsu, *Drunken Ship* (*Yoidore bune*) (Tokyo: Koyamasha, 1949), 125.

30. Katō Rissen, *Complete Collection of Strange Customs of the World* (*Sekai fūzoku kibun zenshū*) (Tokyo: Kōbunsha shuppanbu, date unknown), 10–16.

31. Takami Jun, *Ethnic Peoples* (*Shominzoku*) (Tokyo: Shinchōsha, 1942), 70–71. Takami, *On a Fine Day* (*Aru hareta hi ni*) (Tokyo: Kawade shobō, 1941).

32. Takeda Taijun, *The Banks of the Yangzi River: China and Its Human Wisdom* (*Yōsukō no hotori: Chūgoku to sono ningengaku*) (Tokyo: Haga shoten, 1971), 59.

Index